The French in the Mississippi Valley

# THE
# FRENCH
# IN THE
# MISSISSIPPI
# VALLEY

*edited by*

John Francis McDermott

University of Illinois Press, Urbana, 1965

A grant from the Ford Foundation has helped to defray the cost of publishing this work.

To Gregory J. Nooney

---

*First Friend of the Conference*

# *Foreword*

The papers in this volume, current research by scholars interested in the history of French activities in the Mississippi Valley, range over a vast territory. The opening essay has arisen out of my studies toward a biography of Pierre de Laclède, in the course of which I have become well acquainted with many myths concerning the founder and the founding of St. Louis. Three other papers center on Laclède's city. Charles E. Peterson, architectural historian, has studied the houses of French St. Louis. Dorothy Garesché Holland, descendant of French from Santo Domingo, devotes herself to St. Louis families who came from the French West Indies in the 1790's and later. Charles Guenther, poet and translator of contemporary European poets, presents a hitherto unreported French poet in early nineteenth-century St. Louis.

Two other papers relate closely to St. Louis. Joseph P. Donnelly, S. J., is concerned with Father Pierre Gibault, who served in the French villages of the old Illinois Country east of the Mississippi. Frederic E. Voelker goes west to the Rockies with the French mountain men who were either St. Louisans or worked for St. Louis merchants in the fur trade.

Three papers are principally about lower Louisiana. Samuel Wilson, Jr., architectural historian, has written about colonial fortifications and military architecture. Professor Jack D. L. Holmes, colonial historian, has drawn on his extensive researches in archives in Spain for much new material on French engineers in the Spanish services during the later decades of the eighteenth century. Pierre H. Boulle, who leaves the Department of History at Stanford University to become Assistant Professor of History at the University of Delaware, has based his study of French reactions to the Louisiana Revolution of 1768 on unexploited sources in France.

Two other papers are indeed far wandering. Professor Joseph Ewan, historian of botanical exploration, has written about French naturalists in the broad expanse of the Mississippi Valley, and Richebourg Gaillard McWilliams, Professor at Birmingham-Southern College, has recounted from documentary sources the fantastic tale of Mathieu Sagean, who claimed to have discovered a marvelous kingdom beyond the Rockies.

Finally, three papers will be of special interest to all scholars working in the area, for they describe manuscript resources available for the study of the history of the French in the Mississippi Valley. Father Noël Baillargeon of the Séminaire de Québec and Université Laval tells of letters in the archives of his institution. James M. Babcock, chief of the Burton Historical Collection in the Detroit Public Library, summarizes one of the richest accumulations of local history documents. Winston De Ville of Harper & Row, who was formerly with the Mobile Public Library, writes very informatively about manuscript resources in Louisiana which are little known and little used.

It is hoped that the publication of these studies will stimulate other investigations of French activities in the Mississippi Valley.

These papers were first presented at a conference held in St. Louis on February 13 to 15, 1964, in recognition of the bicentennial of the founding of St. Louis by Pierre de Laclède. The meeting and this volume were made possible by a few friends to whom my colleagues and I return our warm thanks. Gregory P. Nooney not merely contributed with great generosity to the expenses of the conference but with Mrs. Nooney entertained lavishly at a luncheon and a dinner. Joseph Desloge gave liberally as he has so often done before. Mr. and Mrs. Lyle Woodcock made a very substantial contribution. Other helpful friends were the Alliance Française (Groupe de St. Louis), J. Garneau Weld, Morton J. May, Harold Koplar (French Consul at St. Louis), Warren B. Lammert, Dr.

Richard A. Sutter, and the Union Electric Company. A principal sponsor and supporter of the conference was the St. Louis Historical Documents Foundation without whose special contribution it would not have been possible to publish this volume.

Ambassador Hervé Alphand and Madame Alphand honored the conference by coming to St. Louis to attend the dinner session, at which Monsieur Alphand gave an address on contemporary French-American relations. With the ambassador came Monsieur Jean Béliard, consul-general of France at Chicago, and Madame Béliard; Monsieur Roger Vaurs, director of the French Press and Information Service at the French Embassy; and Monsieur René Allewaert, cultural attaché at Chicago.

Quite special guests of honor were Madame J.-L. Chaudruc, representative of the elder branch of the Laclède family, and her husband, who came from France and attended the entire conference. This most appropriate visit we owe to G. J. Nooney and Company, builders of the new Pierre Laclède Building.

George Brooks, director of the Missouri Historical Society; Buford L. Pickens, professor of architecture, Washington University; Robert R. Palmer, dean of the Faculty of Arts and Sciences, Washington University; Professor Elizabeth Schreiber, department of French, Washington University and president of the Alliance Française (Groupe de St. Louis); and John Francis Bannon, S.J., chairman of the department of history, Saint Louis University, were kind enough to act as chairmen of the five sessions. Through the kindness of Dr. Betty Grossman the Thursday meetings were held in the auditorium of the City Art Museum of St. Louis and through that of Provost G. E. Pake those on Saturday at Washington University.

Finally, my thanks to my colleagues for joining in this conference and for the stimulating papers they have contributed. For Mary Stephanie McDermott, my wife, I simply say there are not words enough to express my gratitude for her help in a multitude of details in organizing this affair.

John Francis McDermott
Southern Illinois University
(Edwardsville)

St. Louis
14 June 1964

# Contents

# Myths and Realities Concerning the Founding of St. Louis

## John Francis McDermott

Some years ago a visitor from California gave me the true inside story of the founding of our city of St. Louis. He had returned to the Mississippi Valley to look up his family tree, he told me during a very long conversation on the telephone, and on delving deep into the records, archives, and other sources in New Orleans and St. Louis, he had come to the conclusion that his report "would change the early history of this city considerable." As his story unrolled, it did indeed present a new version of these events that so interest us.

My caller pointed to the blanks and uncertainties in our early history. There was, he insisted, no absolute and positive proof of facts in records as far as St. Louis history is concerned—each historian who had written about it had his own version of what had happened and many records had been lost. Stimulated by hearing from his grandmother a tradition handed down in his family that his people came, as he put it, "from the seed of the kings of France," he concluded that the true story of our city lay in that of his family, which fit the known details so perfectly that it must have originated in the man who had founded the city, Pierre de Laclède Liguest.

My informant believed that he was descended from Laclède whose real name I now learned was Pierre Laclède St. Louis, for—I repeat his words—"as it's recognized he must have been from royal blood (nobility) naturally he must have been from the lines of kings. And if so he was a St. Louis." (Evidently the descendants of Louis IX immediately after his canonization in 1297 took St. Louis as their family name—a fact I had somehow missed in my desultory reading.) There had been in the eighteenth century, he further explained, revolutions, unrest, and difficulties in Europe and possibly Laclède had had to leave France to save his neck. One thing was sure: on escaping to Louisiana he had dropped the St. Louis from his name and in its place had added Liguest.

Being a man of adventurous nature and strong will and a natural born leader, in New Orleans he gained influential friends, formed Maxent, Laclède and Company, opened a branch of the business up here, and made a success. We have all read elsewhere that Laclède was urged to name his village after himself but refused to do so, choosing to call it St. Louis in honor of the reigning King of France. It becomes clear now that he could not name the town for himself because the long arm of his enemies might reach out after him. Besides, please note well, since *he* knew his own true identity, he was actually naming the settlement as much for himself as for his noble ancestor, the sainted king. Perhaps if the troubles blew over in France, he could let the world know the true facts, but at this time, he often declared (according to this family tradition), he was constantly in danger and was careful not to give anyone information about himself. People said, my informant solemnly asserted, that Laclède was a mysterious man.

Well, you know how things were in those days. My narrator believed that, like many another man, Laclède had several women. It becomes a lamentable story. Coming home one night, after a long and tiresome trip (such as he often took), he perhaps celebrated too much and under the influence of wine, women, and song, he let the secret slip, and, just as Samson was betrayed by Delilah, so was Mr. Laclède betrayed, for it was not long after that he was found down the river dead. He was probably murdered. He may have died through jealousy, through the greed of others, or because the long arm of the law caught up with him, but, though my informant was going to keep his ideas to himself for the time being, he was certain that Laclède had been murdered. The clinching proof was that the strong box which he had always guarded so carefully had disappeared—important documents establishing his true identity thus vanished so that no one knows to this day where they are. But the woman who had borne him two children, finding out his true identity, called her children St. Louis after their father's true name. And that brings us to this descendant's return home seeking proofs of his family tradition and the lost fortune in urban real estate which somehow the Chouteaus had managed to acquire. But the personal story of my telephone visitor I shall not go into, for I am concerned at this moment only with the founding of St. Louis.

Fantastic? A melange of nonsense? We insiders can brush aside this confusion twice confounded and laughingly dismiss the outsider who has amused us for a few moments? What will you say, then, to some remarks made in public a dozen years ago by a descendant of Auguste Chouteau, as reported in a local newspaper: St. Louis, he is alleged to have declared, "can be said to have four founders—Pierre Laclede, Auguste Chouteau, Madame Marie Therese Chouteau, or Captain St. Ange, the commandant at Forte des Charte [*sic*], take your choice." With casual assurance and complete indifference to historical fact, physical possibilities, and common sense, this speaker explained that

Laclede, accompanied by his clerk, Chouteau, then 13, selected the site for a trading post in the summer of 1763. They returned to New Orleans for the winter, and in the spring of 1764, when he was ready to set up the post, Laclede was too busy and sent Madame Chouteau, who agreed to operate a hotel at the post up the river to get things started. Because in those days women just didn't lead expeditions, Laclede placed Auguste in charge, knowing that he would do what his mother told him.

The party stopped at Forte des Charte, and, while Madame Chouteau remained there, young Auguste took a band of men to the site Laclede had selected and started felling trees. A few days later St. Ange followed with soldiers and set up a stockade with the felled trees, the first thing to do in an Indian country.[1]

Neither the outsider nor the insider whom I have cited makes pretension to standing as historian or journalist, but even those who have seriously undertaken to write something about the beginning of St. Louis have often allowed themselves the license of filling in any blanks they found in the record. Since no person survived in 1858 who had been present when Laclède in December, 1763, chose the location for his trading post, since no one knew the precise date on

---

[1] *St. Louis Globe-Democrat*, Feb. 20, 1952.

which he marked the trees, since no record existed describing the weather or the actual arrival of the party at the spot, why not make a good story by filling in these interesting details and gain an authentic tone by giving a precise date? Listen to what an avid reader of the once popular G. P. R. James could do with such a scene:

It was on one of those dark, gusty days, that so often clothe, in a western clime, the latter portions of November with a penumbral mistiness, that a party of boatmen, caroling in native sweetness their sweet and simple songs, might have been seen winding around the point of what is now known as Duncan's Island. The day throughout had assumed all the fantastic ebullitions of passion and change, that mark the everchanging footsteps of some spoiled, yet beautiful coquette. One moment suffused with the sweet smiles of love and tenderness, with the dimpling sunshine resting in playfulness on the cheek, an hour of rest too long to last, the frenzy of madness seizes on the brain, and all within is dark and gloomy, with sudden drifts of clouds flitting as shadows along the sunshine of life. So had been the day; one moment, all of the rich glow of an Indian summer, and all of its mild warmth, smiled the affections of love on the earth, to be succeeded by fitful gusts of wind, cheerless and disconsolate. Many had been the changes that had passed along the earth that day. The distant thunder, as it rumbled along its folds of clouds, and the raindrops, as they pattered on the half-withered flowers below, were all succeeded too soon by the rich gorgeousness of an autumnal sky. Such was the day, and such the scene, on the banks of the mighty Mississippi, on the 9th of December, 1763.

The party who were sending forth their songs of joy were none others than Pierre de Laclede and a half a dozen sturdy voyageurs. . . .[2]

The writer of that fine little piece should have combined with it a spot of human interest contributed to another account published in a local directory for 1845. There we can read that the search for the location of a fur trading post became in effect a *fête champêtre*. The actual choice, we are told on the authority of "some of the older [unidentified] inhabitants," was a "mere accident."

. . . when Laclede and his party first set foot on what is now St. Louis, their encampment was made in consequence of there being plenty of *wood* at hand. . . . Their encampment being made, the leaders of the party set themselves about hunting a place for a new settlement. They explored for some distance down the river, and then up as high as the mouth of the Missouri. The result of their examination was that the

---

[2] J. N. Taylor and M. O. Crooks, *Sketch Book of Saint Louis* (St. Louis, 1858), pp. 9–10. I cannot resist adding a further quotation. From Fort Chartres, according to these authors, Laclède "dispatched a couple of young men from New Orleans, Auguste and Pierre Chouteau, with a suitable outfit of men and materials" to begin construction. Not only was the second of these young men not yet six years old but he was still in New Orleans in the spring of 1764!

locality now called "north Saint Louis" was selected, and to this point the commander of the expedition intimated that it was his intention at once to remove. But to this an objection was raised by *the ladies* of the party! They were tired of moving about, had at length become comfortably "fixed" in their new quarters, and they wouldn't budge an inch, not they. If their lords wanted to settle elsewhere, they could do so, but as for themselves, they were satisfied, and determined to remain. Laclede and his followers being men of gallantry, the ladies had it all their own way. . . .[3]

Around the name of the founder, as around that of the town, equally fanciful legends have accreted. Little being known of Laclède's background or his life—you must remember that he died in 1778 long long before these accounts were fabricated—some of his interested descendants made many surprising discoveries about his origin. One great-granddaughter learned that Laclède had first been a page at the court of Versailles and later a *mousquetaire gris* in the service and high in the favor of Louis XV until he fell out with Madame de Pompadour. As punishment he was ordered to America "with, however, a special mission from the King to inquire into the condition of things in that distant colony."[4]

A generation later, another member of the family, retelling this story, improved it by calling Madame de Pompadour the real founder of St. Louis and incidentally gave Laclède a promotion. "In some way that has not come down to us," he wrote, "the Vicompte de Laclede offended that great lady, and she demanded his banishment." Offered his choice between the Bastille and Louisiana, the young man crossed the ocean.[5] Still another descendant advanced Laclède one step higher in the aristocratic world when she described the ancestor as "that far seeing and adventurous French nobleman the Marquis Pierre Ligueste de Laclede who had left his ancestral home in Bedous, France, to seek his fortune across the sea in 'New France.' "[6]

---

[3] W. D. Skillman, *The Western Metropolis* (St. Louis, 1846), pp. 55–56. This story was essentially repeated in the *St. Louis Daily Union*, Sept. 4, 1846.

[4] This interesting "fact" comes from the notebooks of Clementine Papin Carriere, manuscript formerly on deposit in the archives of the Missouri Historical Society. Much of Mrs. Carriere's account of the history of her ancestors (though not this particular statement) is contained in an interview with her published in the *St. Louis Globe-Democrat*, Feb. 2, 1900.

[5] G. Prather Knapp, "The Story of St. Louis," *Service* (house publication of the Mississippi Valley Trust Company, St. Louis), June, 1917, p. 5.

[6] Florence Gratiot Bale, "When the Gratiots Came to Galena," *Illinois State Historical Society Journal*, XXIV (Jan., 1932), 671–672.

Now these tales are gross nonsense but no more so than others which are still repeated by those who will not examine their sources, who will not pass up a good story. Once a statement, however unsubstantiated, once an attractive assumption, however unwarranted, is printed in a book it becomes gospel fact and to eradicate it from the general mind or to forestall its reuse becomes very nearly impossible.

Laclède the man of destiny is such a theme in histories of St. Louis. Because Chouteau in his "Narrative of the Founding of St. Louis" reported Laclède's exclaiming that on this site he was going to found a settlement which might become hereafter one of the great cities of the world, the young Béarnais is pictured in the family chateau at Bedous, "dreaming of his plans to found a colony in the New World." He sailed from Bordeaux, we are told, "with a small company of men from the immediate vicinity of Bedous," all imbued with his enthusiasm. But I fear that, although "by years of planning he prepared himself for the establishment of St. Louis," some slight hitch must have developed in New Orleans since he loitered there for eight years before putting this grand project into effect. If we show now that he actually sailed from La Rochelle and that not one of his fellow passengers ever had any association with St. Louis, will that lead to the abandonment of this romantic story? If we point out that the carpenter Jean B. Ortez, an early settler of St. Louis said to have accompanied Laclède from Béarn to America, was certainly not on the ship with him, will that change the elegant picture we have of the empire builder, devoting himself to extending French colonial power? Let us not count on it. Any day a new popularizer of our history will eagerly rediscover this human interest story and give it once more to the world with added detail.[7]

There is another hoary chestnut crying out for another roasting: "Laclède was a republican at heart. With him democracy came to St. Louis." This theme dear to Americans appeared in histories of the city more than a hundred years ago—and variations on it are still composed today. Early versions present a pretty development of an ideal settlement in the wilderness: there was no law because none was needed. All men were brothers. The founder governed by "the force of his personality." The complexities of life brought in by St. Ange

---

[7] Walter B. Stevens, *St. Louis, the Fourth City, 1764–1909* (St. Louis, 1909), I, xii, 962, 963.

and his soldiers, "who [according to one historian of St. Louis in 1860] did not add to its numbers of industrious inhabitants," led to the institution of more formal government, and "at the general wish of the inhabitants" the captain was "placed at the head of affairs, and exercised all the functions of a commandant-general." Another writer a decade later praised the "sound judgment" of the citizens for conferring on St. Ange his authority as governor. Still a third commentator repeated all this at greater length: "His imperial charter doubtless vested in Liguest discretionary powers of government . . . [but] indisposed to assume political responsibility, he exercised only those civil functions that were essential to his little colony." It was only with the coming of "an indolent soldiery" that the need for government became urgent. "Under the stress of a felt necessity, and without the sanction of Spanish authority, the people unanimously vested in St. Ange the powers of civil government." Thus Laclède and St. Ange, working in an informal partnership, ruled by the will of the people.[8]

It remained for Walter B. Stevens in his centennial history of St. Louis to rephrase this into an expanded composition. Laclède held no commission, Stevens acknowledged, but there was "recognition of his authority by common consent of the governed." His house was the seat of government; civil rule was planned there. When St. Ange, after delivering Fort Chartres to the British, came "without hesitation" to St. Louis, he lived in Laclède's house and consulted him constantly. When Piernas took over as Spanish Lieutenant-Governor, he too took residence "as a guest" in Laclède's house. The firm of Maxent, Laclède and Company "furnished quarters rent free to the officials. The firm must have met the small expenses of government which were not covered by fees. Behind St. Ange and his associates in office was the master spirit of this government, Laclede." Law and order under Laclède's benevolent guidance was "not too elaborate, not theoretic, but sufficient to the needs of a community which did not know whether it was under a colonial flag

---

[8] Richard Edwards and Menra Hopewell, *Edwards's Great West and Her Commercial Metropolis, Embracing a General View of the West, and a Complete History of St. Louis, from the Landing of Ligueste, in 1764, to the Present Time* (St. Louis, 1860), p. 247; Elihu H. Shepard, *The Early History of St. Louis and Missouri* (St. Louis, 1870), p. 14; J. Thomas Scharf, *History of Saint Louis City and County* (Philadelphia, 1883), I, 71–72—this chapter was written by Sylvester Waterhouse, then professor of history at Washington University.

or was to be part of a new nation. When, in 1770, conditions became settled there was nothing that Laclede and his associates had done which required undoing." And now for the grand flourish: "The principle of Americanism was born in St. Louis. The man from Bedous in the Pyrenees is entitled to recognition which has not been accorded to him."[9]

Could ever a sophisticated newsman have been so naïve as Stevens was in this pretty nonsense? This agreeable approach to colonial history had been absolutely demolished by Louis Houck in his *History of Missouri* a year earlier, but that had not had the slightest effect on the journalist who had preferred a good story to mere prosaic fact. Nor has any later presentation of documents stopped later writers from following the same will-o'-the-wisp.

But enough of these unfounded assumptions, this romancing, this uncritical repetition of error and myth. Let me set down concisely the documented facts, the realities about the founding of St. Louis, about Laclède's background, and about his reasons for establishing St. Louis, reasons which foretold the development and the history of this city.[10]

Truth is more precious than fiction and real life more exciting than pretty fancy. We should have more respect for our origins and our past than to turn them into shallow, sentimental thrillers or watered-down treatises on egalitarianism. To reach back through the years and find live men with their human frailties and human courage and achievement makes research high adventure.

Here is a story of commercial enterprise. On his arrival in New Orleans in June, 1763, Jean Jacques Blaise D'Abbadie, the last Frenchman to command in the province, found Louisiana suffering a wild inflation resulting from financial regulations established during the late war. Business was stagnant. Merchants were near bankruptcy. To stimulate business and restore prosperity, D'Abbadie arranged a number of monopolies in various commodities and areas to remain in effect for a limited period of years. To Gilbert Antoine Maxent, a substantial merchant of New Orleans, he granted the exclusive privilege of the trade with the Indian tribes on the Missouri River and the west bank of the upper Mississippi for a period of six

---

[9] Stevens, *St. Louis, the Fourth City*, I, 32 ff., 57, 1066–67.

[10] Full documentation for Laclède's story will be presented in my forthcoming biography of the founder.

years. In the articles of association drawn up by Maxent with Jean François Le Dée and Laclède and Company, it was agreed that Laclède would establish and direct in the Illinois Country a post for the exploitation of this trade.

On or after August 10, Laclède, accompanied by thirteen-year-old Auguste Chouteau as his clerk, left New Orleans with a heavy cargo of trade goods and materials needed for the development of his project. The boat employed on this occasion may have been the one that he owned at his death. If so, it was a boat about fifty feet long, ten feet wide, and of thirty to fifty tons burden and would have required a crew of at least twenty boatmen. Normal time to move such a laden vessel up to the Illinois Country was about three months. The cost would run to five thousand livres or more. There is no record to show that Laclède had more than one boat.

Laclède arrived at Ste. Genevieve (then the only settlement on the west bank of the Mississippi) on November 3, Chouteau later wrote,[11] but he could find no building there large enough to store one-fourth of his merchandise. On November 6 Laclède was at Kaskaskia, attending the auction of the recently confiscated property of the Jesuits. He offered thirty-nine thousand livres but was outbid. At the invitation of Captain Neyon de Villiers, then commandant of the Illinois Country, he stored his supplies at Fort Chartres and made his winter headquarters in the little village of Ste. Anne de Fort Chartres, where he bought a house. In December, accompanied by young Chouteau, he searched the west bank of the Mississippi as far as the mouth of the Missouri for a location suitable for his business and determined on the site of St. Louis, attracted by the rocky, shelving bluff that would place his establishment well above high water, by the easy access at one point (near the foot of present-day Market Street), and by the springs a few miles back which fed the Petite Rivière (later to be known as Mill Creek).

In February Laclède dispatched Chouteau from Fort Chartres with thirty workmen to start work on the trading post. The party "laid axe to wood" on February 15 and began to throw up temporary cabins for the men and a shed for the food and tools. No stockade was built until 1780 for the good reason that there were no hostile Indians. Laclède inspected progress in April, gave his young assistant

---

[11] Auguste Chouteau's "Narrative of the Founding of St. Louis" can most conveniently be found in my edition of *The Early Histories of St. Louis* (St. Louis, 1952), pp. 45–59.

a plan to follow in laying out a village, and named it St. Louis in honor of the reigning King of France. That the eastern part of the Illinois had been ceded to the British was known before Laclède left New Orleans. Uncertainty and alarm spreading among the French villages of this distant area must have increased strongly from that moment in April, 1764, when D'Abbadie's order to evacuate the country reached Captain de Villiers. In June that officer, leaving for New Orleans with most of his troops, was accompanied by eighty inhabitants. Laclède, however, did persuade the families of the workmen and others to move across the river. Within a year forty to fifty families had settled in the new village. Until September 10, 1764, no one in Louisiana—not even the director-general—knew that the western part of the colony had been ceded to Spain. Presumably the news would not have reached St. Louis earlier than November or December. Fortunately for us by this time the village was firmly established and the character of the place determined. St. Louis was destined to be a Spanish colony for nearly forty years, but its population was predominantly French and culturally it was thoroughly French.

St. Ange, formerly in command at Vincennes, turned Fort Chartres over to the British Captain Stirling in October, 1765, and, by orders from New Orleans, withdrew his handful of troops to Laclède's little town, the northernmost in the western part of the Illinois. As French commandant both civil and military power were vested in St. Ange. Until he was relieved by competent authority, first by the arrival of a British officer at Fort Chartres and later at St. Louis by a duly appointed Spanish official, he continued to exercise those powers. Laclède at no time held any military or civil office nor did he pretend to any authority. He remained strictly a private citizen living successively under the laws of France and then of Spain. St. Louis was not a primitive democracy springing up in the wilderness: it was part of a well-established colonial system. If Laclède or any other man in St. Louis had thought of democracy, no record of it has come down to us.

And what of this private citizen, Pierre de Laclède?

First, his name, the form of which long puzzled St. Louisans. He was indeed born Pierre de Laclède, but I hasten to add that the particle is not an infallible indication of nobility. The Laclèdes were not noble. Pierre did not drop the *de*, as so many accounts in print have stated, out of democratic inclination. In fact, he did not drop it at all. Since it was customary for a man to sign himself with his last name only, Pierre's signature commonly appears as *Laclède*, plus the additional name of *Liguest*, customary in his family to distinguish a second son from his elder brother. The correct form of his name was recognized by Auguste Chouteau, who in his narrative referred to him in almost every instance as Monsieur de Laclède.

Though not noble, the Laclèdes were an old family long prominent in the Valley of the Aspe in Béarn, where they had been landowners as early as the fourteenth century and officeholders for generations. Pierre's father was an *avocat* admitted to practice before the Parlement (court) of Navarre. His grandfather Laclède was a *notaire* and served as syndic and adjutant-mayor of the valley. Two of his great-grandfathers had also been *notaires*. His elder brother Jean held his degree in law from the University of Toulouse, was admitted to practice before the Parlement of Navarre, and in 1763 was named master of the waters and forests of Navarre, Soule, and Béarn. Shortly before the Revolution Jean de Laclède did submit a request for admission into the corps of nobility, but this petition was based on the gift to him by Louis XV in 1770 of the royal fief of Saint Sauveur de l'Ousse. Early in the Revolution his house in Pau was burned by the mob. In 1793 he was denounced as a *ci-devant noble* or *anobli*. Imprisoned for eleven months, he survived the Terror to live on the family property at Bedous until 1813. From him the house and lands passed down through the generations until they came into the possession of Madame Chaudruc, whom we are so happy to have with us while we celebrate the founding of our city by Jean's younger brother.

But the Laclèdes were more than a family of successful lawyers and public officials. Pierre's uncle Jean, who was well thought of by Voltaire, was the author of a history of Portugal praised in its day. Jean de Laclède, we are told by his biographer, had a remarkable encyclopedic mind: there was no question of law, rural economy, or forestry that he had not studied. He was particularly interested in the culture of the mulberry and the silkworm and of poplar, flax, and beets. Made a member of the Academy of Sciences, Letters, and Arts of Pau in 1751, he contributed papers on agronomy to its *Annals* and later to the publications of the Société d'Agriculture of the Department of the Seine, of which he was a corresponding member. It is clear that these Laclèdes of Béarn were an interesting as well as a substantial family.

Of Pierre's childhood and education we yet know little. That he was well educated was attested, for example, by British officers who met him at St. Louis in 1766. But without that statement we would yet know from his library that he had a solid background of knowledge and a living interest in the thought of his day. Long ago investigation of early records showed that St. Louis in its colonial days was no mere crude village of illiterate boatmen and *coureurs de bois* buried in the wilderness but a little town with considerable collections of books and many of the other amenities of civilized life.[12] Among the earliest of the private libraries found there was that of Pierre de Laclède. The variety of his interests and activities is well illustrated by the more than two hundred volumes he carried to this distant place and owned at the time of his death in 1778, some of which he had obviously brought from France and others, published in the 1760's, he must have bought in New Orleans or imported from home.

School books on his shelves included a geography for children, a French and English grammar, a French grammar, an abridgment of geometry, an abridged history of France, Petronius' poem on the Civil War, the *Adventures of Telemaque,* a work on French synonyms, and a book on "advice for military youth" (which he may have used at the Académie at Toulouse). As a businessman he had the maritime code, Butel-Dumont's history of commerce in the English colonies, Mirabeau on the theory of taxation, Ulloa on the reestablishment of Spanish commerce, books on finance, maritime contracts, letters of exchange; he owned "the complete merchant," "the complete magistrate," a dictionary of commerce, a work on double-entry bookkeeping, and other volumes useful to a merchant.

As a man of some military interest he had the *Code Militaire* and a work entitled *Military Instruction.* As a country gentleman he had volumes on kitchen gardens, orchards, farming, surgery, medicine, and the care of horses. Like almost everyone else he had that ever-popular guide to everything, *La Maison Rustique.* As a miller he had Belidor on hydraulic architecture. His taste for history led him to own Rollin's ancient and modern histories (twenty-nine volumes in all) and to start home to St. Louis on his last voyage with the twelve volumes of Crevier's *Histoire des Empereurs romains.* He had a

---

[12] John Francis McDermott, *Private Libraries in Creole Saint Louis* (Baltimore, 1938).

twelve-volume collection of travels and volumes of the secret anecdotes so popular in his century. For general reference he could turn
to Corneille's *Dictionary of the Arts and Sciences*, the *Dictionary of
the French Academy*, a geography, and Sobrino's Spanish and
French dictionary in two volumes. Scientific matters were represented by Pluche's *Spectacle de la Nature*, once very popular, by a
work on experimental physics, by an essay on electricity which may
have been a French edition of Benjamin Franklin's study. Most
interesting of all were the books of The Enlightenment which
Laclède owned: the essays of Bacon, the philosophy of Descartes,
Locke's *Essay Concerning Human Understanding*, Feejoo's *Teatro
critico universal* (in Spanish), and Rousseau's *Contrat social* and *La
Nouvelle Héloïse*.

Two hundred volumes do not constitute a large library. What is
significant and illuminating is that Laclède selected these specific
books and carried them across an ocean and a thousand miles up a
river to the confines of a wilderness. When we know what a man
reads, we know something of his mind and spirit.

Laclède came to America for the same reason that brought
many another young man of good family to our shores: as a younger
son he had to look to his own fortune. He did not sail as a gentleman-
adventurer or as a colonizer for the greater glory of France, but as a
man seeking to establish himself in the world, intent on acquiring
wealth enough to enable him eventually to live in comfort in his
native place. Of the eight years he spent in New Orleans we know
almost nothing. He was an officer of militia but his rank has not been
discovered nor do we have one iota of information about any active
military duty he may have performed. In several documents he was
described as a *négociant*, that is, a wholesale merchant, but about his
business activities we have no details. That he was passably successful
is probable, for he associated with the leading businessmen of the
town and with the officials of the colony. That he was hard hit by
the depression at the close of the war seems beyond question.

It is with the organization of Maxent, Laclède and Company
that he actually becomes known to us. Here was a business operation
of great scope and promise. The trade territory was immense. Ener-
getically directed, the business could, within the period of the grant,
bring a fortune, for the vast area assigned to the partners was
virtually unexploited. Laclède moved swiftly and effectively. Within
ten days after the articles of association were drawn up he was on the

way to the Illinois Country, intent on getting his trading house into operation early in the new year. Once he arrived there, even more immediately important than the building of the post was getting outfits into the hands of the traders who would go out to the Indians. It was these arrangements that occupied him so closely in the winter and early spring that he did not take the time to go with the work party to the new site.

Many people today have a vaguely romantic picture of Laclède going out with a few men in a bark canoe to barter with the Indians in their villages. He may have done so, but there is no scrap of evidence to prove it. Laclède was an entrepreneur, the director of a large business. Nearby Indians like the Missouris who came to the post would be traded with directly, but tribes farther away must be visited by traveling merchants. The prime profits lay in outfitting these *marchant-voyageurs*. Prime hazards, too, existed, for these traders might be killed, the furs they were bringing back to St. Louis might be stolen by hostile Indians, the cargoes might be spilled in the river and spoiled, the furs of the season might be few or of poor quality. Returning to the post, the trader delivered his packs of skins and furs to Laclède, who would then reoutfit him, always on credit, and then ship the collections to New Orleans for reshipment to France. The hazards were great at every stage of the business, but the potential profits were great also.

The company was at first very successful. Laclède bent every effort to this end and overlooked no opportunity. The reason for his efforts to induce the French in the old villages to cross the river was partly to strengthen his establishment, partly to build up a retail trade, but even more, I think, to tie these men into the business operation as *traiteurs*. The importance of his settlement and his skill as a trader quickly became apparent to the English. Sir William Johnson, Indian agent in the northern colonies, wrote home to the Lords of Trade in November, 1765, about this Frenchman now established near the mouth of the Missouri "who carries on a vast Extensive Trade, and is acquiring a great influence over all the Indian Nations." Captain Harry Gordon, visiting St. Louis the next summer, noted in his diary that Laclède "takes so good Measures that the whole Trade of the Missouri, That of the Mississipi Northwards, and that of the Nations near la Baye, Lake Michigan and St. Joseph's, by the Illinois River, is entirely brought to him. He . . . will give us some Trouble before we get the Parts of this trade that belong to us out of his Hands."

The records of the company have long ago disappeared so that we cannot follow the operations or judge their success. Prospects were very bright. In October, 1766, Pierre wrote to his brother that if they sold out at this time he would have more than two hundred thousand livres, in those days a goodly sum of money. Luck, however, was against Laclède. Protests in New Orleans against exclusive trading privileges were carried to France and the minister of marine in 1765 ordered cancellation of all grants. This led apparently to loss of interest by Maxent in this trade. In the dissolution of the company Laclède acquired all the assets in St. Louis. By this time St. Louis was firmly established, and Laclède remained as first citizen and principal trader of his town.

Laclède's story, however, is more than that of a business enterpriser. He was the founder of a great city. St. Louis was a planned town, not a chance growth around a mission, not a gathering place of frontiersmen, not a boatmen's landing, not a backwoods settlement. From its earliest days it was a commercial center and a seat of government. In 1764, as now, it was at the crossroads of America and it became immediately the central *terminal* of the continent. Even then traffic did not move through St. Louis but flowed from it down to New Orleans, up the Illinois River, up the Mississippi, up the Missouri, and (soon) up the Ohio. Tiny as it was, it became immediately a wholesale center, a point of distribution, and thus forecast the future development. For the very reason that its location was excellent for the control of trade it had been the obvious choice for the seat of government when the French commandant moved across the Mississippi.

All this Laclède foresaw. He was quite right to declare enthusiastically to the officers of Fort Chartres, as Chouteau has told us, that he "had found a situation where he was going to found a settlement, which might become, hereafter, one of the finest cities of America— so many advantages were embraced in this site, by its locality and its central position." What St. Louis is today we owe to the enterprise and foresight of Pierre de Laclède. Let us honor him with a true and faithful account of what he was and what he did. This is the high adventure of research. This the founder of our city deserves.

# The Houses
# of French St. Louis

## Charles E. Peterson

Of St. Louis—river port, fur-trading center, and provincial capital of upper Louisiana, founded just two hundred years ago—it has been possible to build a documented picture. Although the last colonial structures disappeared beyond the memory of those now living, real estate and other records when carefully analyzed yield a surprising amount of information. Then, too, there remain for close examination a number of eighteenth-century buildings in the Illinois Country on both sides of the Mississippi, especially in Ste. Genevieve. Though few in number, these contemporary structures do much to explain the French builders' terms used in the records. A few early artists' views and some travelers' descriptions add to our understanding.

Before completing in 1949 a little volume on St. Louis,[1] the

[1] That study first appeared in the April, July, and October issues of the *Missouri Historical Society Bulletin* for 1947. Two years later it was published under one cover with a postscript, the whole entitled *Colonial St. Louis: Building a Creole Capital* (St. Louis, 1949). The present essay lifts some of the

writer made a quick survey of the St. Lawrence country, a tour of wooden-built Normandy (before it was ravaged by war), and a visit to the early architectural remains in New Orleans and rural Louisiana. Afterward he visited a number of islands in the West Indies from the Virgins to Curaçao, finding in many places, especially in those colonized by the French, architectural features which relate in some way to early St. Louis. A second expedition to Eastern Canada early this year was particularly rewarding.

It would be gratifying to be able to report that these studies have now been completed and all questions resolved. But it must be confessed that whenever one horizon was reached, another region inviting exploration appeared beyond it. For every question answered, new ones have arisen. But serious interest in architectural history has greatly increased in the last twenty-five years and more investigators are working in the archives of two continents. It is hoped that this essay will assist in arriving at a more complete understanding of French colonial buildings as they were built here two centuries ago.

## A TOWN RECONSTRUCTED FROM ITS DOCUMENTS

First, the houses of colonial St. Louis will be described,[2] and then their architectural derivations explored.

From various counts of the buildings and scattered census figures it has been determined that the average house sheltered about

text of 1949; where this is done the citing of sources, painstakingly set forth in the original, has been omitted.

Related essays are "French Houses of the Illinois Country," *Missouriana*, I (Aug.–Sept., 1938), 9–12, and "Early French Landmarks Along the Mississippi," *Antiques*, LIII (Apr., 1948), 286–288.

[2] The detailed knowledge we have of the disappeared town is mainly derived from land records. City real estate acquires great value and public and professional agencies care for the documents that prove ownership. Notarial records from the earliest days have survived here in numbers, and a transcription and cross-index of them was made twenty-five years ago under my direction. Ten persons worked with great care and accuracy for two years on the project. Fortunately these records are unusually specific in some architectural particulars.

Besides the strictly local papers, a limited amount of information on St. Louis as the capital of upper Louisiana had been made available from the archives of Seville and other places. Local collections from Louisiana and Canada to France were found to hold endless amounts of supporting data which have not even yet been exhausted by historians. Then, too, the French of France have been getting interested in the vernacular architecture of their five persons.[3] As to size, they varied considerably and probably no two were exactly alike. In the earliest days there were many small and temporary huts, but there were also large houses like that of the notary Labuscière which was sixty-six feet long. Late in the colonial period some tiny cabins were built. In general, however, the tendency was for house dimensions to increase as the village grew and developed, and the prosperity of certain families like the Chouteaus, the Cerrés, and the Robidoux is reflected in the growing size of their mansions.

Nearly all of these houses were of one story. A few had basements (*caves*) underneath and others could claim attics (*greniers*). The mansions of Auguste and Pierre Chouteau were raised on high basements in the style of Louisiana and the New World tropics so that today we would call them two-story houses (Illus. 6A, B).

## Roofs and Galleries

Two striking characteristics of these houses reveal their architectural ancestry in Canada and Louisiana; these were the steep French hip (*pavillon*) roof and the porch or *galerie* of the South. Casement windows swinging in on hinges also contrasted with the vertical sliding windows of contemporary Anglo-Americans.

The distinctive *pavillon* roof of Normandy, steep at the long sides and almost vertical at the ends[4] is found in the older country buildings of Quebec Province and was brought by Canadian carpenters to the Illinois Country.[5] The steepness of the roof had been more or less dictated originally by the angle necessary to shed water from thatch, but the form was carried along by tradition after the use of shingles became general. The attics of the Guibourd, Amoreaux, and Bolduc houses in old Ste. Genevieve down the river show the fine Norman trusses used to support such roofs (Illus. 10A,

villages, no longer confining themselves to *Les Monuments*. The gaps are gradually closing in.

[3] When large trading parties returned to the town from the fur country, many houses must have been crowded, for there were no regular inns or hotels.

[4] As much as 52° and 72° as found in Ste. Genevieve.

[5] The majority of St. Louis mechanics were of Canadian origin. Of the seven carpenters in the St. Louis militia of 1780 four were natives of Canada, two of France, and one of the Illinois Country. Of the six masons, five were of Canadian origin and one local (*The Spanish Regime in Missouri*, ed. Louis Houck [Chicago, 1909], I, 184–189).

B, C, D). John Reynolds who came in 1800 to live in the Illinois Country found them characteristic.[6]

The porch or *galerie* was much in evidence at St. Louis and seems to have been used on one, two, three, or all sides of most houses. This was a Louisiana feature described by the traveler C. C. Robin:

. . . the heat of the climate makes porches necessary. All houses have them—some on all sides, others on two sides only, and rarely, on only one side. These porches are formed by a prolongation of the roof with the pitch broken into two planes—just the opposite of our mansards. These roofs are supported by little wood columns with a pleasing effect; ordinarily these porches are given a width of eight to nine feet. The width of the porches offers several advantages, it prevents the sun's rays from striking the walls of the house, thus keeping them cooler; it offers a good place to walk (on the shady side), to eat, sit out in the evening with company and often, in the warm spells of summer, to sleep on. In a large number of houses the two ends of these porches are walled in to make private bedrooms, thus giving two rooms at either end of the house.[7]

Robin could have added the necessity of keeping rain out of the plastered walls[8] and used the same description for St. Louis houses. General Collot's illustration "French Habitation in the Country of the Illinois"[9] delineates a typical house with an all-around gallery. The St. Louis archives mention them from the earliest years, speci-

---

[6] Quoted in *Old Cahokia*, ed. John Francis McDermott (St. Louis, 1949), pp. 45–46. "The roofs of the dwelling house were uniform and peculiar. They were [p. 46] made of rafters and lath for sheeting. These roofs had no gable ends perpendicular, but were shingled on the ends as well as the sides. The ends sloped considerably towards the centre of the building, so that the shingles would lie on the lath. No nails were used to fasten the shingles to the lath. Holes were bored in the shingles and pegs put in them. With these pegs the shingles were hung on the lath, and the holes and pegs covered so completely that no one would know at a distance that the shingles were not nailed on. The outside [topmost?] course of shingles was generally nailed, and then one course bound another, until the whole roof was solid and good; never leaking one drop. The shingles were generally made of white oak, and lasted many years."

[7] Quoted in Peterson, *Colonial St. Louis*, p. 20, n. 7.

[8] ". . . galleries . . . are not costly but of great utility since they preserve and embellish the building" (report of Governor Vaudreuil, New Orleans, Apr. 28, 1753, in Leonard V. Huber and Samuel Wilson, Jr., *Baroness Pontalba's Buildings* [New Orleans, 1964], p. 12).

[9] This copper plate, no. 21, was bound with Georges Henri Victor Collot, *A Journey in North America* (Paris, 1826). Presumably it was executed from a field sketch by Charles Joseph Warin, the young engineer who accompanied Collot to St. Louis in 1796.

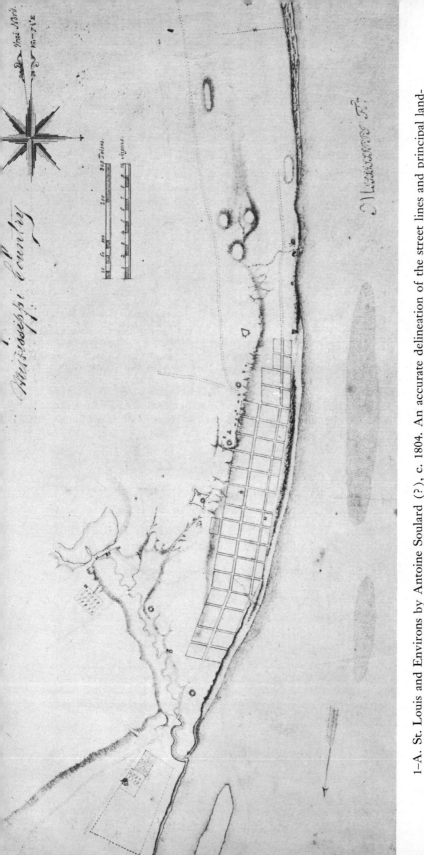

1–A. St. Louis and Environs by Antoine Soulard (?), c. 1804. An accurate delineation of the street lines and principal landmarks near the town. The latter are mainly the remnants of fortifications minus the enclosing stockade which had disintegrated a few years earlier. (*Corps of Engineers, U.S. Army, Washington.*)

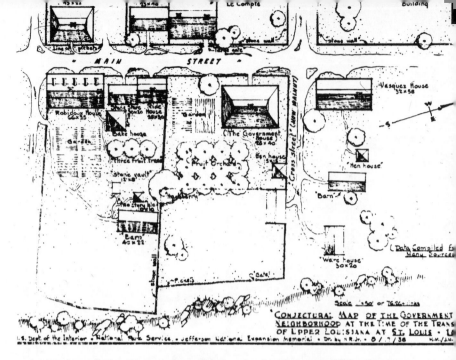

1–B. Setting of the Government House, St. Louis, 1804. This plotting of house, outbuildings, and enclosures shows how the town lots had been developed between the principal street and the river bluff after forty years. It was painstakingly compiled from documentary sources to guide diorama makers in portraying the formal act of transfer of upper Louisiana to the Americans. (*Drawing by Henry Rice, Jr.*)

1–C. *Logement* of Dumont de Montigny, New Orleans, Before 1744. An enclosing stockade was required for all dwellings in the towns as a protection against Indians. Montigny's improvements, shown in this sketch by his own hand, included the *maison principalle*, an outside kitchen with slave quarters and an oven, a *pavillion*, a ladder by which the chickens could reach the tree for the night, and various landscape features, including two gardens. (*Ayer Collection, Newberry Library.*)

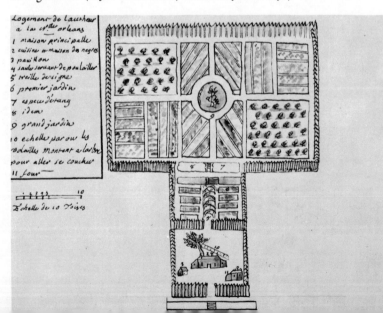

1–D. Palisade Enclosure, St. Louis or St. Charles, Missouri, 1818. House lots, or *emplacements*, in the Illinois Country villages were customarily enclosed by *pieux debouts*. These were easy to build but difficult to maintain unless made of rot-resisting mulberry or cedar. (*Sketch by Maria von Phul. Missouri Historical Society.*)

1–E. Palisade Enclosure, Shoal River House, 1889. Example of a palisade with sharpened stakes, a type of fortification used by the American Indian even before the coming of the white man. This was a Hudson's Bay Company post at Swan Lake in the far North. (*Photograph by J. B. Tyrrell. Geological Survey of Canada.*)

2–A. French Habitation in the Illinois Country, 1796. General Georges Henri Victor Collot visited the West in 1796 with a young "subengineer" Charles Warin, who made topographical records. It is presumably on one of these that Tardieu l'aine based this engraving published in Collot's *Journey* thirty years later. The vertical *poteaux en terre* should have been spaced somewhat apart; this was probably a misinterpretation of the field sketch. (*Collection of the writer.*)

2–B. Typical *Poteaux en Terre* House (Front). This scale model, made by National Park Service museum preparators from drawings furnished by the writer, may be examined at the Jefferson National Expansion Memorial, St. Louis. The *poteaux en terre* of the main walls along with typical French roof trusses, are revealed in the cutaway portion. (*National Park Service photograph.*)

2–C. Typical *Poteaux en Terre* House (Rear). When plastered over and whitewashed—as these houses usually were—they were almost impossible to distinguish from stone structures. The doors are glazed and the windows casement style, both closed with board shutters. (*National Park Service photograph.*)

3–A. The Giroux House, Charlebourg, P.Q., 1939. Here is an almost perfect specimen of a very old French Canadian frame with a shingled pavilion roof. The nearly vertical slopes at the ends are topped with little finials covering a vulnerable point in the shingling. The high plate of the main frame makes for low seated dormers. (*Author.*)

3–B. "Chouteau's Fort," Bonfils, Missouri. This rather mysterious country house in St. Louis County was demolished about 1903. It had typical lines as to roof and *galerie*. The dormers were probably later additions. (*Old photograph by Goebels of St. Charles. Missouri Historical Society.*)

3–C. Louisiana-Type House, St. Moc, P.Q., 1939. The low-pitch hip roof and the *galerie* indicate a southern inspiration for this St. Lawrence Valley specimen. (*Author.*)

3–D. Derivation of the Typical Illinois Country Roof Lines. The pavilion roof of France and Canada with a light gallery wrapped around it produced the characteristic Illinois Country forms. (*From Charles E. Peterson, "Early Ste. Genevieve and Its Architecture,"* The Missouri Historical Review, *XXXV* [*Jan., 1941*], 227.)

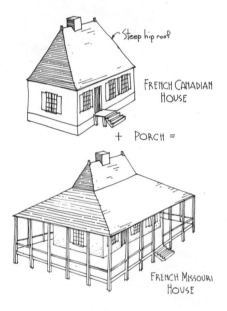

3–E. Chief Factor's Quarters, Norway House, Manitoba, 1890. Another example of the Louisiana influence with hipped roof and *galerie*, in this case at a northern fur-trading post. (*Photograph by J. B. Tyrrell. Geological Survey of Canada.*)

4–A. Remains of the Jacques Noisé House. The plaster has fallen from these walls (built before 1780) revealing the vertical posts—round in the earth and hewn flat above grade. The pavilion roof and neat limestone chimneys remain, although the galleries have been torn away. Alexander McNair, an early Missouri governor, lived here. (*Old photograph. Missouri Historical Society.*)

4–B. Remains of the Bienvenue House, 1870. Built in 1786, the house, when photographed, had already lost its tall roof and *galerie*. The *poteaux en terre*, clearly visible, were *pierrottée*, or filled in between with stone and mortar. Some latter-day patching with brick is also evident. (*Photograph by E. Boehl. Missouri Historical Society.*)

5–A. Dodier-Sarpy House. The roof *galerie* and chimney of this little frame house, believed to have been built in 1766, are characteristic of the Illinois Country. The gabled wing on the right is probably a kitchen of the Anglo-American period. (*Old daguerreotype. Missouri Historical Society.*)

5–B. Lorraine-Lisa House. This record was made while the main roof remained but the gallery had been torn away. The double glazed doors are typically French, but the double hung sash show Anglo-American influence. (*Old photograph. Missouri Historical Society.*)

6–A. Laclède-Chouteau House, 1841. Erected at the first founding of the town in 1764, this great stone house served as the headquarters for Maxent, Laclède and Co's fur-trading operations. Late in the eighteenth century it was remodeled for the use of merchant Auguste Chouteau. (*J. Child lithograph. Missouri Historical Society.*)

6–B. Pierre Chouteau House. This great eighteenth-century stone house with two-story gallery rivaled the plantation houses of lower Louisiana which it resembled. A fur trader's house (1785?), like that of brother Auguste Chouteau, it was surrounded by a stone wall. (*Old painting. Missouri Historical Society.*)

7–A. The Robidoux-Sanguinet-Benoist House. On the left overlooking the river may be seen the stone house of Joseph Robidoux, a fur trader from Montreal originally. The design of the chimney tops, the casement windows (dimly seen), and the front gallery betray the presence of an old French house surrounded by later additions. (*Old photograph. Missouri Historical Society.*)

7–B. The Robidoux-Sanguinet-Benoist House. In this view little more than the chimney tops can be seen of the original house, but the unique two-story bakehouse with pyramidal roof is clearly revealed in the rear. (*Old photograph. Missouri Historical Society.*)

8–A. Bequette-Ribault House, 1937. The red cedar logs of the main walls are hewn flat above grade but left in the round below. Through the years the clay *bousillage* has been tunneled by wasps. (*Author.*)

8–B. St. Gemme-Beauvais House, 1939. Here the logs are filled in with a *pierrotage* of stone and lime mortar. (*Author.*)

8–C. St. Gemme-Amoreaux House, 1937. Underneath the gallery—and beneath the finish of hand-split lath and plaster—may be seen the *poteaux en terre*. (*Author.*)

9–A. Cahokia Courthouse, Cahokia, Illinois, Before 1893. The low-seated French frame, *pierrottée*, shows clearly in this view made before it was disassembled and moved to the 1893 World's Fair in Chicago. Thought to date from the mid-eighteenth century and associated with the Lapancé and Saucier families it became a courthouse under the American regime of the 1790's. (*Missouri Historical Society*.)

9–B. Bolduc House, Ste. Genevieve, Missouri. This view shows the house as recently restored by the National Society of the Colonial Dames in Missouri and surrounded by a palisade in the eighteenth-century manner. A similar restoration in diorama form was made several years earlier and may be seen in St. Louis at the museum of the Jefferson National Expansion Memorial. (*Courtesy Colonial Dames*.)

9–C. Guibourd House, Ste. Genevieve, Missouri. Like most of the old French houses in Ste. Genevieve this one had undergone modernization at various times with weather boarding and double-hung, windows. Especially notable in this house were the original casement windows on the rear and the Norman roof trusses. (*Old photograph. Missouri Historical Society.*)

9–D. Pierre Menard House, Kaskaskia, Illinois. Only because it was located on high ground, the Menard House survived the river which destroyed the old town. Built around the year 1800, this house is a transitional hybrid combining a French frame and gallery with Anglo-American trim. (*Old photograph. Missouri Historical Society.*)

10-B. St. Gemme-Amoreaux House, Ste. Genevieve. (*Author, 1937.*)

10-A. Bolduc House, Ste. Genevieve. (*Author, 1937.*)

10. Roof Framing, Illinois Country. These four examples of Norman-Canadian trusses embellish attics where they are seldom seen. Dormer windows seem to have been rare, if they were used at all. The attics, unfinished and unheated, were used only for storage.

10–C. Jacques Guibourd House, Ste. Genevieve. (*Author, 1937.*)

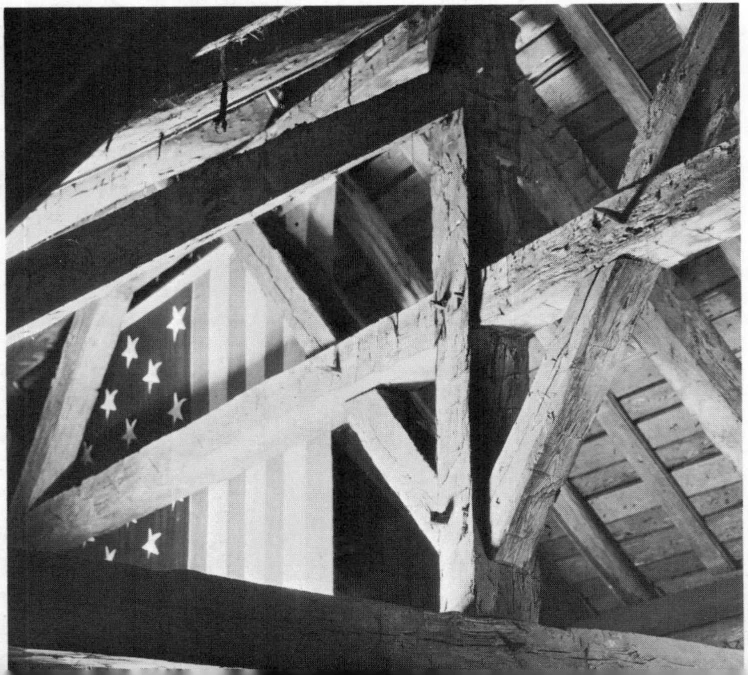

10–D. French Trusses, n.a. (Recueil de Planches de l'Enclycopedie, *Paris, 1783, Plate 3, except as noted.*)

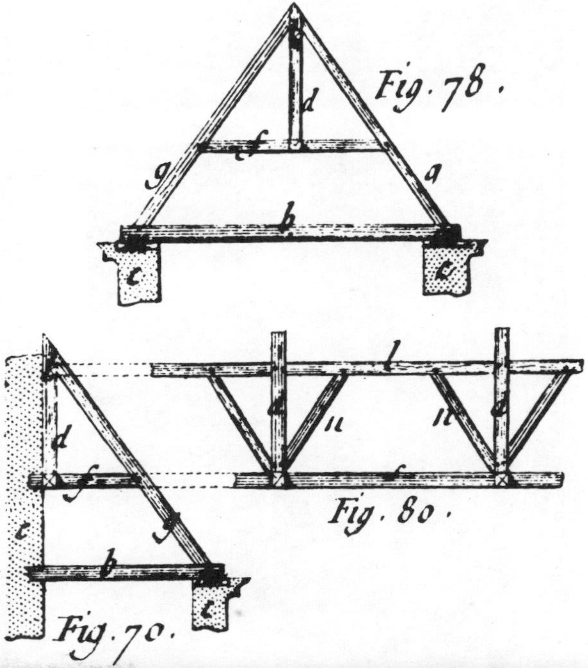
Fig. 78.
d
f
g
a
b
c
c
l
n
n
d
f
g
b
c
c
Fig. 80.
Fig. 70.

11–A. Bolduc House, Ste. Genevieve, Missouri, 1937. In the south frame the *poteaux* are spiked to the plate and filled in with *bousillage*. Note unique log floor. (*Author.*)

11–B. Lamarque House, Old Mines, Missouri, 1937. Here the *poteaux* are mortised and pegged to the plate. Sides of posts hacked to retain bousillage. (*Author.*)

11–C. Herbst House, Florissant, Missouri, 1937. Above the puncheon floor of the attic may be seen the *poteaux* as they meet the plate. The stone filling is loose; perhaps it was laid in mud which has leached out. (*Author.*)

11–D. Boyd House, Ste. Genevieve, Missouri, 1937. Here we see one wall remaining from a house being demolished. Its crude workmanship of round logs probably indicates a late date and the decay of early French craftsmanship.

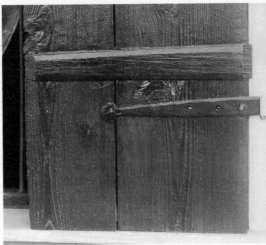

12–A. Casement Windows, Guibourd House, Ste. Genevieve, Missouri, 1937. Casements *swinging in* on hinges are typical of French buildings generally; this house has the only remaining examples in the Illinois Country. The type was early superceded by double-hung sash. (*Author.*)

12–B. Shutter Details, Bequette-Ribault House, Ste. Genevieve, Missouri, 1937. Board shutters swinging outward are held together by a dovetailed and tapered batton made in the Continental manner. The strap hinge, swinging on a pintle driven into the window frame, could be Anglo-American. (*Author.*)

12–C. Some Door Latches. All old French door latches the writer has found in the Illinois Country are of a type called a "single cusp Suffolk latch" by Albert H. Sonn, *Early American Wrought Iron* (New York, 1928), I, 27, plates 18, 81. These may well be imports from Continental Europe. (*Drawing by Frank R. Leslie. National Park Service.*)

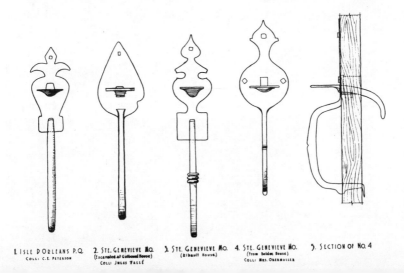

1. ISLE D'ORLEANS P.Q.
COLL: C.E. PETERSON
2. STE. GENEVIEVE MO.
(Excavated at Guibourd House)
COLL: JULES VALLÉ
3. STE. GENEVIEVE MO.
(Ribault House)
4. STE. GENEVIEVE MO.
(from Solder House)
COLL: MRS. OBERMULLER
5. SECTION OF NO. 4

13–A. Leveau House, Chenal, Louisiana, c. 1919. This frame house, recently demolished, was set up on cypress blocks but otherwise resembled contemporary houses on the middle Mississippi. Note swirling of the shingles at the roof hips. (*Photograph. Courtesy Owner Leveau, 1938.*)

13–B. "Lafitte's Blacksmith Shop," New Orleans, 1938. Fires caused great losses of New Orleans houses late in the eighteenth century, and few early ones are left. This low frame building is one of the better examples in the Vieux Carré. It is believed to have been built after 1781 by Simon Durocher. (*Author.*)

13–C. Nogging Detail, "Lafitte's Blacksmith Shop," 1938. Revealed where the plaster finish has fallen off is the brick "nogging" which prevented vermin from living in the walls and had value as fireproofing and insulation. The Louisiana term for this was *"briquetée entre poteaux."* (*Author.*)

13–D. Bousillage Detail, Old Frame Cabin, vicinity, Paincourtville, Louisiana, 1938. Horizontal sticks were let into the upright timbers and then *bousillée.* The mixture was made of mud and Spanish moss (*barbe espagnol*) and whitewashed for cleanliness and appearance. (*Author.*)

14–A. Indian Post House, Hispaniola, Sixteenth Century. This lithographic view of a typical Indian house in Hispaniola was published in Oviedo y Valdes, *Historia General y Natural de las Indias* (Madrid, 1851), vol. I. It is thought to have been derived from a field sketch by Oviedo himself. This writer believes that the representation is out of drawing; among other things the main posts are far too heavy. It does show, however, curtain walls of light poles, probably bound with vines, and a thatched hip roof, probably covered with palmetto. (*University of Pennsylvania Museum.*)

14–B. Post Houses, Turn Bull Pen, Jamaica, 1933. Posts in the ground with curtain walls of whitewashed daub-and-wattle, the whole thatched with palm fronds, make up a house widely typical of the Caribbean. (*Author.*)

14–C. Post Houses near Gonaïve, Haiti, 1961. Much like the Jamaica houses, the thatched post house is still built generally in North Haiti by descendants of French slaves. (*Author*.)

14–D. Old House in Port-au-Prince, Haiti, 1961. Except for the huge dormer (probably for admitting goods to be stored in the attic and of a design common in the early Danish houses of St. Croix), this house would have been much at home in the Illinois Country. (*Author*.)

15–A. "VEUË DU CAMP DE LA CONCESSION DE MONSEI-GNEUR LAW," New Biloxi, 1720. This portion of a manuscript drawing of Jean Baptiste Michel Bouteux depicts various provisional structures at the new settlement on the Gulf. Their construction appears to be of *poteaux en terre* as described in contemporary Louisiana documents. (*Ayer Collection, Newberry Library.*)

15–B. A *Jacal*, or Mexican Hut, San Antonio, Texas. Palisadoed house walls were not uncommon in nineteenth-century Texas buildings and may have been a heritage from the local Indians. One or more of these structures still stands in San Antonio. (*Old photograph. Courtesy Marvin Eichenroht, AIA.*)

15–C. House at Plaisance (Placentia) Newfoundland, Before 1722. A house of *piquets* typical of the early fishing settlements at Placentia harbor. A sheep is grazing on the moss-covered roof. (*La Potherie*, Voyage de l'Amérique, *1723. Public Archives of Canada.*)

15–D. Unidentified Structure at Louisbourg, Cape Breton Island, 1740. From a facsimile of a watercolor signed "Verrier," this is a portion of an engineer's cross-section of the harbor beach. Lack of cross bracing has made buttresses necessary. (*Public Archives of Canada.*)

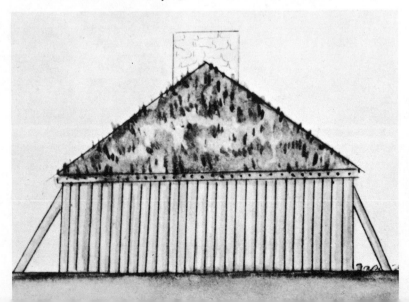

16–A. Farm House near Foulbec, 1938. The upright posts in the Illinois Country buildings are spaced like those of Normandy from which the technique came via Canada. In the New World such structural members were covered over; here they are exposed for decorative effect. (*Author.*)

16–B. City-Type Houses, Rouen, 1938. Here the similar framing is employed in multistory buildings. Where the plaster has fallen off, the packing of stone (*pierrotage*) is clearly seen. (*Author.*)

fying widths varying from four to nine feet. The ends of these were sometimes enclosed, as Robin noted, and combined with the lean-to, or *appentis,* found on many houses. The roof form of these galleried houses was distinctive and attractive (Illus. 2A, 3B). Some examples found in eastern and northern Canada show that the idea had spread from the tropics where it originated to points far beyond the Illinois Country (Illus. 3C, D).

The thatching of roofs was common in France and Canada, and in 1710 we find that all the buildings in Detroit were covered with grass.[10] Documents of fifteen years later show that the houses at La Balise at the mouth of the Mississippi,[11] the new houses of Kaskaskia,[12] and the hut of the Sieur de Bourgmond at his little fort far up the Missouri River[13] were similarly roofed (*couverte en paille*). As late as 1798 the St. Louis archives mention a man "to cut straw for roofing,"[14] and John Reynolds wrote that thatching was common across the river as late as his time: "The covering of the houses, stables, &c., was generally of straw, or long grass cut in the prairie. These thatched roofs looked well, and lasted longer than shingles. They were made steep and neat."[15] Thatching continued in use at Prairie du Chien, Wisconsin, until an ordinance was passed against it in 1822.[16] It could still be seen on a few barns along the St. Lawrence as late as 1939. In St. Louis it was used for the roofing of the very first huts but was relegated to barns and other outbuildings in later

[10] "Cadillac Papers," *Michigan Pioneer and Historical Society, Reports and Collections,* XXXIII (1903), 494.

[11] "PLAN DU FORT DE L'ISLE DE LA BALISE" annotated ground plan *c.* 1726 at the Newberry Library, Chicago, cataloged "Carte Marine #83, Sec. 2."

[12] Chester, Illinois, Randolph County Courthouse, *Kaskaskia Manuscripts.* These were microfilmed by Historian Edward A. Hummel of the National Park Service, Omaha, for the writer. Many house descriptions beginning in the 1720's are scattered through these papers.

[13] Paris, Archives Nationales, *Colonies, C13C, 4:117–125 I.*

[14] St. Louis, City Hall, *Recorded Archives* (MS) (hereafter *STLRA*), IV:2, 266.

[15] *Old Cahokia,* ed. McDermott, p. 45.

[16] ". . . there shall be no houses or other buildings covered with straw in the village south of Fort Crawford and if any so covered the covering shall be taken off on or before the first day of September next, or the owner thereof shall pay a fine of five dollars for every week the straw is permitted to remain thereon" (By-Laws Enacted and Passed by the Warden and Burgesses for the Borough of Prairie des Chiens this 20th day of March 1822 [typescript courtesy of Dr. Peter L. Scanlan]).

years. It was a makeshift at best and a great fire hazard in the dry air of the Midwest.

Shingles (*bardeaux*) were easily available in North America where there was plenty of straight-grained wood from which to make them. In St. Louis they were the most popular roofing material. Both split and sawn types were used and they were fastened down either with shingle nails (*clous à bardeaux*) or wooden pegs (*à cheville*).

*La Nouvelle Maison Rustique*, a popular reference book for the gentleman farmer of the eighteenth century, stated that shingles (*bardeaux*) were used in France "where tile is scarce and wood is common" and points out that their light weight would effect a saving in roof framing.[17] The abundant timber of the New World encouraged their use; Father Charlevoix, arriving from France in 1720, remarked upon the prevalence of shingle-covered roofs in Canada; the slated Jesuits' church at Quebec was the only building he noted which did not use them.[18] Although prohibited by fire ordinances,[19] they continued in general use. In 1734 the Abbé Navières stated that, with three or four exceptions, Quebec buildings were still roofed with "wood cut in the fashion of slate."[20]

Shingles of that time were much like those of today. Knives for splitting them are mentioned in lists of tools;[21] they were probably like the iron "frow" of the Anglo-American builder driven by a club. The rough shingle was then held on a "horse"[22] while it was dressed. Thirty blocks (*billes*) of oak for making shingles are mentioned in the Ste. Genevieve archives.[23]

Bark was sometimes used for temporary roofs. For example, one

---

[17] *La Nouvelle Maison Rustique* (anon.) (4th ed., Paris, 1786), I, 37.

[18] P. F. X. Charlevoix, *Letters to the Duchess of Lesdiguières* (London, 1763), p. 23.

[19] Pierre-Georges Roy, *La Ville de Québec sous le régime français* (Quebec, 1930), II, 242.

[20] Roy, *La Ville de Québec*, II, 137.

[21] For 1770 see *STLRA*, III:2, 357. For 1793, *STLRA*, V:1, 78–83.

[22] Henry C. Mercer, *Ancient Carpenters' Tools* (Doylestown, Pa., 1929), pp. 11–14.

[23] Missouri Historical Society, *Deeds*, #29. The rough split shingles were probably smoothed with a drawknife. Original examples preserved on two old French houses, the Dubreuil house at Quebec (built 1719) and the Pierre Menard house near Kaskaskia (built *c.* 1800), have their butts beveled. This is likewise true of eighteenth-century Philadelphia shingles (illustrated, Mercer, *Ancient Carpenters' Tools*, p. 17).

St. Louis kitchen had such a covering (*couvert d'écorse*) in 1785[24] and so had a barn in 1799.[25] *Merrains* were also used for roofing toward the close of the eighteenth century. They were probably either clapboards or the long, riven "shakes" of the Anglo-American frontiersman. The early St. Louis translators thought they were the former. That they were not shingles is shown by the following excerpt from the records describing: ". . . a house of posts in the ground thirty feet by twenty, floored above and below, covered with shingles [*bardeaux*], with a penthouse also of posts in the ground and covered with clapboards [*merrains*]. . . ."[26]

## DOORS AND WINDOWS

Specifications for construction in this period show that most houses had two doors—allowing for one on the street and one opening on the yard in the rear. The type of door generally used is not known. An old photograph of the Lorraine-Lisa house (Illus. 5B) shows that it had double-glazed "French" doors, but it was probably not a typical house.[27] The fact that when the villages across the river were abandoned the first St. Louis settlers salvaged the doors and windows for their new settlement suggests they were well made and better than the home-made doors generally used by the Anglo-American pioneer in the West.

From the records, the average house had four windows. Ordinarily these seem to have been glazed. The French colonies in both Canada and Louisiana had imported window glass from their earliest days, and even remote St. Louis seems to have had it available most of the time. By 1798 it was a regular article of trade with Clamorgan, Loisel & Co., and in 1802 the Cerré estate had a large quantity on hand, both in boxes and ready-set in sash. These would normally have been hinged casements, single or double. Two pairs of twelve light sash could still be seen in the Guibourd house in Ste. Genevieve

---

[24] *STLRA*, I:1, 122. The Grignon house at Green Bay, Wisconsin, was covered with many layers of white cedar (*Thuja*) bark (*Wisconsin Historical Society Proceedings*, 1912, p. 181). The bark of the paper birch (*Betula*) was commonly used in Canada in all periods.

[25] *STLRA*, I:2, 392.

[26] *STLRA*, V:1, 189–193.

[27] The writer has noted that exterior doors with some glass in them are notably favored in many old Franco-American communities even though no very old examples have survived.

a few years ago (Illus. 12A). These sash were protected by shutters (*contrevents*) of solid wood swinging outward against the walls of the building. The old shutters on the Ribault house in the same town, with their typical wedged and pegged battens, resemble those of continental Europe rather than those of Anglo-America or England (Illus. 12B).

The house exteriors had little paint but were much brightened by the use of whitewash (*eau de chaux* or *lait de chaux*) burned from the local limestone.

Of the interiors of these houses we know very little. Only one floor plan has been preserved—a crude sketch of the upper floor of the Auguste Chouteau mansion, which shows it to have had a large central room (probably called *la salle*) and small rooms or *petites chambres* opening off at the four corners, a floor plan familiar to those of Louisiana. In the building contracts that have been found the ceiling height as specified averaged eight feet. The amount of interior woodwork used for decorative effect is hard to estimate. The joiners in the village could have made fine paneling from the local walnut (excellent examples can still be found in Canada), but a few wooden mantelpieces and one corner cupboard are the only items mentioned in the archives. Ceilings were normally of exposed joists revealing floorboards above and the walls were plastered and whitewashed. Floor surfaces varied from the bare earth to highly polished walnut boards. Furniture was listed in quantity and variety in the many household inventories which have been preserved.

## DEPENDENCIES AND ENCLOSURES

Real estate documents often name the outbuildings which stood on the same lots or *emplacements* to serve these houses. For instance, a warranty deed for Nicolas Barsalou's small frame house on a standard-sized lot, included a thatched barn (*grange*), an old outside kitchen (*cuisine*) with a built-in oven (*four*), a hen house (*poulailler*), and a small milk house (*laiterie*). The whole, enclosed by a fence of channeled oak posts, was divided into yard and garden. Louis Perrault's large stone house on a double lot had a separate building serving as a kitchen, another large building at one gable end of the house divided into a shed (*engard*) and storehouse (*magasin*), together with an outdoor oven, latrine, and other useful items. There were also a large garden and orchard (*verger*) of fruit trees, the whole enclosed with a cedar and oak post fence. In such groups there might also be found a granary, stable (*étable*), slave quarters (*cabane à nègre*), pigsty (*cochonniere*), pigeon house (*pigeonnier*), outside cellar (*caveau*), or a well (*puits*). But in all cases the house remained the place of business as well as of residence, and it dominated the village landscape.

The streets were laid out at right angles, as was customary under Spanish authority, and they divided the town into standard blocks of 240 by 300 feet, French measure (Illus. 1A). These in turn were divided into four equal building lots, or *emplacements*, each 120 by 150 feet.

It was customary for each owner to enclose his lot with palisadoes, called at the time *pieux en terre* (stakes in earth) or *pieux debout* (stakes upright). This was an old practice among the French in these frontier towns. When New Orleans was laid out it was ordered that all of the property holders *"must have their houses or land enclosed by palisades within two months or else they will be deprived of their property and it will revert to the company. . . ."* A similar practice was followed in the early villages of the upper Mississippi, including Kaskaskia and Ste. Geneviève. The advantage of having all the private lots enclosed is obvious. By merely barricading the ends of the streets in an emergency it would be possible to have a continuous enclosure all around the village for defense. In any case fences were needed to keep out domestic animals and, being hard to climb, they afforded a measure of privacy and of discouragement to visiting Indians who were often drunk and troublesome. While the enclosure of individual lots is not positively known to have been compulsory at St. Louis, it was required by the 1767 instructions for establishing the settlement at the mouth of the Missouri: "Outside the houses must run an encircling pointed fence, which will be constructed by each owner at his own expense, in order to prevent the savages from making any sudden rush at night and surprising them."[28]

These stockades were preferably made of mulberry or cedar posts, but oak and other woods were also used. There was also in use the channeled post (*poteau cannelé*) fence usually of mulberry posts and cottonwood boards. Several of the more pretentious residences were surrounded by stone walls, sometimes with loopholes for de-

---

[28] *The Spanish Regime*, ed. Houck, I, 16.

fense (Illus. 6A, B). The records make it clear that these enclosures were used until the end of the colonial period, though not always maintained in good condition.

The palisade fences required an enormous amount of wood and were continually in need of replacements which became more difficult as the nearby forests were used up. There are none standing today, but examples are illustrated in Dumont de Montigny's early eighteenth-century drawings of settlements along the Mississippi (Illus. 1C).[29] The von Phul sketches include two examples in St. Louis or St. Charles in 1818 (Illus. 1D).[30] A photograph of a Hudson Bay post at Swan Lake in the Far North shows this type of enclosure used there as late as 1889 (Illus. 1E).[31]

## WALL CONSTRUCTION: THE PALISADOED WALL

One of the most notable and basic features of the Illinois Country buildings was their wall construction, and the remainder of this essay will examine that subject. The several types used were distinctively French, and they were almost always specified in contemporary documents. There were four general categories which are listed here in order of numbers, the most common first. They were (1) the palisadoed wall, (2) the stone masonry wall, (3) the framed wall, and (4) the wall of horizontal logs.

Fortunately, from a relatively early date, the French records were fairly explicit about the type of construction used. For instance, in the Ayer Collection at the Newberry Library, Chicago, there is a professionally drawn and annotated plan of about 1726 which locates the wooden buildings at La Balise, a post at the mouth of the Mississippi. It distinguishes each type of construction rather precisely. At La Balise there were, first, the frame building (*en bonne charpente sur sole*, literally of good carpentry on a sill) which included the church, the commandant's house, a kitchen, a guard-house, one barracks, two dwellings, and a pigeon house. Second, there was the structure of posts in the ground (*poteaux en terre*) which included one other quarters structure, a temporary powder house of cypress posts, a hen house, and another building. The posts

---

[29] Originals in the Ayer Collection, Newberry Library, Chicago.
[30] Reproduced in Charles van Ravenswaay, "Anna Maria von Phul," *Missouri Historical Society Bulletin*, X (Apr., 1954), opp. p. 368.
[31] Public Archives of Canada, Ottawa.

of these were probably hewn neatly to allow a good exterior finish like the framed houses. Last of all were the lowly structures of unhewn round posts or stakes (*pieux en terre*) which included twenty-three small *barraques* and a shed. Fortunately for the architectural historian, such distinctions were carried, with some variations, up through the rest of Louisiana and appeared in the records of colonial St. Louis.

As an economical construction type the *poteaux en terre* wall came into general use throughout the Illinois Country. In the year 1723 we have records of two houses built as far apart as Kaskaskia (founded 1703) on the Mississippi River and the Fort d'Orléans well up the Missouri. The former was a house twenty-two by thirty feet built by François la Plume for the Lieutenant Pierre Melique;[32] the latter, a crude hut in a temporary fort described by the Sieur de Bourgmond as: ". . . a house of round posts in the ground [*pieux en terre*] and not framed [*de charpente*]—without ceiling, floor, or chimney—the fire being made in the middle of the floor Indian fashion and a roof of grass supported on rafters just as God grew them in the woods, being neither squared nor finished."[33]

One of the better types of palisadoed house was illustrated by General Collot as typical of the Illinois Country. Although the construction procedure was never described, to this writer's knowledge, the walls had to be built by first digging a trench and standing the logs upright in it a few inches apart. These were then fastened at the top by a plate and the trench backfilled with earth. The interstices between the posts were filled in with mud and grass (*bousillée*) (Illus. 11A, B) or with mortar and stone (*pierrottée*) (Illus. 8B, 11C).[34]

Specifications have been preserved describing these houses. In a St. Louis contract dated April 23, 1768, Peter Tousignan bound himself to build a *poteaux en terre* house for Surgeon Jean B. Valleau of the Spanish service. This house was to be fourteen by eighteen feet (outside measure) of round oak logs with an interior partition of small squared posts. The house was to be well floored and ceiled with hewn cottonwood planks (*madriers de liard, équarés à la hache*)

---

[32] Natalia Maree Belting, *Kaskaskia Under the French Regime* (Urbana, Ill., 1948), p. 33. The house had floors, three doors, and a gallery.

[33] Paris, Archives Nationales, *Colonies, C13C, 4:117–125 I.*

[34] In Louisiana locally available materials for this kind of work were mud and Spanish moss or brick and mortar. An oyster shell cement was sometimes used on the Gulf coast.

with butt joints (*à joints quarres*). Two doors, two windows, and two pairs of shutters were specified. The builder was required to furnish all the ironwork (*ferrures*) and nails needed; the consideration was sixty hard dollars.[35]

Some of the better-built houses were entirely of mulberry logs (*Morus rubra*) which the French called *mûrier*. Others had mulberry only for the principal posts—those at the corners and alongside doors and windows—such as the house of Louis Lambert, built 1769. Red cedar (*Juniperus virginiana*) was also highly thought of for its rot-resisting qualities.

Two St. Louis examples, the Jacques Noisé house (built before 1780) (Illus. 4A) and the Bienvenue house (built 1786) (Illus. 4B), stood until the age of photography. In a ruined state, their wall construction is clearly revealed. There are still three remaining in old Ste. Geneviève: the Bequette-Ribault, the St. Gemme-Amoreaux and St. Gemme-Beauvais houses (Illus. 8A, B, C). The latter all seem to date from the eighteenth century and owe their existence to having been built of rot-resisting red cedar.[36]

The writer has retraced French colonization back through the Gulf coast settlements with still incomplete but promising results. Dumont de Montigny, who spent several years on the lower Mississippi, left us the best account of the type in the early part of the eighteenth century:

In regard to cabins; they do not require much craftsmanship and their method of construction is very quick. First one takes as many poles [*perches*] or forked logs [*fourches*] as are judged appropriate to the length and width desired for the cabin. These forked logs ought to be at least a dozen feet long. They are planted in the ground at regular intervals two and a half feet deep and joined together by plates [*traverses*] laid on top. Thus is formed a rectangle of which the short sides make the width of the cabin, taking the place of a gable. In the middle of the two short sides, one raises two other forked poles to the height of sixteen to eighteen feet on which is placed the ridgepole [*faite*] to which are nailed the rafters, the latter being properly spaced and falling on the plates to which they are also nailed. The framework [*carcasse*] of the cabin is thus raised. It is closed in with cypress stakes [*pieux*] driven a foot into the

---

[35] *STLRA*, IV:3, 525.

[36] These three houses were described and illustrated in Charles E. Peterson, "Early Ste. Geneviève and Its Architecture," *The Missouri Historical Review*, XXXV (Jan., 1941), 223–227. The first was measured for the Historic American Buildings Survey in 1938 and the second about 1957.

The lack of land title data for Ste. Geneviève houses makes it impossible to trace their origins with certainty.

ground and fastened above to the plates [*traverses*] with nails, allowing for doors and windows in the walls. Finally it is covered, as I have said, with cypress bark or palmetto [? *lantanier*] leaves and, *voila*, a cabin has been built. One can see that in a country as well wooded as Louisiana there should be no difficulty of procuring shelter since one can build a house in twenty-four hours.[37]

Montigny, by his own account, was describing a hasty type of construction for a warm climate. The *poteaux en terre* wall construction of the Illinois Country was closely related but detailed in a sturdier way for permanent buildings and reflecting the background of Canadian housewrights who had to build against heavy winters.

The first more or less permanent French settlements on the Gulf coast were Biloxi (1699 and 1710) and New Orleans (1718). Here again the founders were of mixed origin, including Canadians. The typical house was one of *poteaux en terre*, pine logs being used at Biloxi and cypress at New Orleans (Illus. 15A).

## POST HOUSES IN THE CARIBBEAN

It is possible that the *poteaux en terre* wall construction of St. Louis ultimately came from the shores of the Caribbean or the Gulf of Mexico. Post houses were customarily built by the natives in those tropics,[38] and there is still a widespread survival of examples on the islands from Curaçao to Jamaica and Haiti, especially in territory developed by the French. In most places this peculiar type of construction is rapidly disappearing, but over a period of thirty years I have photographed examples on a number of islands. The best place to see them now is on the north coast of Haiti, where the descendants of slaves still build much as they did two centuries ago (Illus. 14B, C). A closely related structure of Mayan origin is still being built on the Yucatán peninsula.

Among the aborigines the relatively peaceful Arawak-speaking Indians seem to have characteristically built the more permanent

---

[37] Jean François Benjamin Dumont de Montigny, *Mémoires historiques sur la Louisiane* (Paris, 1753), II, 64. The manuscript of this work is preserved in the Ayer Collection, Newberry Library, Chicago. It bears the title *Mémoire de Lxx Dxx officier ingenieur, contenant les evenements qui sont passés à la Louisiane depuis 1715 jusqua présent,* [1747] etc.

[38] The evidences of prehistoric times uncovered by archaeological investigators and the contemporary descriptions and artists' views that we have inherited from the first contacts of the white man are far from complete in the matter of detail.

houses (Illus. 14A). The Caribs, warlike and nomadic, did not produce substantial dwellings.[39]

The white man built post houses in the New World from an
early date. The Spanish planted their first settlements during the time
of Columbus. Theodor de Bry, *Americae pars quinta* (Frankfurt am
Main, 1595), illustrates a scene in which Diego de Nicuesa's expedition of 1509 is building thatched houses on the shores of the Isthmus
of Panama. The roofs are clearly supported on posts in the ground,
but the construction is sturdy in contrast with the Indian houses
standing nearby. The same author in *Indiorum Floridam provinciam
inhabitantium eicones* (Frankfurt am Main, 1591), after a Jacques le
Moyne drawing, illustrates a somewhat similar house being erected at
Fort Caroline on the Florida coast by the ill-fated Huguenot expedition of 1564.[40]

The Spanish used post construction in Jamaica before they
ceded that fine island to the English in 1655. Sir Hans Sloane noted it
was used there in order to withstand earthquakes.[41] Edward Long
writing later left us more detail: ". . . a certain number of posts of
the hardest timber, generally *lignum vitae*, brazilletto, or fustick, of

---

[39] Irving Rouse, Yale archaeologist, wrote that the Arawaks in Hispaniola
(the western part of which was St. Domingue—modern Haiti) built two
typical dwelling types—a small round hut with a conical roof and the *bohio*,
a rectangular gabled house supported by posts in the ground. He reprinted the
illustration from Oviedo y Valdes, *Historia general y natural de las Indias*
(Madrid, 1851), I. The author of the latter died in 1557; just how reliable was
the 1851 lithograph would be difficult to say. But it is one of the few old
illustrations that has turned up and it unmistakably delineates a construction of
posts in the ground.

Rouse, in excavating the villages of these people, did not seem to have
found posthole remains in the earth. His sources were evidently literary rather
than physical. See *Handbook of South American Indians* (Washington, D.C.,
1949), p. 525.

J. Davies, *The History of Barbados, etc.* (London, 1666), p. 292, wrote
that the Indian huts were built of "pieces of wood planted in the ground.
. . . The Caribeans do also make use of small Reeds fasten'd across for the
Palisadoes which are instead of walls to their Habitations." I have not yet found
a really good detailed description of one of these houses.

[40] The accuracy of these illustrations needs to be checked, if that is
possible.

[41] Hans Sloane, *A Voyage to the Islands Madera, Barbados, Nieves, S.
Christophers and Jamaica* (London, 1707), I, xliv, xlvii. Sloane was in Jamaica
in 1687–88.

Captain William Jackson, an English privateer who raided Jamaica in
1640, wrote that the Spanish town houses were "built for ye most part with
Canes, overcast with mortar and lime and covered with Tyle" (Sybil Williams,
"Spanish Town," *The Capitals of Jamaica* [Kingston, 1955], p. 5).

about 18 feet in length and 6 to 8 inches in diameter, being first well-seasoned and hardened in smoke, were fixed at proper distances to the depth of 2 or 3 feet in the ground; then a wall of brick, enclosing these posts, was carried up with very strong mortar to the plate, which was pinned with wooden spikes to the tops of the posts. . . ."[42] This was a *poteaux en terre* type related to the construction of the Illinois Country and of St. Louis.

The French began their settlements at the mouth of the Amazon, spreading northwards via Cayenne, St. Christophe (now St. Kitts), Martinique, St. Martin, and St. Domingue (now Haiti). By 1680 they had substantial colonial populations on all those islands.

Post houses had become the vernacular at Cap François, leading port of St. Domingue, by the end of the seventeenth century. Père Labat, a Dominican visitor of 1701, noted that the town had been burned down twice by the Spaniards and the English shortly before but was soon after rebuilt. ". . . nothing could have been easier because all the houses were built of forked posts in the ground palisadoed or enclosed with split palmetto trunks called in that country palmetto-tails [fourches en terre, palissadées, ou entourées de Palmistes refendus, comme on appellée en ce pais-la les queües ou les guanisnes des Palmistes]."[43] Even the parish church was built that way with the sides consisting of a palisade only breast high. Cap François was already a principal stop for ships on the way to the Louisiana coast. The newer settlements there, as we have seen, were likewise to be built of *poteaux en terre*.[44]

In what is now the United States this type of construction eventually reached as far as Fort Frederica, Oglethorpe's Georgia settlement in the 1730's, and to California in the West.[45] A few

---

[42] Quoted in Frank Cundall, *Historic Jamaica* (London, 1915), p. 8.

[43] Père Labat, *Nouveau voyage aux isles de l'Amérique* (La Haye, 1724), II, 221.

[44] *Baties de palissades*, in old and new Biloxi of pine stakes, in New Orleans of cypress (Dumont de Montigny, *Mémoires historiques*, II, 49). He noted however that at New Orleans they were starting to build brick buildings and frame buildings nogged with brick.

The reports of the engineers in the French colonies are explicitly written and often handsomely illustrated by fine drawings. Eventually the archives of Paris may be expected to yield documents before the year 1700 which will close the gap between the post houses of the Caribbean Indians and the *poteaux en terre* houses of the Louisiana French.

[45] Rexford Newcomb, *The Old Mission Churches and Historic Houses of California* (Philadelphia, 1925), p. 79.

32

specimens were recently standing in San Antonio, Texas (Illus. 15B).[46] None of these, however, had the strong walls of close-set posts as in the Illinois Country. The southern house was essentially a house of widely spaced posts with a curtain wall of wattles, light horizontal or vertical sticks.

PALISADOED HOUSE WALLS IN CANADA

Looking northeast to the chain of French fur-trading and military posts along the Great Lakes we find that the palisadoed house was used at Detroit. An expedition led by the Sieur de la Mothe Cadillac was mounted at Montreal in June, 1701, and established Fort Pontchartrain on the Detroit River that summer. Within the fortification was built a village of houses described as small and of upright stakes plastered with mud and thatched with grass, all but two being of this construction. We must conclude that it was a familiar type in lower Canada.[47]

---

[46] Amos Stoddard, *Sketches, Historical and Descriptive of Louisiana* (Philadelphia, 1812), p. 195. Some of these structures, known locally as *jacals*, were recently standing in San Antonio. Marvin Eichenroht, A.I.A., photographed one for the writer at 141 South Street in April, 1964.

   Within the last one hundred years the U.S. Army built structures in this manner at posts in scattered parts of Texas. One report mentions four buildings built in 1869 at Fort Richardson on Lost Creek in Jack County "of pickets, on what was known as the stockade principle, the pickets being cut in length of 11 feet, and sunk two feet in the ground. Three of these buildings . . . were 85 feet in length by 20 in width, and one . . . 100 feet in length by 20 feet in width, all being of a height of 9 feet in the clear (to the eaves) and 15 feet to the ridge" (Joseph H. Toulouse and James R. Toulouse, *Pioneer Posts of Texas* [San Antonio, 1936], p. 59). The year before at Fort Quitman the troops had built quarters for themselves "by placing sticks perpendicular in the ground and closing the crevices with mud" (Toulouse and Toulouse, *Pioneer Posts*, p. 133).

   A house of this type is illustrated as "Native Indigenous" in *Historic San Antonio, 1700–1900*, comp. San Antonio Chapter, American Institute of Architects (San Antonio, [1963]).

   There has recently been a revival in the West of post structures encouraged by the modern development of effective wood preservatives. See "The Versatility and Value of Pole-type Buildings," pamphlet issued by J. H. Baxter & Co. (San Francisco, 1963).

[47] Cadillac's expedition loaded "iron and tools to enable them to house themselves conveniently, to fortify themselves." They erected a wooden fort one arpent square within which were built quarters for the commandant and the missionary, a church, quarters for the soldiers, and a warehouse. By 1703 there was a tavern and by 1708 a windmill for making flour. In 1707 small private building lots were parceled out along the named streets, and the fort

For a long time the writer was unable to trace this construction type as far as lower Canada, but a breakthrough eventually came with the discovery of more documentary references. Some of these go back well into the seventeenth century.[48] For instance, on June 11, 1673, in an exchange of property at the Côte St. Louis near Montreal between Jean LeRoy *dit* Deschats and Michel André *dit* St. Michel there is mention of a cabin and stable *de pieux en terre* roofed with bark.[49]

This distinctive wall type was commonly found farther east. Lahontan, who was at Plaisance or Placentia, a fortified fishing establishment on the southern shores of Newfoundland,[50] in 1693

had to be extended to contain them. In 1707–8 the houses were reported to number 63 *or* 120. Lands for cultivation were laid out along the river in strips generally two by twenty arpents.

Oak timber was favored for building—"even and hard and heavy as iron." All structures were of upright logs except the chapel and the warehouse, which were of horizontal logs ("Cadillac Papers," *Michigan Pioneer and Historical Society, Reports and Collections*, XXXIII [1903], 107, 131, 136, 152, 236, 244, 340, 373–381, 414, 425, 426, 428, 494).

It should be noted that a number of military and political leaders, and presumably some of their assistants, were active in both Canada and Louisiana at the beginning of the eighteenth century, and there was ample chance for them to pick up construction ideas at either place.

[48] The documents from which this section was written were located by A. J. H. Richardson of Ottawa. Mr. Richardson, formerly with the Public Archives of Canada and now head, Research Section, National Historic Sites, an indefatigable scholar and longtime correspondent, has been most generous in his assistance.

[49] Montreal Court House, *repertoire* Benigne Basser, no. 926 (Public Archives of Canada transcript M.G. 8, C3, XIX, 3869).

Robert-Lionel Séguin, *Les Granges du Québec du XVII<sup>e</sup> au XIX<sup>e</sup> siècle* (Ottawa, 1963), made a diligent survey of the early French notarial documents. He reports (pp. 4, 19, 23, 25) a thatched stable "de pieux en terre" (Montreal, 1684), two sheds "de pieux en terre" (Montreal, 1703), a barn "de pieux de Cedres plante enterre" and roofed with bark (Montreal, 1730), and a barn and stable "en peauteaux en terre" (Chambly, 1759). The Canadian notaries in general do not seem to have been as meticulous about construction terms as those of the Illinois Country. It will be noted that in these lists of farm buildings the palisadoed wall is always found in the lowliest structures of each group.

[50] The settlement at Placentia enjoyed a fine protected harbor with wide beaches convenient for drying fish and became a principal headquarters for the great fisheries on the Grand Banks. As early as 1594 there were more than sixty sail of French Basques and others operating there and by 1655 a fort had been erected. In 1667 a governor, one hundred and fifty soldiers, and sixty families were sent out from France to reinforce the place ("Placentia, Newfoundland/Agenda Paper 1962–45," undated, unsigned; prepared for the Historic Sites and Monuments Board of Canada).

wrote that "les maisons sont de pieux" and, in another place, "les cabanes sont de pieux."[51] This, of course, does not prove that the *pieux*, or logs, were arranged vertically, but to clarify this we can turn to the inventory of Placentia buildings made nineteen years later when the island was being surrendered to the British. In a descriptive list of privately owned structures submitted by Iberville to Pontchartrain on August 27, 1714, there is mentioned on the property of one St. Martin a structure with "un coste d'epiquette[s] plantés pour commencer une Cabane, Environ soix$^{te}$ Piquets."[52] I can read this only as "about sixty pickets planted in the ground as the beginning of one side of a cabin." Practically all the other buildings were likewise of *piquets*. An engraving published by Bacqueville de la Potherie, an early Plaisance visitor, gives us a crude delineation of one of these houses, unmistakably with walls of *piquets* (Illus. 15C).[53]

The use of palisadoed construction was carried over to Louisbourg on Cape Breton Island when the old Placentia colony was moved to that location. We have, incidental to an engineer's cross-section of a beach at Louisbourg, a watercolor drawing of a hut of *piquets plantés* dated 1740 (Illus. 15D).[54]

In 1769 Lord William Campbell reported that the houses on the islands of St. Pierre and Miquelon (which, incidentally, still belong to France) were "all built with Spruce Picketts very small" and "There are no Storehouses here but what are very small and built with Picketts on the Stony Beach as all the Houses are."[55]

Examples were to be found along the St. Lawrence in the

---

[51] *The Oakes Collection, New Documents by Lahontan,* ed. Gustave Lanctot (Ottawa, 1940), p. 52.

[52] London, Public Record Office, Board of Trade. Newfoundland L 17 (MS, microfilm at Public Archives of Canada, Ottawa), p. 343.

In several other structures on this list there were noted interior partitions of *piquets*. In some cases—like that of the governor's house—the walls were made of "piquets Escarrés"—in other words, they were hewn square. They were specified as "rondes," or in their natural round form as cut from trees, for some cruder structures.

[53] Claude Charles le Roy Bacqueville de la Potherie, *Voyage de l'Amérique* (Amsterdam, 1723), I, 26.

[54] "PLAN DU FAUXBOURG DE LA PORTE DAUPHINE A LOUISBOURG . . . le 12 Janvier 1740/Verrier." Copy in Public Archives of Canada, H3/240-Louisbourg-1740.

[55] Campbell to Lord Hillsborough, July 8, 1769, Public Archives of Canada, ser. A, LXXXV, 207.

eighteenth century; witness the report of one Edward Harrison who inventoried the improvements at the King's Posts on the north side of the river in 1786. Harrison was quite able to distinguish the various construction types employed, and he described many structures as "of upright pickets" and some of mixed construction. The provision store at the Seven Islands—a hybrid—was, in Harrison's words, "built of Logs in front piece sur piece and of upright logs at each end."[56] From these scattered references it will be seen that palisadoed walls were being used in lower Canada until nearly the end of the eighteenth century. Current searches in various Canadian archives will, it is hoped, complete the story.

FRAME CONSTRUCTION

The frame house was not common in St. Louis; there were only seven of them after forty years of building—less than three per cent of the houses in the village. Such a house was known locally as a *maison de poteaux sur sole, sur une solage,* or *de colombage.* Morticing the *poteaux* into a sill (instead of running them down into the ground) required much more pains and skill than the popular palisadoed house, and it customarily entailed the building of a foundation (Illus. 5A, B). The advantage of frame construction lay in separating the structural timbers from the rotting dampness of the earth. For this reason, most of the Mississippi Valley French houses which have survived are of frame construction, even though they were, when built, of the least common type.

The frame houses of lower Normandy, ancestors of those in Canada, may be commonly seen in both the metropolis of Rouen and in the farm houses of the district. Similar walls are also abundant in Les Landes of old Gascony just north of the Adour River. An early example at Quebec City was the Récollet house built in 1620. "The body of this lodging," wrote Father Denis Jamet at the time, "is built of good strong framing [*de bonne et forte charpente*] and between the heavy timbers is walling 8 or 9 inches thick up to the roof—of good stone."[57] Peter Kalm, the Swedish traveler visiting Baie St. Paul

---

[56] Ottawa, Public Archives of Canada, *King's Posts,* 1762–86. Bound MS RG4/A1/S–1A, p. 52. *Pièce sur pièce* refers to walls of horizontal logs. There were two types, as we will see later.

[57] Roy, *La Ville de Québec,* I, 75.

in 1749, remarked on the church which was then considered one of the oldest in Canada: ". . . the walls are formed of timber, erected perpendicularly about two feet from each other supporting the roof. Between these pieces of timber, they have made the walls of the church of black slate. . . ."[58] The type became common in lower Canada. At Louisbourg, the great French fortress-town built 1714–44, frames were both nogged with brick[59] and *pierrottée* with stone.[60]

Framed houses appear early in the Illinois Country records with a contract for two houses *sur solle* to be built at Kaskaskia by Mathurin Charante for Lieutenant Melique in 1725, the wall posts to be five by seven inches.[61] Six years later Charles Rogue contracted to build the local presbytère *sur solle*, the posts to be seven inches thick.[62] The first commandant's quarters at Fort Chartres was a large double house, thirty by fifty-five feet, with a walnut frame, *bousillée*, built 1727.[63] Of the early French frames standing today the so-called Cahokia Courthouse, an eighteenth-century dwelling that went to the World's Columbian Exposition in Chicago and was many years in returning, is a well-known example,[64] as are the Bolduc[65] and Guibourd[66] houses in Ste. Genevieve and the Pierre Menard house near the old site of Kaskaskia (Illus. 9A, B, C, D).

Some notable examples in lower Louisiana might be cited. In New Orleans the great three-story Ursuline Convent, designed by Alexandre De Batz and begun in 1733, was of frame nogged with

[58] Peter Kalm, *Travels into North America* (London, 1771), II, 483.

[59] ". . . construit en bois de charpente dun Pied de carissage et en Brique entre les Potteaux." This is delineated on a sheet entitled "PLAN DES TERRAINS MAISONS et concessions Apparten^{ts} a la Veuve de S. Lartigue Baillif de Lisle Royale."

[60] ". . . construit en Bois de Pin de charpente denviron 1 pied de carissage et du Moilon entre les Potteaux" ("PLAN DES TERRAINS MAISONS").

[61] Chester, Illinois, *Kaskaskia Manuscripts. Commercial Papers*, vol. I, Oct., 1725.

[62] Chester, Illinois, *Kaskaskia Manuscripts. Commercial Papers*, vol. II, Feb. 1, 1731.

[63] Paris C.B.B.1.

[64] Charles E. Peterson, "Notes on Old Cahokia, Part III," *Journal of the Illinois State Historical Society*, XLII (Oct., 1949), 326–330. The building, restored by the State of Illinois, is now open for inspection as a public museum. Most of the timbers are replacements.

[65] Peterson, "Early Ste. Genevieve," pp. 224–225. The Bolduc frame is *bousillée*.

[66] Peterson, "Early Ste. Genevieve," pp. 231–232.

brick.[67] The so-called "Lafitte's Blacksmith Shop," a humble frame on Bourbon Street (now doing duty as a saloon), is one of the best known still standing in that city (Illus. 13B, C). "Madame John's Legacy," an old house on Dumaine Street is another example—in this case the frame is raised high over a ground story of masonry. Of framed plantation houses "Whitney" and "Homeplace" on the west bank of the Mississippi well above the city are two of the best preserved.

In St. Louis the Julien Le Roy house on La Grande Rue Royale sold on October, 14, 1768, to Antoine Hubert, *négociant*, is the first mentioned in the archives. It was about twenty-two or twenty-three feet square with a stone chimney, floor, and ceiling and had a roof covered with shingles.[68] The walls of these framed houses were *bousillée* or *pierrottée* like the palisadoed walls.

In a contract of 1770 Antoine Sans Souci, *maître maçon*, bound himself to build the masonry parts of a frame house for Jean Salé *dit* Lajoye for one hundred livres in peltries. The work included the foundations, the *pierrotage* between the posts and a chimney. Sans Souci, incidentally, was obligated to furnish four barrels of the lime and one man to help the owner haul the stone.[69]

Another type of framed structure was known in the Illinois Country though not often used there. That is the frame with upright posts widely spaced and filled in between with hewn horizontal planks (*madriers*) or logs. The verticals were channeled posts (*en cannelé*). One barn and a horsemill in St. Louis were known to have been constructed that way; perhaps there were a few houses of the type, too. They were common in Canada where the softwood conifer logs were abundant and easily hewn and fitted.[70]

---

[67] Samuel Wilson, Jr., "An Architectural History of the Royal Hospital and the Ursuline Convent of New Orleans," reprint from *Louisiana Historical Quarterly*, XXIX (July, 1946), 3–46. This huge structure failed and had to be replaced with one of masonry by 1747. See also Samuel Wilson, Jr., "Louisiana Drawings by Alexandre De Batz," *Journal of the Society of Architectural Historians*, XXII (May, 1963), 76–77.

[68] "Batie sur sole ou Colombage . . . planchée haut et Bas couverte En Bardeaux, avec une Cheminée En pierre" (Missouri Historical Society, *St. Louis Archives* [MS], instrument no. 13).

[69] *STLRA*, IV:3, 526.

[70] This type of construction does not seem to have a distinctive name in either French or English until the term "Red River frame" was coined in the last century. The French of Canada used the term *de pièce sur pièce* which

The frame of channeled vertical posts with board fillers was standard for barn construction in Les Landes of old Gascony until recently.

STONE MASONRY WALLS

Stone was readily available at St. Louis from the limestone cliffs at the river's edge and was used throughout the colonial period, both to build entire houses and for the foundations and chimneys of others. The first permanent building—Laclède's headquarters—was of masonry, and during the next forty years there was an average of one a year built. At the close of the colonial period—in 1804—stone houses comprised about one-quarter of those in the town.

Stone masonry had the desirable qualities of resistance to fire and rot, and it was firmly in the Canadian building tradition. As early as 1720 most of the houses of Quebec were of stone. A succession of bad fires had prejudiced the government against wooden houses built in numbers close together and a characteristic row house built in masonry was developed there and in Montreal.

Masonry houses began early in the Illinois Country with the erection of a stone house by the lead-mining operator Philippe Renault at his concession above Fort Chartres about 1722–23.[71] Natalia Belting cites a number of contracts for building stone houses in Kaskaskia a generation before the founding of St. Louis. One of these, the Louis Turpin house, was described when sold as being of three stories.[72] The construction of the great Fort Chartres in the 1750's must have brought numbers of stone masons to the frontier.

Although a number of small barns and outbuildings at St. Louis were built of stone, that material was mostly reserved for the larger

also refers to log walls notched at the corners. As a building type the Red River frame spread west to the Pacific Ocean and north to the Arctic. Its origin is being further investigated by the writer.

The writer located and photographed a number of examples in the area St. Vincent-de-Tyrosse—Tartas—Roquefort—Luglon, north of the Adour River in June, 1964, after this paper was first drafted. Some of these structures appear to be quite ancient, but one example, with circular sawn timbers, was dated as late as 1896.

The houses associated with these barns had brick nogged frames, but their general design was much like the typical houses of the Pays Basque.

[71] *Mississippi Provincial Archives, 1701–1729*, ed. and trans. Dunbar Rowland and Albert Godfrey Saunders (Jackson, Miss., 1929), II, 407.

[72] Belting, *Kaskaskia Under the French Regime*, p. 36.

dwellings. To name some of the most prominent stone houses, Laclède's, mentioned above, was twenty-three by sixty feet in size. The house of Labuscière (built before 1772) was sixty-six feet long, the Clamorgan-Chouteau house (about 1785), forty-five by sixty-five feet, and the Papin-Gratiot house (about 1796), thirty-six by fifty-two feet. These would have been considered large houses in any Anglo-American village of the time.

Exposed ledge rock was plentiful, and prospective builders helped themselves along the river bank. The only additional material needed for masonry was lime for mortar and plastering. This was made by simply burning the local limestone over a hot wood fire. The kiln (*fourneau à chaux*) was not difficult to build. The master mason Roussel had one in 1787, J. B. Hubert another in 1795, and Hyacinthe St. Cyr two in 1801. Where the masonry was protected against rain, it could be laid up in mud, and many buildings, including large ones, were so built.

Elsewhere I have published the contract specifications for two St. Louis houses of stone—the Joseph Labrosse house built in 1767 by the irascible Jean Marie Pepin, *maître maçon*, and the one for Hipolite Bolon, Indian interpreter, by James Clamorgan.[73]

Unfortunately none of the French stone houses of the Illinois Country still stand. Those of Kaskaskia were swept away by a caprice of the Mississippi River; those of St. Louis by the prosperity and growth of the American period. The great Laclède-Chouteau mansion, citadel of the founding fathers, did stand long enough to be portrayed by lithographic artist J. C. Wild and the Robidoux stone house on Main Street appears on two early photographs (Illus. 6A, 7A, B).

## Log Walls

Comparatively few log houses were put up in St. Louis during the colonial period. Two early exceptions were the house of Joseph Robidoux who had just come from Montreal where such houses were very common[74] and a two-story log building ten feet square on Louis Ridé's lot, which may have been a tobacco barn.

---

[73] Peterson, *Colonial St. Louis*, pp. 33–34.

[74] Jean Baptiste Ortez, joiner, a native of Béarn, France, who had come to St. Louis six years earlier, agreed to build a small log house for Robidoux, a shoemaker. The consideration was five hundred livres in beaver or deerskins (typical trade items) plus three pairs of shoes. The specification calls for Ortez

The phrase *de pièce sur pièce* was used to describe the two above-mentioned buildings. At St. Louis the term implied *hewn* logs, which in Canada were either let into upright corner posts and tenoned *or* were dovetailed (*en queue d'aronde*). Late in the century the *maison en boulins* appears in the St. Louis records. This was the hasty cabin of round logs brought in by the Anglo-American frontiersman. It was never much used in St. Louis but was commonly found in the outlying villages of Florissant and Nouvelle Bourbon. By this time the forests were disappearing fast, and it was soon more convenient in St. Louis to build an American frame or brick masonry house than one of logs.

The origin of the log cabin as it came from Canada is obscure. Buildings of *pièces sur pièces* are mentioned in the records of the St. Lawrence settlements as far back as the 1600's. But which type of corner construction—the most distinctive detail of craftsmanship—was used is not yet clear. The field is wide open to investigation. The secrets still belong to the mechanics who built so competently but seldom left us written records. Not the least difficulty of the investigator will be getting owners of the remaining houses to pull off some of the boarding which both protects and hides the fabrics. Underneath lie the clues to the origins of Canadian log construction.[75]

to erect a house twenty by twenty-five feet on a stone foundation (*sur une solage en maçonne*) to be well floored and ceiled and the walls of cottonwood, ash, or walnut logs (*en pièce sur pièce de bois de liard, frene ou noyer*). The house was to have a nine-foot plate (*de quarré du solage*) and seven feet from floor to ceiling. There was also specified a board partition (*une cloison en planche*) twenty feet long and a cross partition ten feet long making two *petites chambres*. The owner was obligated to provide the masonry, the lathing and the roofing; Ortez "to furnish anything connected with the carpenter work . . . to deliver the house ready for lathing."

It is not so surprising to later find John Coons, the first American carpenter and joiner in St. Louis, building himself a horizontal log house on Main Street about 1786 and selling it to another American resident a few years later.

[75] Ramsay Traquair, *The Old Architecture of Quebec* (Toronto, 1947), is an admirable work, but it does not go deeply into the matter of wooden wall construction. Traquair noted (p. 50) that the Paradis house at Charlesburg, evidently a very early house, had a "wood-filled frame wall in place of the usual *colombage pierrotté*," but he was not able to examine the building completely. It has since been pulled down.

At this writing doubts have been cast on the age of a number of buildings formerly thought to be the oldest in Canada. Early Canadian building construction has been a neglected subject, and apparently few of the fabrics have been carefully investigated.

# St. Louis Families
# from the French West Indies

## Dorothy Garesché Holland

---

As we all well know, St. Louis was settled by the French: those who
came from the south, up the river with Pierre Laclède and Auguste
Chouteau; and those who came from the north, down from Canada,
many of them settling first on the Illinois side of the Mississippi
River. But there were other French among the early St. Louisans,
those who came from the east, who had fled from Santo Domingo
and taken refuge at first along the eastern seaboard. A second group
came from the West Indies later on, from Guadeloupe in the 1840's.
Little has been written about the French from the West Indies;
books on early St. Louis mention a few from Santo Domingo, but the
information in this paper has been compiled largely from family
memoirs and letters and conversation with their descendants.[1]

---

[1] Consult Richard Edwards and Menra Hopewell, *Edwards's Great West
and Her Commercial Metropolis Embracing a General View of the West, and
a Complete History of St. Louis, from the Landing of Ligueste, in 1764, to the
Present Time* (St. Louis, 1860); Louis Houck, *A History of Missouri* (Chicago,
1908); J. Thomas Scharf, *History of Saint Louis City and County* (Philadelphia, 1883); Paul Beckwith, *Creoles of St. Louis* (St. Louis, 1893); Beatrice
Clark Turner, *The Chouteau Family* (St. Louis, 1934).

Most of the French from Santo Domingo left the island during the 1790's, driven out by the frightful uprising of the slaves; some of them were of the second and third generation of the family born there, the sons and daughters of wealthy plantation owners. After the 1697 Treaty of Ryswick ceded to France the western half of the island, the French colony there had increased tremendously. Some of those who came, chiefly from the seaports of western France, were younger sons who saw an opportunity to make their own fortunes, raising sugar and coffee on the immensely fertile plantations; some were Huguenots, who were deprived of many opportunities in France.

With the uprising of the slaves in 1791—the slaves they had imported from Africa and in many instances treated so shamefully— the plantation owners' world of unbelievable luxury collapsed; many of them were slaughtered before they could escape; thousands managed to flee, some with only the clothes they wore. How many came to this country is not certain; Moreau de Saint-Méry, the chronicler of the refugees from Santo Domingo, states that in 1794 there were twenty-five thousand French in Philadelphia alone,[2] including those from the colonies and those who had escaped the Revolution in France. In her scholarly book, *French Refugee Life in the United States*, Frances Childs quotes Gilbert Chinard as estimating the number of those from Santo Domingo as ten thousand.[3] Most of them came as emigrés, without passport, some intending to remain here, others waiting for the first opportunity to return to France. Many did return when Napoleon removed the restrictions against them in 1803 and allowed them to repossess the property taken away at the time of the Revolution. How many came west, it is impossible to say; there is direct information about only a few families. Those who did come came from the Philadelphia area; from casual references in their letters it is clear they were all acquainted with one another. Besides their Santo Domingo background they had much in common, for they had lost their often considerable fortunes and were determined to make a fresh start on the frontier.

The best known of those who came from Santo Domingo was

---

[2] M. L. E. Moreau de Saint-Méry, *Voyages aux Etats-Unis de l'Amérique 1793–1798*, trans. and ed. Kenneth Roberts and Anna M. Roberts (Garden City, N.Y., 1947), p. 88.

[3] Frances S. Childs, *French Refugee Life in the United States* (Baltimore, 1940), p. 63.

William Valentine Du Bourg, who became the Roman Catholic
Bishop of Louisiana and the Floridas. He had been born in Santo
Domingo, educated in France, ordained a priest at the Seminary of
Saint Sulpice, and had arrived in the United States in 1794, where he
served as president of Georgetown University and founded a school
for boys, St. Mary's, in Baltimore. As much has been written about
Du Bourg, only the highlights of his work in St. Louis will be
mentioned. On a visit to France in 1817 he obtained a promise from
Mother Madeleine Sophie Barat to send some of the nuns, the religious of the Sacred Heart, to St. Louis to found a school for girls,
which was done in 1818 by Mother Philippine Duchesne and four
other nuns. Mother Duchesne conducted the first free school west of
the Mississippi and from her log house in St. Charles have emerged
three elementary and high schools and Maryville College in the St.
Louis area, plus many other schools in various parts of the country.
Bishop Du Bourg founded the St. Louis College for boys, from
which has developed Saint Louis University, one of the largest
private universities in the country.[4]

A man of great culture and learning, Bishop Du Bourg owned an
impressive library described by John Paxton, compiler of the first St.
Louis directory in 1821, as ". . . an elegant and valuable library,
containing about 8000 volumes, and which is without doubt, the
most complete, scientific, and literary repertory of the western
country, if not of the western world. Though it is not public, there is
no doubt but the man of science, the antiquary, and the linguist will
obtain a ready access to it."[5] No doubt some of the volumes formed
the nucleus of the Saint Louis University library; there is no proof
as to the whereabouts of the remainder.

Probably the first to come to St. Louis from Santo Domingo was
François or Francis Barousel[6] who was here in 1796 and died in Ste.
Genevieve in 1797. Apparently he was unmarried, as his will left
everything he owned in the United States to Nicholas Lesconfleure,
his business partner in Philadelphia, and all of his possessions in

---

[4] John F. Rothensteiner, *History of the Archdiocese of St. Louis in Its
Various Stages of Development from A.D. 1673 to A.D. 1929* (St. Louis, 1928), I,
238–239, 300–307.

[5] Quoted in John Francis McDermott, *Private Libraries in Creole
St. Louis* (Baltimore, 1938), p. 20, n.

[6] Tesson and Barousel information from a descendant, George H. Hall,
and from Tesson Collection MSS, Missouri Historical Society, St. Louis. The
French manuscripts were translated by Mrs. Nettie Beauregard.

France to his brothers and sisters. His niece, Victorine Barousel, came to St. Louis several years later. Victorine had lived near Port-au-Prince on the western side of Santo Domingo and after the death of her parents, who had left her very well-off, she had made her home in Baltimore with her guardians, Monsieur and Madame Souty. An intimate friend, Madame Pescaye, begged that Victorine be allowed to live with her in St. Louis, and so the young girl came west. When she was 18, in 1811, she married Michel Desravines Tesson, also from Santo Domingo.

Michel Tesson had been born at Cap François in 1789; apparently his parents had died or been murdered in the uprising, for when his sister, Madame Moulter, was slain after seeing her husband and infant killed by slaves, Michel was rescued by a faithful slave and hidden in his cabin for three days. He managed to make his way to Philadelphia where he stayed with a man named Boucherville, but being a restless youth he decided to go farther west. He heard that in St. Louis he would find French and Spanish people, and as he spoke both languages fluently, he decided to move there. He established a business and sent for his two older brothers, Pierre and Francis, who were newspapermen in Boston and in Charleston, South Carolina. Michel and Victorine Tesson had only two children who lived; his brothers have no descendants. There are many Tessons in St. Louis who are descended from another family but not related to those from Santo Domingo.

In 1829 Michel Tesson went to France and visited his unknown relatives. There is a delightful letter, dated Agen, April 4, 1829, from his uncle, the Comte d'Asselin, to Michel's wife in St. Louis. The count wrote that he had once hoped to embrace his brother, but since he had been deprived of that joy, God has granted him the favor of meeting his nephew, left an orphan at the age of four. "I had been fancying to myself continually that a child of four years of age, deprived of his father and mother, without support, without a protector, without means of education, could turn out to be only a downright clodhopper . . . whom his family in France would never be able to introduce into society." Then he describes how the nephew appeared at his door one evening and of his delight in knowing him. The letter continues: "This dear nephew is not only presentable but is a relative who does honor to his people, one whom they introduce with eagerness and who honors them."

A Santo Domingan who has many descendants in St. Louis and

elsewhere, the Vicomte Jules de Mun,[7] arrived here after several harrowing experiences. Born in the Croix-des-Bouquets area near Port-au-Prince, he was the son of the Vicomte Bernard Jacques de Mun, who had come to the island, fearing the impending French Revolution, and lived there on valuable property owned by the family. After several years the worst seemed to be over and the de Muns returned to France so that the children could be educated. When the Revolution was renewed with increased fury, the parents were forced to flee to England, as there was a price on their heads. They left two of the boys, Jules and Auguste, with a nurse, Atilie, to whom they promised to send money for their passage, money which never reached them. At one point Atilie had to hide the boys in a cellar to avoid capture and then to disguise them as peasant children. On starting to make their way from Paris to Calais, as they approached the Place de la Révolution, they stopped to make way for several tumbrels of people who were on their way to be guillotined. Much to the consternation of the nurse Jules recognized one of the ladies bound for execution and cried out "Oh, there is Maman's friend!" As they made their way to the Channel, Jules would play his fiddle and collect a few sous which they used to buy food—the fiddle incidentally remained in the family until a few years ago.

When Jules de Mun was a young man, he, his widowed mother, and brothers and sisters went to Cuba, where after five years they petitioned for permission to become citizens. However, Jules changed his mind and sailed for the United States; there is a letter from his brother Antoine, dated Havana, June 10, 1809, to Jules at Burlington, New Jersey. Burlington was a favorite settlement of the Santo Domingans, among them Madame and Mademoiselle de Saint-Mémin, mother and sister of the well-known artist, who conducted a small school for girls.

But de Mun did not stay long in the East; on April 6, 1810, his friend, Jerome Keating, wrote him from Philadelphia, addressing the letter to St. Louis: "You should congratulate yourself on the decision you made, seeing how the few occasions which present themselves to young people to travel or to place themselves, do not offer you any opportunity, and to remain in the shop where you were would never

---

[7] De Mun information from de Mun Collection, Missouri Historical Society; "The Journals of Jules De Mun," *Missouri Historical Collections*, V (Feb. and June, 1928), 167–208, 311–342; conversations with de Mun descendants, Mrs. Mary Ambrose Birdsall and Mrs. Charles Lamy. De Mun letters were translated by Mrs. Max Meyer.

had led to anything. With what pleasure, my friend, I will see you make a trip to us." Jerome Keating was the nephew and adopted son of John Keating, one of the partners of de Noailles in the Azylum venture, the settlement originally intended as a refuge for the unhappy Marie Antoinette. John Keating had married Eulalie des Chapelles from Santo Domingo, and they had passed their brief married life in Wilmington where there was a colony of Santo Domingans.

Perhaps Jules de Mun did make that trip to Philadelphia, for in July of that year his brother addressed a letter to him at that city, in care of Garesché and Ravesies. But in October he was receiving his mail at Ste. Genevieve, the Mississippi River village some sixty miles south of St. Louis, where he opened a small store. His mother wrote him there in March, 1811: "I assure you, my dear Jules, that it would be difficult to express the pleasure it gave me by telling me that you were enjoying good health, and in seeing you pleased with the country you have traveled. I have since then learned of all the difficulties you encountered, but after all, that is over . . . you are satisfied with your start."

On May 22, 1811, Jerome Keating wrote again from Philadelphia: "You should congratulate yourself on the course you have chosen—there are now, I believe, few resources here for a young man who is starting out in business. You have left Miss Eliza *brocart* as Madame Bauduy says for broken heart, she does not forgive you for having left her. Miss Charlotte is in the same state."

To judge from the portrait of Jules de Mun it is easy to see why the young ladies of Philadelphia pined for him. But there were other young ladies nearby. Jules's sister had written that she knew how he longed to visit St. Louis and see *les élégantes*. The French grapevine was functioning efficiently, and in January, 1812, Jules's mother wrote that she heard he had been dancing with a "pretty young lady." In February she wrote again, urging him to marry the young lady and reminding him how difficult it is to find someone ". . . who is suitable in everything as this one is. All that she lacks is money, but you are young, you are thrifty, and have a business which cannot help growing every day. You can live for six months or a year with her father—during this time you can find a little house." Like a good French son, Jules took his mother's advice, and in March the letters of congratulation began to arrive; all of the family were pleased at the engagement of Jules and the lovely Isabelle Gratiot, a granddaughter of Pierre Laclède and Madame Chouteau. He continued with his store at Ste. Genevieve until 1816 when he set out on a fur-trading expedition with A. P. Chouteau and others. They were arrested by the Spanish governor at Santa Fe and imprisoned for forty-eight days. Jules kept a journal of his trip, in which he recounted the many hardships they suffered.

When he returned to St. Louis, he found a special invitation from Louis XVIII, asking him to return to France, but he decided to take his family to Cuba. There he was near his mother and his sister, Madame Depestre, his cousins the d'Orbignys, and other friends from Santo Domingo, including the members of the Bauduy, Garesché, and des Chapelles families. After a ten-year residence on the island the de Muns returned to St. Louis; he was made secretary to the United States Board of Commissioners, adjusting titles to French and Spanish land grants; he was also register of the St. Louis land office and recorder of deeds until his death.

There is an interesting postscript to the account of Jules de Mun; several years ago one of his numerous descendants, a student at Smith College, went to Paris for her junior year. Her hostess, the Countess de Vogües, received her with open arms. She herself was born a de Mun and noticing on the girl's passport that her middle name was de Mun was delighted to welcome one of the hitherto unknown American branch of the family.

The Gareschés of Philadelphia, in whose care the letter to Jules de Mun had been sent, were brothers, Jean Pierre and Vital.[8] They had been born near Port-au-Prince in Santo Domingo and taken to La Rochelle in 1791, where they lived for about four years. They and their mother then rejoined in America their father, Jean Garesché du Rocher, who had been obliged to leave France hurriedly as he was about to be imprisoned by the Jacobins. He settled in Wilmington, Delaware, and the boys finished their education in Philadelphia under the tutelage of Abbé Carles, one of the priests who had been at Azylum, and at St. John's College, Baltimore. After the death of their father, the two young men established themselves as merchants in Philadelphia, having salvaged some of their fortune by the sale of sugar from the Santo Domingo plantation. They

---

[8] Dorothy Garesché Holland, *The Garesché, de Bauduy and des Chapelles Families: History and Genealogy* (St. Louis, 1963).

married two of the daughters of another Santo Domingo planter, Pierre de Bauduy de Bellevue, or as he signed his name as soon as he came to America, Peter Bauduy.

Peter Bauduy had gone into partnership with another young Frenchman, Eleuthère Irénée du Pont, and acted as sales manager while du Pont superintended the manufacture of gunpowder. The two men also established a woolen mill, in which business Peter's two sons-in-law invested. The antagonism which had marked the relationship between Bauduy and du Pont almost since the beginning finally became intolerable, and in 1816 the two men parted company, each to run his own powder mill. In 1819 Peter Bauduy decided to move to Cuba and sold the powder business to Vital and John Peter Garesché. Lacking the skill of E. I. du Pont, who had been trained in chemistry under Lavoisier in France, the Greschés found in 1837 that the manufacture was not producing enough income to support two growing families. A letter from Vital's oldest son, Julius, then a student at Georgetown University, asked about his father's plans: "Lately, when dining with messrs Bayard and Milligan, the former said to me, 'You are aware, no doubt, that your father intends, when spring comes, to migrate to Missouri?' I replied that I had often heard you speak of the matter and believed you intended to go but did not know you had decided on doing so . . . tell me, my dear father, whether this is true or not; for I feel so very uncertain."

It was true and the spring of 1839 saw Vital Garesché, his wife Mimika, and five of their six children arrive via steamboat at the wharf of St. Louis; the eldest son, Julius, was then at West Point. The Garesché brothers had decided that Vital, who had four sons, should be the one to go West—there were more opportunities for young men there. The family owned land in Missouri, some in St. Louis and a large tract at the confluence of the Missouri and Mississippi rivers, a piece of property they vainly expected would be extremely valuable some day. Vital Garesché had been West before; as examiner of the Western Land Offices he had come to St. Louis in 1833 and from there had gone on horseback through Missouri, Arkansas, Mississippi, and Louisiana, investigating the offices, often corrupted by dishonesty, and installing a new system of keeping the books and records. Vital Garesché's health was ruined by these arduous trips, and he died of consumption in 1844, five years after coming to St. Louis. Many years later his brother, John Peter, and his wife Cora arrived in St. Louis, where several of their surviving children lived, and both of them died here.

Like so many of his child-compatriots, Étienne Nidelet, or Stephen Nidelet as he became known, was taken to Philadelphia shortly after the 1791 uprising of the slaves.[9] He had been born in 1789 at Port-au-Paix on the western coast of Santo Domingo. His widowed mother, the Countess Elizabeth la Forge de Nidelet, remained there for several years, spent some time in Cuba, and finally arrived in New Orleans in 1809. In the letters from Stephen Nidelet to his mother while she lived in New Orleans, there is frequent mention of friends from Santo Domingo and their relatives in Philadelphia.

In many of his letters Stephen begged his mother to sell all of her slaves except Bridget, who would be useful in Philadelphia, and constantly urged her to join him. Finally the reason for her delay came out—she was fearful of the sea voyage. Her son sent her news of their relatives, the Chaprons, of the Gernous, their good friends, of Mesdames Drouet, Teisseire, Brugierre, of Mr. Rasilly, of Mr. and Mrs. Tetrel, and of Aunt Chaussaulme. By 1818 Madame had apparently conquered her fear of sea and was living in Toulouse, where her son wrote her, expressing his hopes of her safe arrival and his grief at parting with her.

Stephen Nidelet was in partnership with his cousin; they owned the firm of Chapron and Nidelet, silk merchants. In 1826 Stephen was married to Celeste Pratte of St. Louis, daughter of Bernard and Emilie Labbadie Pratte, and a descendant through her mother of Madame Chouteau and Pierre Laclède. Family tradition holds that at the marriage the bride was still so youthful that she took her dolls with her on the honeymoon. After living in Philadelphia for a time they came, or returned to, St. Louis, where he died in 1856. There is a charming letter from Stephen Nidelet to his wife—a letter typifying the chivalry and courtesy of the cultured Frenchman:

To my dear Celeste,

I have thought of the time I was seated by your side before dinner and you were darning stockings. I gazed on you and felt a peacock's pride, in silence leaned toward you, and neither spoke a word. Your industry in darning was all I observed and I kissed your lily cheeks for it. Your fine

[9] Information on Stephen Nidelet from Nidelet Collection, Missouri Historical Society, and from Mrs. Charles E. Michel, Jr., Nidelet descendant. Letters were translated by Mrs. Nettie Beauregard.

eyes, half-filled with tears bespoke a meek spirit, added to your good wishes for me to join the church . . . To be so charmed as I was then had never before occurred. A sudden shower made blind my eyes, I neither saw nor heard, but was in ecstacy by the words and sound I heard.

The family of Eustache Paul,[10] at one time lieutenant-governor of Santo Domingo, was among the first to come to St. Louis from the island. His wife and children were in France at the time of the uprising, and although he managed to escape, he died at sea. Madame Paul stayed in Paris so the children could be educated—the girls at the Ursuline Convent, the boys at the École Militaire Polytechnique. In 1801 Sophie, the younger daughter, married Fleury Generelly, who brought his bride, her mother, and her older sister, Algaé, to this country, where the two brothers joined them later. They lived in Baltimore and in Philadelphia, and in 1808 Algaé was married to a French physician, Dr. Edward Coursault. Algaé had been born in Santo Domingo in 1781 and had served as Lady of Honor to Queen Hortense of Holland, stepdaughter of Napoleon.

In 1809 the two brothers, René and Gabriel Paul, came to St. Louis; their sister was certainly here about this time, for she was listed as a member of the choir at the Church of St. Louis of France. René Paul had been an officer and an engineer in the French navy under Napoleon; in St. Louis he became the first city engineer, surveying and mapping the city in 1823. He also made surveys in the Indian Territory, and both he and his brother were active in the affairs of the old Cathedral parish. Their wives were sisters, Eulalie and Louise Chouteau, daughters of Marie Thérèse Cerré and Auguste Chouteau, descendants of Madame Chouteau and René Chouteau of New Orleans. Their brother, Henri Chouteau, later married Madame Coursault's daughter, Clémence, whose daughter Beatrice became the wife of Colonel John O'Fallon Clark, son of General George Rogers Clark and nephew of General William Clark, territorial governor of Missouri and explorer of the Lewis and Clark expedition.

Perhaps others came from Santo Domingo to St. Louis, but research and inquiries have thus far uncovered no more. The Santo Domingo French had several qualities in common: they were well educated, many of them in France; they were men and women with cultured tastes. The very books they brought with them were in-

---

[10] Beckwith, *Creoles of St. Louis*, pp. 25–26; Turner, *The Chouteau Family*, pp. 99–100; Scharf, *History of St. Louis*, I, 136.

dicative of their education—volumes of history, of poetry, both English and French, of the works of the French philosophers. On the island they had lived in great luxury, but when forced to leave their rich plantations, they took their ill fortune philosophically; instead of wallowing in self-pity, they turned to almost anything to earn a living. Parents who had been raised with the expectation of inheriting enormous fortunes now were anxious that their children grow up able to support themselves. Long before she was married, the future wife of Vital Garesché had been admonished by her mother, Juliette des Chapelles Bauduy, in a letter sent to her while she was a pupil at Madame Rivardi's boarding school in Philadelphia, "I see that fortunes are sometimes so precarious that I think all fathers and mothers would be wise to give to their children some means of earning a living whatever might happen. I see nothing more useful to a woman who has suffered reverses than a great skill in music. This is why I wish very much that you apply yourself and try for perfection at the piano."[11]

This then was the spirit of the Santo Domingans—whether emigrés without passport or emigrants with everything in order. They were in a new world; they were making a fresh start. The son of a once wealthy plantation owner slept on the ground during trips for the land office; the titled scion of an ancient family tended store in a Missouri village. And with it all they brought a polish, an air of sophistication, to St. Louis that caused the historian Scharf to say: "The French population improved and refined itself after 1788; another reinforcement in population and manners was derived from the slaves outbreak in San Domingo which expelled the wealthy planters."[12]

Almost all of the characteristics of the French from Santo Domingo were found in those who came here from Guadeloupe in the 1840's. They had much the same educational and cultural background, and they too had left the easy life of the plantation. But there were no Huguenots among them—all were devout Catholics but Catholics who read even the freethinkers and who accepted their religion by reason as well as faith. Fortunately there is a firsthand story of the coming of the Guadeloupe French to St. Louis; Edward de Lauréal, who came here with his wife and six daughters, read such

---

[11] Holland, *The Garesché, de Bauduy and des Chapelles Families*, p. 69.
[12] Scharf, *History of St. Louis*, I, 308–309.

an account to the Missouri Historical Society in 1873. He recounted
how

On February 8, 1845, about 10 o'clock in the morning Pointe-a-Pitre,
the Capital of the colony, was destroyed by an earthquake more violent
than any previously known. What the reeling earth spared the fire seized
upon. The number of dead crushed beneath the ruins or calcined by the
flames was so great that there were not sufficient persons to bury them;
and as a matter of necessity the remains were transported to the open sea
and entombed in the deep. . . .

Their wounds scarcely healed they [the colonists of Guadeloupe]
began to breathe when of a sudden they found themselves menaced with
ruin from another cause in the face of which strength and energy were
paralyzed. In the month of March 1848 a sinister rumor spread like a pall
over the country and caused a thrill of terror throughout. . . . A war
vessal appeared on the horizon; it came bearing to the colony momentous
news. A revolution had broken out in France, the king, Louis Phillippe,
driven from his throne, had been compelled to seek refuge in England.
. . . The new agents of power in the colony, doubtless to give proof of
their zeal, casting aside every precaution so indispensible nevertheless
under such grave circumstances, suddenly proclaimed the abolition of
slavery.

Mr. de Lauréal described the terror the colonists had felt at the
thought of another revolution. Many had lived through the one in
France in 1791. Others had heard of the frightful suffering and
tortures the colonists in Santo Domingo had undergone. Fortunately
the slaves in Guadeloupe were not of the same savage breed—perhaps too they had been better treated than those unhappy wretches
in Santo Domingo. At any rate their chief reaction to sudden freedom was to cease working. The colonists, however, felt that violence
might break out any moment, and many decided to leave the country at once. To resume the de Lauréal narrative:

The unanimous thought had America for its object. By a singular
chance, St. Louis, in Missouri, was the converging point of all projects of
emigration. Consequently, in the month of July, 1848, there were seen
disembarking at St. Louis the first families, wandering in search of a
security which their native country no longer afforded them.

Soon these families were followed by a great number of other emigrants, so that in 1849 an agglomeration of French from Guadeloupe
formed almost a little colony. They had every reason to congratulate
themselves on their reception on American soil.

But almost immediately after their arrival the emigrants were doomed
to undergo a rude trial. The cholera, which during the spring and summer
of 1849 desolated St. Louis, did not spare them. Their numbers were
sadly diminished.

But this time again courage was not wanting in the colonists from Guadeloupe. Then were these people accustomed to the elegances of luxury, the comforts of an easy life, seen to make courageously the sacrifice of their past in burying its souvenirs in the depths of their hearts and to begin a life of fatigues and rude occupations to which they were far from having been accustomed. More than one mother of a family thrown entirely upon her own resource, by a prodigy of economy and courageous patience, was enabled to bring up her offspring and to place her children in a position to contract alliances with honorable families of her adopted city.[13]

Where this account of Edward de Lauréal stops, the story is taken up by his youngest daughter, Adèle, Mrs. Nicholas Hornsby. After mentioning her own family, Mrs. Hornsby told of some of the others from Guadeloupe:

The family of Mr. Alfred Bouvier and that of his brother-in-law, Mr. Gilbert, arrived in St. Louis when the cholera epidemic was at its worst in 1849. They took a house in Walsh's row where Mr. Edward de Lauréal was already established.

Mr. Gilbert, his mother-in-law, Mrs. Egiman, and five of his children, fell victims to the plague a few days after their arrival, and all died within a short time of each other. Such a calamity would be most trying under any circumstances, but on arriving in a strange land where the language was unfamiliar, it was a blow that few could have withstood. Mrs. Gilbert and Mrs. Bouvier, however, were superior women and rose above their misfortunes. Being highly educated, they opened a school for girls which was patronized by St. Louis' exclusive set. Mrs. Bouvier distinguished herself as a music teacher and Mrs. Gilbert as an instructor in French. . . .

Two other ladies that came from Guadeloupe at this time were Mrs. Ladevais and Mrs. Du Clos, whose husband died shortly after reaching St. Louis. Mrs. Du Clos when young was a beautiful woman and impressed the Prince de Joinville as such, he saying that the prettiest thing he had seen in Guadeloupe was Mrs. Du Clos.[14]

Mr. de Lauréal and his wife, known respectively to their descendants as "Papa Dor" and "Mama Té," were greatly beloved by all of their numerous family. Their son-in-law, Robert Bakewell, wrote of them in 1903:

Mr. de Lauréal married his first cousin, Octavie de Lauréal, who survives him at a very great age, retaining, however, until quite recently, to a great degree, her very remarkable energy and activity of body and mind. Whilst this is being written, she still lives, beloved and revered by all those who have the privilege of her intimate acquaintance and especially

[13] Edward de Lauréal, "Emigration from the French West Indies in 1848," *Missouri Historical Collections*, II (July, 1906), 13–16.

[14] Adèle de Lauréal Hornsby, "The French Emigres from Guadeloupe," *Missouri Historical Collections*, II (July, 1906), 17–22.

by a numerous circle of descendants to the fourth generation. Of her may be truly said, in the language of Holy Writ, "her children rise up and call her blessed. . . ."

Mr. de Lauréal was a man of high principle, of great refinement, and of varied accomplishments. His education, as was the case with all the wealthy colonists, was had in France. . . . Amongst other accomplishments, Mr. de Lauréal was an amateur painter in chalks of great merit, and his landscapes and portraits adorn the houses of his friends and descendants and were highly appreciated by such competent judges as the late Mr. [E.] de Franca, the famous portrait painter of St. Louis.[15]

Today, sixty years after that was written, the watercolors of "Papa Dor" are still prized by his descendants and the descendants of his friends.

Among the Guadeloupe French who came to St. Louis was a large contingent who were related and intermarried, comprising members of the Boislinière, Tétard, Bonnet, Dupavillon, Cherot, Bourdon, and de Pombiray families. Dr. Dupavillon is mentioned in the life of Mother Elizabeth Seton;[16] he had been sent to Baltimore as a very young man to complete his education. Here he met and fell in love with a classmate's sister, Anina Seton. Notes were passed between the young people by Anina's brother until finally both mothers became concerned, chiefly on account of the youth of the two; Anina's mother forbade any further friendship with the almost unknown suitor, and Dupavillon's mother summoned him back to Guadeloupe where she could select a wife for him in proper French fashion.

Many years later when this young Frenchman had acquired a wife, a degree in medicine, and a large family,[17] the Dupavillons left Guadeloupe for St. Louis but, hearing of the cholera raging there, they stopped off at Cape Girardeau and remained several years until St. Louis was judged safe. In the meantime Dr. Dupavillon died, but his family went on to St. Louis. One daughter returned to Guadeloupe but her descendants, the Renard family, came to St. Louis later.

[15] Hon. Robert A. Bakewell, "Edward de Lauréal," *Missouri Historical Collections*, II (July, 1906), 23–25. Also information from Evremond Hornsby, de Lauréal descendant, and Mrs. William K. Morrison, wife of a descendant.

[16] Katherine Burton, *His Dear Persuasion* (London, New York, Toronto, 1940), pp. 181, 205.

[17] Some of the information in the following paragraphs was taken from the Hornsby article; however, most of it was given by Dr. Joseph Boislinière Grindon and his sisters, Mother Pauline Grindon, R.S.C.J., and Mrs. Anselm Murphy.

Adrien Tétard, born in Guadeloupe and educated in France, was the friend of Victor Hugo, de Musset, and Lamartine; his poetry is judged to be very fine, most of it contained in one volume, *Souvenirs*. After coming to St. Louis, he worked in the Belcher Sugar Refinery, where he is said to have revolutionized the method of refining sugar. Later he became deputy recorder of deeds.

The Bourdons were descended from Captain Jean Marie Louis de Bourdon, godson of the Empress Josephine. There was another St. Louis connection with the Martinique-born empress: her sister had married a brother of Filassier de Richebois, ancestor of the Grindon family, to be mentioned later.

Of those who came from Guadeloupe, perhaps the best-known was Dr. Louis Cherot-Boislinière. When he arrived in St. Louis he already held two degrees, one of them in law from the University of Toulouse, and he received his M.D. at St. Louis University in 1848. His career in St. Louis was almost instantly successful, and, elected in 1858 the first coroner of St. Louis, he held that position for two years. He served as president of the St. Louis Medical Society and was the author of many valuable papers on medical subjects. It was due to his persuasion that the Sisters of Charity opened St. Anne's, the first maternity hospital west of the Alleghenies. Dr. Boislinière had many interests, was widely read in the classics, and never lost his appreciation of fine literature; he was an artist and musician and on his deathbed asked for the score of a favorite high mass and planned his funeral.

Dr. Boislinière's son Louis also became a doctor, and one of his daughters, Lina, married a cousin, Dr. Joseph Grindon, who became one of the leading dermatologists in St. Louis; his son, Joseph, Jr., is a doctor today. From the descendants of Dr. Boislinière have come some interesting stories about the family life in Guadeloupe and about their early days in St. Louis, stories told them by their parents, who in turn heard them from the first generation to live here.

One story from the island concerns the enormous pile of sheets always ready at the back door of the servants' quarters. The Negroes worked naked in the heat of the sugar plantations and as they came in would quickly wrap themselves in the sheets. Another delightful bit of lore concerns the three presents a Guadeloupe child received at baptism—a slave approximately his own age, a newborn monkey, and a newly planted coconut tree. Tradition held that whenever the child was lonely he could sit in the shade of the tree with his slave and his monkey for companionship.

A favorite anecdote is that of an elderly aunt, Tante Amélie, who had great difficulty learning English and never mastered it. Volunteering one day to purchase a little bell to be used at the table to summon the servant, she started out on her quest repeating to herself, "Small bell, small bell." But one mishap after another befell her, and she returned home without the bell, berating the stupid St. Louis salespeople, not one of whom could find her a "smell ball." Another aunt, Tante Angeline, was a great reader, who, when she was seventy-five and in her last illness, began the study of Spanish in order to read Cervantes in the original. Among the gentlemen of the family there always existed the chivalry for which their country was famous; a lady's lack of beauty was never mentioned, one spoke of the beauty of her soul and she was referred to as "une belle âme."

Many of the descendants of the West Indies French lived to an advanced old age, many into their nineties, still hale and hearty until a short time before their death. One maiden lady in her ninety-first year was planning two more trips to Europe, one to the Scandinavian peninsula and the other to Vienna for the music festivals. Her sister, when she was also in her nineties, was making notes for a book about Franklin D. Roosevelt, and carried packing cases of pamphlets, periodicals, and books with her from place to place.

There are today in St. Louis and elsewhere many descendants from these two groups who came here from Santo Domingo and Guadeloupe. Those of Jules de Mun are numerous, although none are of that name; the descendants of his daughters, Isabelle Walsh and Julie Chenié, include Smiths, Corleys, Lamys, and Crosbys. One of Michel Tesson's two children, Cora Polskowski, had no children; his descendants are Halls and Forsythes. Four of the children of Vital Garesché have descendants, at least forty by the name and many others including Brodheads, Housers, Dietrichs, Benoists, Coudons, Archers, and Jordans. Stephen Nidelet has one descendant by that name and others by the names of Michel, von Phul, and Keeler. There are probably none of the Paul family by that name, but among many descendants are Chouteaus, Dyers, Clarks, Adreons, and Turners. It was impossible to trace all of those who came from Guadeloupe, but it is thought that many of the families who settled here have died out. However, there are numerous descendants of the de Lauréals: Morrisons, Bolands, Hornsbys, Bakewells, Munroes. The Grindon family is descended from Dr. Boislinière and the Renard family from Dr. Dupavillon.

All of those interviewed for the writing of this paper have great affection for their forebears and a pride in their French heritage; all have bred into them the strong feeling of family unity, the unity which extends to the fifth and sixth degree of kinship. Many remember with amusement the concern with one's health and the health of all the family; the old letters are full of details of illness and the remedies prescribed. There are still a few ties with France, either with the descendants of those who returned after the Revolution or the descendants of those who remained there. Wedding invitations still arrive, and occasionally a death notice—one of those large double folds of paper with an inch-wide black border, in which all the family join in informing the recipient of the death of one of the members. St. Louisans still visit the Paris apartments and the country châteaux of distant cousins, for there is still a strong feeling of the bonds of kinship and the heritage of French blood.

In many a St. Louis household is a memento carried with care from Santo Domingo or Guadeloupe, a household treasure some woman insisted on saving even when fleeing from an earthquake or insurrection. There are many portraits and miniatures, some exquisitely done by professional artists, some by skillful amateurs of whom there were many among the educated French. A silver fork and spoon, part of a set made in Paris in 1760 and brought by a young man and his bride to his Santo Domingo home, is a cherished possession of one of his descendants, along with a faience inkwell also brought from the island, and a leather wallet carried by a Huguenot ancestor, in the pocket of which is still tucked away a calendar of 1763 with all of the Protestant saints days marked. A gold pencil is engraved with the names of the four generations of doctors who have owned it. One of the Guadeloupe families has quantities of exquisite Meissen china which has survived many moves, including that perilous one from the island. Pieces of mahogany furniture from the islands made by the slaves skillful in cabinet work lend a gracious air to St. Louis homes; there is Guadeloupe jewelry formed of long strands of coral set with gold nuggets and cameo-like earrings believed to come from Santo Domingo. One woman still uses her great-grandmother's darning egg, an island gourd.

One might search in vain for a truly great man among the families from the West Indies: they produced no president, no famous soldier, no outstanding man of science or inventor, no great writer. But during the years there have been many who added considerably to the growth and culture of St. Louis; men who founded and built up industries and businesses; men who served the community as doctors and lawyers, army officers, civic leaders, and educators; women who set an example of charity and service to those in need.

Perhaps the best summing-up of the French from the islands was written by Adèle de Lauréal Hornsby in 1878:

. . . let us consider briefly what manner of people these were, who have their share in forming the social and civic life of this city of ours.

Many of them were descendants of the old French nobility, possessing its fine traits and few of its failings. They were welcomed and gave to the land of their adoption the best that was in them, examples of refinement and of the highest principles born of a deep religious conviction. Long will their influence be felt by those who have known and loved them.

As to those creole women they were models for mothers, wives and daughters. Accustomed to a life of ease in their native homes, they courageously went to work to help in the support of their families and aided in encouraging and inspiring their husbands. They brought up their sons to be good citizens and their daughters to walk in their footsteps.[18]

---

[18] Hornsby, "The French Emigres from Guadeloupe," p. 22.

# An Early St. Louis Poet:
# Pierre Francois Régnier

## Charles Guenther

It was not extraordinary that among the French immigrants who
arrived in upper Louisiana nearly two centuries ago, some were
gifted in arts and letters. Yet it was unusual that a French poet as
talented as Pierre François Régnier settled here and practiced his
craft, far from the cultural base of Paris where he might have commanded a wider audience.[1] Pending further research on his earlier and
later life, Régnier—a military man, miner, linguist, and schoolteacher
—belongs to a brief period in St. Louis and Ste. Genevieve history.
The only dated documents thus far directly connected with him are

[1] As far as I can ascertain, this is the first paper ever presented on Pierre
François Régnier; his known poems are here published for the first time.
Grateful acknowledgment is extended to the Missouri Historical Society for
granting me use of the poems, letters, and other manuscripts by and about
Pierre François Régnier quoted or referred to in this paper. I owe special
thanks to Mrs. Grace Lewis Miller of St. Louis who, knowing my interest in
French poetry, called my attention to Régnier and to the Craighead Papers
several years ago. To Mrs. Elizabeth Kirchner and other staff members of the
St. Louis Mercantile Library Association and to the St. Louis Public Library,
I am indebted for assistance in searching through many sources including un-
cataloged collections.

certain manuscripts among the private papers of Major Alexander Craighead in the Missouri Historical Society. These documents, in French, span less than a year, from September 29, 1811, to August 13, 1812. If we accept these papers, which inform us of his marriage at Santo Domingo, and several additional sources referring to "Francis Regnier" and "Francis Regnire," we can reconstruct a bare outline of the poet's life from July 27, 1802, to November 2, 1821.[2]

While we do not yet know the dates of Régnier's birth and death, the few facts we have about him indicate several things: he was born in France and was well educated; he probably had served as an officer in the French army; he might have come to upper Louisiana by way of Philadelphia with French settlers who had lost their plantations in the Santo Domingo uprisings after the island came under French control at the end of the eighteenth century; he worked for a time (1811–12) as a part owner or manager of Old Mines; and in 1821 he opened a private, coeducational day school in St. Louis, supplemented by evening tutorial instruction.

The earliest dated document in the Craighead Papers bearing Régnier's autograph is a four-page letter written from *Vieille Mine* (Old Mines) at 2:00 A.M., September 29, 1811, and addressed to Craighead "at the mine at Shibboleth." This letter encloses a satire on "the new mine" (*la nouvelle mine*). Régnier must have risen early, unable to sleep, to write the poem, and then the letter in which he playfully scolded Craighead: "I have a grudge against you, Craighead, too serious a grudge to keep to myself—and I'm getting up early on purpose to tell you about it. Every day you're throwing insinuations at me, always telling me that, like you, I court the belles and secretly make love . . . *having a desire for something isn't the same as the enjoyment.*" (How like T. S. Eliot is Régnier in this observation!) We may assume from Régnier's letter and poem—and from a light note sent to Craighead from "Hq Palace Royal, Old Mines," signed "Wilson, rex"—that the mines had none of the comforts of the Creole drawing room.

Régnier's next surviving letter was written at Old Mines on January 30, 1812. It was addressed to his "friends and companions" and, like the poem dated three days earlier, it eulogized the late

---

[2] References in the Craighead Papers show that Major Craighead was entrusted with Régnier's legal and literary documents. Craighead was a partner in the firm of Wilson, Craighead and Company (later Dodge, Wilson and Craighead) which handled general merchandise.

Grand Master Shrader of the lodge of Freemasons at Ste. Genevieve. Régnier was active in that lodge (Louisiana Lodge No. 109), which was the first established west of the Mississippi. It had come into being in 1807–8 after a group of settlers in Ste. Genevieve successfully applied to the Grand Lodge of Pennsylvania for a warrant for its establishment. Otho Shrader was the first master, and Dr. Aaron Elliot and Joseph Hertick were wardens. The membership included Pierre Chouteau, Bartholomew Berthold, and others who later became prominent St. Louis merchants. The Ste. Genevieve lodge declined and in 1816–17 ceased to exist, owing partly to the rapid growth of St. Louis. Shrader was evidently held in high esteem by his fellow Masons. Régnier was greatly affected by the news of his death, and in his four-page letter wrote, "So I address this to you my friends, in order to consecrate the memory of the best friend we have lost."[3]

About two weeks later, on February 12, 1812, Régnier addressed a letter from Old Mines to Craighead at the Shibboleth Mine. This is perhaps the most important letter in the Craighead Papers bearing on Régnier's life. In it he wrote that on the previous day, bad weather and nightfall had kept him and Louis DeMun from reaching the mine (*Vieille Mine*). They had lost their way about 10 P.M. and were "soaked, numb with cold and all worn out." Régnier informed Craighead that he was anxious about his wife Félicité, who was soon to be delivered of a baby in Ste. Genevieve, and that he was going on to that village. Régnier said he would stay there a few weeks until his wife was out of danger. (Their only daughter, Adele, was subsequently born on February 26.) "For the time being," Régnier added, "I am passing as a villager without land or lead, and yet I command nearly $3,000 piastres." In closing, he wrote, "I am taking my books with me to work on my accounts in

---

[3] Cf. George Frank Gouley (grand secretary), *The Official Record of the A.F. & A.M. of the State of Missouri, 1821–1840, inclusive* (St. Louis, 1877); and William Frederick Kuhn (past grand master), *Centennial History of the Grand Lodge, Free and Accepted Masons of Missouri: 1821–1921* (St. Louis, n.d.). Gouley and Kuhn both give the Grand Master's name as "Strader," possibly transcribed in error from old manuscript records. He is believed to be the Hon. Otho Shrader (or Shröder, Schrader, etc.), a judge who lived in the Ste. Genevieve–St. Louis area in the early 1800's. Régnier's spelling of the name is hard to decipher. Kuhn concludes in his introduction: "In 1809–10, the Grand Lodge of Pennsylvania granted a warrant to form and open a Lodge of St. Louis under the name of St. Louis Lodge No. 111. No record or any information as to names of the officers or the career of this lodge are known."

the village and settle them so that my absence may not go forgotten by all the friends I believe I had at the mine and especially you. . . ." Meanwhile, on February 5, Nicolas Wilson had written from Ste. Genevieve to Craighead at Mine Shibboleth and sent a message that Régnier's "family is well."

The next surviving document surprises us, since it follows by less than three months the letter of February 12 in which Régnier expressed concern for Félicité. It is a four-page declaration of mutual consent by Régnier and Louise Félicité Vallée to separate and live no longer as man and wife. This agreement was drawn up at Old Mines on May 10, 1812. It was signed by both parties and witnessed by Craighead and Ed. D. Devillmonte. Under its terms Régnier, who had married Félicité in Santo Domingo on July 27, 1802, would have custody of his two sons, Adolphe (the elder) and Alfred. Félicité agreed to turn over their daughter Adele to Régnier as soon as the girl was five years old. Meanwhile Adele, who was to be baptized the next month, was to be provided for by Régnier at the rate of ten piastres a month. Neither party to the agreement was to disinherit the children. Mme. Régnier took custody of all household goods in the house of the presbyter at Ste. Genevieve. She could not leave the country without forfeiting her rights under this agreement, nor did Régnier wish to permit the removal of his daughter or the family's Negro servant Lisa (Adele's nurse). It was also stipulated that their divorce action would be publicly announced at some time and place in the future.[4]

The separation must have affected Régnier very deeply, for on the same date we find him writing a four-page letter "to his friends" (no doubt to present his side of the case to society), recalling his ten years of marriage to Félicité. He explained that a few disputes and incompatibilities of disposition had sometimes arisen, and that Félicité, who was born to a life of ease, had found their difficulties too much to bear. He wrote of the countless abuses she had heaped upon him ("reproches sans nombre que Madame Régnier m'a prodigués"). He admitted that his own conduct was not perfect, yet insisted that his outbursts and fits of anger, for which she still blamed him so unjustly, were only the result of her indifference toward him.

---

[4] That this action in 1812 was only a legal separation becomes clear five years later when a summons to François Régnier to appear at Jackson, Missouri, before the Circuit Court to answer his wife's divorce suit was published in the *Missouri Gazette*, Feb. 1, 1817.

Gradually in this letter Régnier worked himself into a fever of invective, first against Félicité, then against womanhood in general. "A woman's arms consist only of words," he complained; "when she wants to hate, they are made only of the most monstrous malignity." He continued to rail like this for several more pages until he apparently exhausted his energy and writing space. At the end he inferred that Félicité simply did not want to live with him any more. Lacking any testimony by Félicité in her own defense (or perhaps to Régnier's offense), we cannot pass judgment on their separation or fix the blame on either spouse. This is the last extant letter by Pierre François Régnier.[5]

To these glimpses of his life we can add only that in 1821 he was teaching school in St. Louis. The city directory for that year (Paxton's Directory) lists him as a "teacher of French, south Church, N.W. corner south F." This is confirmed by bilingual (French and English) advertisements which appeared in the *Missouri Gazette* in September, 1821, informing the public that he was continuing "teaching Reading, Writing, and Arithmetic" and that he had expanded his curriculum to include Greek, Latin, and various other courses. He also announced that, besides operating a day boarding school, he intended "to devote his leisure hours" to instructing night classes.[6]

---

[5] A little later Craighead apparently had difficulties of his own, financially, perhaps for overextending credit. In a letter dated July 16, 1814, James Adams in Pittsburgh notified Craighead that the latter's balance had been attached by the sheriff for a note of his in the hands of Bakewell and Company.

[6] The complete English text of these advertisements is as follows:

"The subscriber having already advertised in February last, his intention of establishing a French school in Mr. Didier's house, Church-street, has the honor of informing the public that he now resides in the house formerly occupied by F. M. Guyol, in the same street, where he continues teaching Reading, Writing, and Arithmetic by demonstration. In consequence of the encouragement hitherto manifested by the parents of the children entrusted to his care, & of the arrangements lately formed with Messrs. Sullivan & Duvelus, he moreover informs the public that from the first of September inst. the Greek, Latin, and English languages, together with Reading, Writing, and Arithmetic with book keeping by demonstration, will be taught in his seminary; and that he will pay the best possible attention to the education and morality of his pupils. His house enables him to receive children of both sexes in commodious and separate apartments. The charges for tuition will be proportionated to the age, proficiency, and disposition of his pupils, and regulated with the parents or guardians of the children at his house. Boarders by the month or year, or demi-boarders will be received at very moderate prices. The school for both sexes shall be opened at nine o'clock in the forenoon, and continued till twelve o'clock; and in the afternoon from two till five. In the summer

64

There are sixteen manuscript poems in French among the Craig-head Papers.[7] At this point, fact ends and conjecture begins. While most of the manuscripts may be ascribed to Pierre François Régnier, their original authorship is questionable, despite Régnier's signature or Masonic symbol on them. Tentatively we may assign about half of the poems to Régnier. Yet even these few reveal him as a poet of wide sensibilities. Like the late E. E. Cummings he was able to express many moods, from satire and gaiety to tenderness and grief, in various forms, rhythms, and diction.

The earliest dated poem in the Craighead Papers is a clever, rollicking lyric of five seven-line stanzas, each ending with a refrain on "the new mine," with an extra couplet between the third and fourth stanzas. Régnier sent this poem to Craighead from Old Mines in a letter dated September 29, 1811. This poem is written to an old tune with the refrain, "Disons le mot, disons le mot, le petit mot, pour rire." In this poem, as in the letter, Régnier lightly chides Craighead—"the Cupid of the new mine"—for courting the belles. The poem is full of double meanings and suggestion. ("Mine," for example, means "face" as well as "mine.") In the final stanza the

season the regulations will be varied.

"Exclusive of the aforesaid literary branches he will, to the best of his abilities, impart the elements of history, Mythology, Geography, & other sciences. To those wishing to receive private lessons in the French, or English language, the best possible satisfaction will be rendered at very moderate prices.
FRANCIS REGNIER."
(*Missouri Gazette*, Sept. 5, 1821)

"The subscriber hereby respectfully signifies to the public his intention to devote his leisure hours, viz. from 5 to 7 o'clock P.M. to the instruction of such gentlemen as may feel an avidity to acquire a satisfactory, radical knowledge as well of the French & English Languages, as of Arithmetic Book-Keeping, &c. His apartment is comfortable, and well adapted to the contemplated purpose. In the prosecution of his literary occupations, his primary object shall be, to impart as well to his night as to his day-scholars an education, rather substantial than ostentatious. Those who may entertain a desire to avail themselves of the present proposal, are respectfully invited to communicate their intentions as soon as possible. When a number sufficient to justify both his own employment and that of his co-operators will have been completed, he assures his friends and the public in general that his exertions in rendering every practicable satisfaction to the gentlemen aforesaid shall be as well uniform as strenuous. His school shall be regularly opened at the above-mentioned time, and continued in succession (Saturday excepted) throughout the week.

"Charges for Tuition, $2½ per month, payable in advance.
FRANCIS REGNIER."
(*Missouri Gazette*, Sept. 26, 1821)

[7] The full texts of twelve of the poems are printed in the appendix to this paper. My transcription of some of these poems is provisional, for the manuscripts are almost impossible to decipher.

poet writes that he would like the "old mine" if his "take" of mineral were equal to Craighead's:

> Ah! si mon tôt de minéral,—
> au tien, du moins, était égal—!
> j'aimerais la vieille mine—;
> pour le bien fondre, mon ami—
> je n'aurais pas besoin des vi——
> des vigoureux, des vigoureux—
> De la nouvelle mine.

Régnier added a postscript: "Good-by, good day, and good health—excuse my foolishness. Sincerely—." ("À Dieu—bon jour—et bonne santé—excusez mes folies. Tout à vous—.")

Next in order, dated December 27, 1811, are two poems on one sheet, written at Old Mines: "À ma femme Créole de St Domingue" ("To my Creole wife of Santo Domingo"), numbered 83, and an acrostic on the name of Nicolas Wilson, numbered 76. In the former, Régnier casts doubts on his wife's character—although he writes, "I thought it virtuous." The poem ends bitterly, "Good-by, you and all your lovers." Régnier dedicates the acrostic to Wilson with "My thanks for various favors that I have received from him and my reflections on his character." He splits the "W" of "Wilson" into two "V's" to begin the eighth and ninth lines with the word "Vive": "Long live Wilson and his good Character/Long live especially his constant friendship." Both of these poems are rather illegible and seem to have been hurriedly composed or copied.

Another poem in the collection is dated January 27, 1812. It is dedicated "To the Memory of Brother Shrader, Late Grand Master of the Ste. Genevieve Lodge" ("À la mémoire du Frère Shrader—décédé Grand-maître de la loge de Sainte-Geneviève") and is signed "by a lodge brother" ("par un frère de la loge"), with a Masonic symbol at the end. The poem is conventional in tone and consists of two quatrains of alternately rhymed alexandrines. Here is a translation:

> Let's not forget the friend whom we have lost;
> We're bound to miss that master we esteem.
> Of all Freemasons, by his constant zeal,
> He merited respect and won renown.

> O you whose days are ended now by Fate,
> O worthy Shrader who adorned our temple!
> Know that you'll always live among your friends,
> Since you've left them your virtues for example.

One of the best poems in the Craighead Papers is Régnier's "Élégie" to Félicité, written on two pages of a single manuscript sheet, dated June 14, 1812, at Mine Shibboleth, a month after the separation. It is signed "François Régnier fils." In a footnote to Craighead, Régnier directed that the poem "be deposited with the papers which were entrusted to him for me and my wife" ("aux soins de l'ami Craighead—pour être déposé avec les papiers dont il est chargé pour moi et ma femme"). The elegy is fifty-six lines long—fourteen quatrains of alternately rhymed eight-syllable lines.

Briefly, the poem reflects Régnier's unhappiness and disappointment in his marriage. He plays ironically on the name Félicité. He describes himself as a victim of Félicité and concludes that his hope is no longer in his wife's arms but in death. Altogether it is a very introspective and moody poem, marked by the self-pity common to many Romantic poets. Here is a prose transcription in English:

### Elegy

O you whose name tempted me, Felicity, whom I still love, whatever fate embitters you, listen to the voice which implores you.

How could I hate you? It's even impossible to forget you. Your husband's every desire was to make you responsive.

Alas, I dared to believe in happiness and I was beginning to forget my sorrows. Good Lord, how wrong I was! How heavy are my chains!

*Felicity* reigns in my heart, and yet I'm her victim. . . .

You alone could make me love life again; I'd even sacrifice it for you, yet my own wife is my enemy.

Wife and mother, must you be unfaithful to your vows? Love caused all my distress and love made you cruel!

Another has my Felicity and may praise the charms of her love—never sincerely—has he appreciated the tears?

Far from my heart is any feeling of vengeance or betrayal; but if you cherish a lover, how can I overcome jealousy?

Discouraged by my Sorrow, I don't know what more I can do; far from desiring your misfortune, I'd like to please you.

I take my children in my arms, sometimes, to conquer my sadness . . . . They and their mother soon bring back all my feelings of tenderness.

For you I had the courage to forgive and forget everything! But agree to love me again; I want only your heart as a pledge.

For three children whose childhood we must love and protect, together in friendship let's seek true enjoyment.

If love made us unhappy, let friendship—more reasonable for us from now on—bind us again; our happiness would last.

But what hope! O the severity of my fate isn't too distressing. . . . Not in your arms, but in death I see what's left for me.

Besides the acrostic to Nicolas Wilson, there is an acrostic in the collection addressed to "Alexandre" Craighead (Régnier uses the French spelling). This is dated August 13 or 15, 1812. (The top and bottom of the manuscript, showing date and signature, are torn and illegible.) The poem has a unique structure, consisting of two stanzas of nine lines each, irregularly rhymed. The first thirteen lines are ten-syllable verses, variations of iambic pentameter, but the next line, which is partly illegible, seems to be longer, and the last four lines are in French alexandrines. The irregularity shows perhaps that the poem was not written in one sitting, that Régnier found the last stanza difficult or could not contain his expression in the shorter line. All of these factors might have affected the building of the last stanza.

We seldom find a good serious poem among acrostics, and Régnier's are no exception. By its special construction, the acrostic is more artificial than most verse forms and may be considered a kind of minor tour de force. The most interested reader is the recipient, and he is seldom too critical of the quality of verse that happens to be strung out after the letters of his name. Traditionally, the acrostic is flattering and the poet protests it is not. So Régnier addresses Craighead: "Don't take me for a sycophant;/in this state, true honor/governs my pen, and not flattery." Xenophon enters the poem to become the "x" in "Alexandre": "Even Xenophon had praised your candor." The most sincere line in the poem is probably line ten: "As a Mason, you know how to act as a brother."

Another manuscript bearing Régnier's signature and dedicated "To my friend Craighead" is titled "My Reflections on the Nine Parts of Speech, or Words Received in Discourse" ("Mes réflexions sur les neuf parties de l'oraison, ou les mots reçus dans le Discours"). This poem is forty lines long—five stanzas of eight lines, alternately rhymed. The meter is iambic tetrameter and trimeter. Although signed by Régnier, the poem seems to be the kind of verse every schoolboy knows by heart and which comes from some anonymous source. Since it is light, functional verse, the question of authorship is not very important. The singsong verses are easy to learn and have a few clever twists. The third stanza goes, "The noun, the pronoun, the adjective,/and the verb and the adverb/offer nothing positive enough/to cheer my glass./But the word 'preposition'/awakens my spirit;/and for the Conjunction/I'm capable of folly."

One remaining poem among the manuscripts of less doubtful authorship is addressed to Régnier's sons, Adolphe and Alfred. This is a two-page composition of forty-eight lines, undated but signed. The manuscript itself is folded as a letter and addressed, "À mon ami—À Craighead." At the top of the poem is the inscription "En vers libres" ("In free verse"), a phrase which meant something quite different to the Romantic poets than to the later Symbolists (Laforgue, Maeterlinck, Gustave Kahn) and Imagists. The lines are in fact predominantly iambic pentameter and are alternately rhymed. The "freedom" of the verse lies in its departure from the classical couplet. In this poem, as in the "Élégie," Régnier wrote that he lived for his sons—his "charming young sons"—and loved them in spite of his wife's infidelity. Several lines are in a style reminiscent of Ronsard: "Your mother . . . /was unfaithful to me for another—/yet some day she will love Régnier."

A poem titled "To All Husbands in My Situation" ("À tous maris, dans ma situation") is of more questionable authenticity, although its theme certainly bears on Régnier's plight. It consists of five twelve-line stanzas (if we adjust the arrangement of the fourth stanza, which is divided in ten lines). The lyrics are composed to an old military tune, "Soldats français, c'est pour la foi." The style of this poem resembles the free verse of Verhaeren and Henri de Régnier, and the rhymes are light and mincing:

> Joli minois, peut quelquefois,
> Nous entraîner à la folie—;
> quand l'amour marche en tapinois,
> le plus sage souvent s'oublie.
> De deux beaux yeux
> je suis bien mieux
> —amoureux;
> s'ils me disent, "je t'aime"—
> mais si leurs feux
> trompent mes vœux
> je ne peux—
> souffrir leur stratagème.

> A pretty face, sometimes,
> leads us to lunacy;
> when love walks stealthily
> the wise man loses his mind.
> I'm smitten
> much more
> by two pretty eyes
> if they tell me, "I love you."
> But if their fires
> cheat my desires,
> I can't
> put up with all their schemes.

The third or pivotal stanza applies more to Régnier's separation from Félicité:

> Ami, qui sembles, comme moi,
> par moments, regretter la femme,—
> ne compte pas plus sur sa foi—
> qu'elle ne compte sur ta flamme.
> Quoiqu'il en soit,
> tout homme *adroit,*
> s'il m'en croit,——
> doit par philosophie—
> savoir, qu'il doit—
> en tout endroit
> loin de soi—
> chasser la Jalousie.

> My friend, you're just like me,
> sometimes you miss your girl,
> but don't count on her being true
> any more than she can count on you.
> Though he be hers,
> every *smart* man,
> if I'm to be believed,
> must philosophically
> understand
> that he must chase,
> every place,
> a haunting Jealousy.

Another light song, a "Drinking Song" ("Chanson à boire"), appears on a manuscript sheet with a poem on the Cardinal de Bernis. The "Drinking Song" has four eight-line stanzas with the refrain,

> Ayez toujours du bon vieux vin
> Et buvez à pleins verres!

The theme of infidelity runs through the second stanza, which goes, "Chloë, the object of all your desires,/At last became unfaithful /And one day leaves you/For a more successful lover!/There's no great mystery/In how to dispel your sorrow!/Always have some good old wine/And drink with glasses full!"

The poem "On the Death[?] of the Cardinal de Bernis" ("Sur la mort[?] du Cardinal de Bernis") consists of four quatrains of iambic pentameters, with alternately rhymed lines. The poem describes the transience of human grandeur and ends, "I shall become more fortunate than you" ("Je deviendrai plus fortuné que vous"). This piece is particularly interesting because it may support our assumption that not all of the poems in the Craighead Papers were composed in 1811–12. The Cardinal de Bernis (François-Joachim de Pierre de Bernis) was born in 1715 and died at Rome on November 3, 1794. It is most likely that the poem was written soon after the cardinal's death, and may be dated 1794 or 1795.

Five other French poems in the Craighead Papers are quoted in full in the appendix. These poems are "Reflections on Man's Fate" ("Réflexions sur Circonstance[?] des Hommes") and four poems covering both sides of a single manuscript sheet: "Let us taste pleasures here" ("Que l'on goûte ici de plaisirs"); "Charming flowers, leave Flora's fields" ("Charmantes fleurs, quitter les prés de flore"); "I saw Love, a charming child" ("J'ai vu l'amour un enfant plein de charme"), and "Melody" ("Ariette"). These five poems, as well as the "Drinking Song" and the poem on the Cardinal de Bernis, are all unsigned and of uncertain authorship. While I have not searched exhaustively, I have gone through many sources in an attempt to identify the poems. They may belong to another period—with the Pléiade poets, for instance. In several texts the conditional ending is not clearly legible and may be read as either the old or modern form. Many other questions arise. For example, the Lisette mentioned in "Charmantes fleurs" may be the Lisa who lived with the Régnier family.

Régnier must have written many more poems than the few we can attribute to him among the Craighead Papers. Until other work turns up or until the doubtful manuscripts can be authenticated, we should not hasten to pass judgment on his life and work. We can only assume he is a minor poet in France's long literary history. Yet, how many major poets did France produce between Chénier and Lamartine?

Unfortunately a certain narrowness of taste on the part of anthologists has blocked them from regarding French writings since Pénicaut as "American."[8] Yet, how significant Régnier is, or could be, to us as a poet of upper Louisiana! Whether his verse stands comparison with the work of poets like Philip Freneau and Joel Barlow may be open to question. But Régnier may find a place with these poets some day when French writing in America is viewed as a natural part of our polyglot heritage.

APPENDIX

French poems in the Craighead Papers composed by, or attributable to, Pierre François Régnier. Poems marked with an asterisk (*) are not included in this appendix because they present great difficulties of transcription.

Acrostiche (à Alexandre Craighead)
*Acrostiche (à Nicolas Wilson)
À la mémoire du Frère Shrader
*À ma femme Créole de St Domingue
Ariette ("De prendre femme un jour dit-on")
À tous maris, dans ma situation
Chanson à boire ("Mes amis, je veux, aujourd'hui")
"Charmantes fleurs, quitter les prés de flore"
Élégie ("O toi! dont le nom m'a séduit")
*En vers libres ("Être père de ces jeunes enfants")
"J'ai vu l'amour un enfant plein de charme"
La nouvelle mine ("Sur les plus beaux trous que j'ai vus")
Mes réflexions sur les neuf parties de l'oraison
"Que l'on goûte ici de plaisirs"
Réflexions sur Circonstance[?] des Hommes
*Sur la mort[?] du Cardinal de Bernis

---

[8] Richebourg Gaillard McWilliams also notes this long-existing trend in the introduction to his translation of Pénicaut's narrative. Certain historians, too, he adds, totally ignore French dominion in the South, whether from a social, political, or literary viewpoint (*Fleur de Lys and Calumet* [Baton Rouge, 1953], pp. xv–xvi).

Acrostiche

13[15?]–8–1812

A à l'amitié, ton âme est toute entière
L l'or et l'argent, ne font point ton bonheur—
E en toi, je trouve, un charmant caractère
X Xenophon même eut loué ta candeur.
A ami Craighead! ma muse est ton amie—
N ne me prends point, pour un adulateur—
D dans cet état, le véritable honneur—
R règle ma plume, et non le flatterie—.
E être sincère, est tout par un grand cœur.

C comme maçon, tu sais agir en frère—
R rien ne t'arrête, une faveur d'ami—
A aussitôt que, . . . *du sein de la misère*—
I il peut par toi, quelque soit son ennui—.
G grace à [ . . . ] dans, retrouver [ . . . ] un appui—,
H heureux, ou malheureux . . . toujours la bienfaisance
E est pour l'homme un devoir . . . mais riche et vertueux . . .
A à toi, je dois la palme . . . au jour! . . . puissant mes yeux
D du ciel, pour mon ami, doubler la Récompense!


[N'oublions point l'ami. . . . ]

January 27th, 1812.

À la mémoire du Frère Shrader—décédé
Grand-maître de la loge de Sainte-Geneviève

N'oublions point l'ami, que nous avons perdu
nous devons regretter, ce respectable maître. . . . .
de tous les franc-maçons—par son zèle assidu—
il mérita l'estime—et se fit reconnaître.

O toi dont le Destin—vient de finir les jours!
O vertueux Shrader! ornement de ce temple—!!!
crois que pour tes amis, tu revivras toujours—
quand tu leur as laissé, tes vertus pour exemple.

par un frère de la loge.
PFR


arriette [ariette]

de prendre femme un jour dit-on
l'amour conçut la fantaisie
on lui proposa la raison
on lui proposa la folie

quel choix fera ce dieu fripon
chaque déesse est fort jolie
il prit, pour femme la raison
Et pour maîtresse la fôlie.


—à tous maris, dans ma situation
Sur l'air militaire . . .
*Soldats français c'est pour la foi*

près d'une Belle, ah! quel plaisir!
Et surtout . . . quand elle vous aime.
combien dans le moindre dessin
la jouissance est-elle extrême!
un rien suffit,
lorsque l'esprit—
est séduit;
pour enchaîner notre âme.
mais quel ennui!
pour un mari.
—mal uni—,
de vivre avec sa femme.

Joli minois, peut quelquefois,
nous entraîner à la folie—;
quand l'amour marche en tapinois,
le plus sage souvent s'oublie.
De deux beaux yeux,
je suis bien mieux
—amoureux;
s'ils me disent, "je t'aime"—
mais si leurs feux
trompent mes vœux
je ne peux—
souffrir leur stratagème.

Ami, qui sembles, comme moi,
par moments, regretter la femme,—
ne compte pas plus sur sa foi—
qu'elle ne compte sur ta flamme.
Quoiqu'il en soit,
tout homme *adroit*,
s'il m'en croit,——
doit par philosophie—
savoir, qu'il doit—
en tout endroit
loin de soi—
chasser la Jalousie.

pour gouttes des plaisirs parfaits—
Dieu, ne nous a pas mis au monde;
que n'a-t-il, de tous ses bienfaits—
permis que le vin seul abonde?
avec le vin,—on veut fort bien—,
      au chagrin,
faire en tout temps la guerre—.
faute de vin. . . . . margoûs[?] sans fin—
      -le destin,
quand il nous est contraire.

oser, vous vanter le wiskey—
serait prêtes, peut-être à rire—
du vin, c'est dit-on l'ennemi—
J'aime assez pourtant son empire. . . . . .
du bon wiskey,
des mieux, choisi—
peut aussi,
charmer notre existence—
peur d'en manquer,
vaut-mieux trinquer
Et garder—
prudemment le Silence.-


## Chanson à boire

Air: [?]

Mes amis, je veux, aujourd'hui,
Vous donner des conseils bien sages:
Si jamais le tort ennemi,
Vous accabloit de ses outrages
Amis, pour vaincre le destin
Suivez mes conseils salutaires:
Ayez toujours de bon vieux vin
Et buvez à pleins verres!

Chloé, l'objet de tous vos vœux,
Enfin devint-elle infidèle
Et pour un amant plus heureux
Un jour vous abandonne-t-elle!
Pour dissiper votre chagrin
Il ne faut pas de grands mystères!
Ayez toujours, etc.

Si la [ . . . ] pour vous
Des jours de bonheur, d'allégresse
Et si le retour le plus doux
Est le pris de [ . . . ] paresse[?]
Amis, pour finir le destin
Suivez mes avis salutaires,
Ayez, etc.

Sans le bon vin point de bonheur;
Croyez-en mon expérience:
De nos chagrins c'est le vainqueur,
Il ajoute à la jouissance
Ainsi toujours le verre en main
Les destins nous seront prospères.
Ayons donc toujours de bon vin
Et buvons à pleins verres.


[charmantes fleurs. . . . ]

charmantes fleurs, quitter les prés de flore
je vous prépare, un plus heureux destin,
orner l'objet, que j'aime et que j'adore,
suiver ses pas, et mourir[?] sur son sein.     *bis*

quand vous verrez—ma charmante Lisette
vous bénisez mille fois, votre sort—
pour imiter sa constance parfaîte—
vous ne voudrez, la quitter, qu'à la mort.     *bis*

de la beauté, vous êtes le simbôle,
un jour, hélas, vous voit naître et mourir,
que ma Lisette, appécune[?] à votre écôle!
que la sagesse, est d'en savoir jouir.

*Fin.*


### Élégie

O toi! dont le nom m'a séduit,
Félicité! que j'aime encore,
quelque soit le sort qui t'aigrit,
écoute la voix qui t'implore.

Comment pourrais-je te haïr?
t'oublier, est même impossible.
De ton époux tout le désir,
était de te rendre sensible.

Hélas! j'osais croire au bonheur,—
et déjà j'oubliais mes peines,
grand-Dieu! quelle était mon erreur!
Combien sont pesantes mes chaînes!

*Félicité* règne au mon cœur,
et pourtant, je suis sa victime. . . . .
ah! de l'aimer avec fureur,
peut-elle bien me faire un crime?

toi seule à jamais tu pouvais—
me faire encore aimer la vie,
pour toi je la sacrifierais— . . .
et ma femme est mon ennemie . . .

Épouse et mère, à tes serments—
Dois-tu devenir infidèle?
l'amour causa tous mes tourments,
et l'amour t'a rendu cruelle!

un autre à [*sic*] ma Félicité,
de l'amour peut vanter les charmes.—
jamais de la sincérité,—
a-t-il apprécié les larmes?

loin de mon cœur, tout sentiment,
de vengeance ou de perfidie—
mais si tu chéris un amant,—
comment dompter la jalousie?

Découragé par ma Douleur,
je ne bien plus sais[?] qu'il faut faire—
bien loin de vouloir ton malheur,—
à toi seule, je voudrais plaire.

dans mes bras—je prends mes enfants,
parfois pour vaincre ma tristesse . . .
eux et leur mère, en tous mes sens,—
bientôt rappellent la tendresse.

tout oublier et pardonner,
pour toi . . . j'en avais le courage!
mais consens encore à m'aimer;
je ne veux que ton cœur pour gage.

pour trois enfants, dont nous devons
aimer et protéger l'enfance;—
tous deux—dans l'amitié, cherchons—
la véritable jouissance.

Si l'amour nous fit malheureux:
que l'amitié, plus raisonnable—.
désormais—resserre nos nœuds—!
notre bonheur serait durable.

mais quel espoir!—ah! de mon sort,
la rigueur n'est trop funeste . . .
non dans tes bras—mais dans la mort,
je vois le parti qui me reste.

François . . . Régnier fils

Mine Shibouleth—
14 juin 1812
_____
        aux soins de l'ami Craighead—pour être déposé
        avec les papiers dont il est chargé pour moi
        et ma femme.————————————

[j'ai vu l'amour. . . . ]

j'ai vu l'amour un enfant plein de charme
hélas, j'osais le presser sur son cœur
   que cet enfant m'a fait verser de larmes
   ah! étiez-vous, à sa feinte douleur!      }      *bis.*
[c?]

Depuis longtemps, je déteste mes gaînes,
et je les vois, s'augmenter chaque jour
   et chaque jour s'offrent nouvelles peines
   voilà—dit-on, les bienfaits de l'amour    }      *bis.*

O douce paix! que l'amour m'a ravi
viens sur mon cœur y reprendre les droits
   toi seule, fis, le bonheur de ma vie
   de la raison quand j'écoutais la voix    }      *bis*

[La nouvelle mine]
Sur l'air: Disons le mot, disons le mot, le petit mot, pour rire—

"Sur les plus beaux trous que j'ai vus,
ou que des yeux, j'ai parcourus;
ma Muse est si badine—,
que je n'ose dire en chanson—
combien j'admire tous les Con————
tous les contours, tous les contours,                de la nouvelle mine!

"il en est, de tant de couleurs,—
il en ainsi tant de piocheurs,
que je crains que ma pine——
n'y fouille jamais tous les trous
avec autant d'ardeur que vous—
pouvez le faire, pouver le faire,                à la nouvelle mine.

"Messieurs, qui régler les terrains,
qui les tenez tous en vos mains,
je lis sur votre mine. . . . . . .

Dans certains trous—ah! qu'il est bon!
De voir se fourrer[?], jusqu'aux fon——
jusqu'aux fondeurs, jusqu'aux fondeurs,—
       de la nouvelle mine.

"pourquoi régler aussi—par vous seul, tant de trous,
"si j'en avais ma part, je serais moins jaloux.

"Ami, pour qui sont ces couplets—
je veux bien taire, tes hauts faits—!
mais . . . rire à la sourdine—
sans doute n'est pas défendu;
quand des belles. . . . tu fais . . . le Cu—
le Cupidon, le Cupidon—
       de la nouvelle mine.

Ah! si mon tôt de minéral,—
au tien, du moins, était égal—!
j'aimerais la vieille mine—;
pour le bien fondre, mon ami—
je n'aurais point besoin des vi——
des vigoureux, des vigoureux—
       -De la nouvelle mine.

À Dieu—bon jour—et bonne santé—excusez mes folies.
         Tout à vous—.
         PFR


Mes réflexions sur les neuf parties de l'oraison,
ou de mots—reçus dans le Discours.

   "Nous ne parlons commencement
   ici, que de grammaire—:
   Amis, laissons donc un moment,
   l'école de l'arrière—;
   Sur les neuf parts de l'oraison,—
   que je suis las d'écrire:
   Si j'entreprends une chanson,—
   Ce n'est bien que pour rire.

   L'article me fournirait bien,
   plaisante chose à dire—:
   mais, comment trouver le moyen
   de pouvoir y suffire?
   Sur l'*article*, qui fait le sourd—:
   Songeant fait des prouesses;—
   Moi, pour ne pas rester à court,
   J'épargne les promesses.

"Le nom, le pronom, l'adjectif,
et le verbe et l'adverbe—:
n'offrent rien d'assez positif,
pour égayer ma verre—.
Mais le mot préposition,—
Éveille mon génie;
Je suis pour la Conjonction—
Capable de Folie.

Je le crois bien, me direz-vous—
chacun de compagnie,—
qui n'aimerait pas entre nous,
Cette aimable partie?
Sans elle, adieu mille douceurs,
qui charment notre vie—.
Vive l'union de deux cœurs!
Vive une tendre amie!

"Ce n'est pas encor tout pourtant
il reste la neuvième:
cette partie, assurément
parle assez d'elle-même—
Amis, que les plaisirs sont doux
quand au sein de L'ivresse—
l'interjection vient en nous—
redoubler la tendresse! ! !

/s/ Pierre François Régnier

à l'ami Craighead


[que l'on goûte ici de plaisirs. . . . ]

que l'on goûte ici de plaisirs
1  où pourrions-nous mieux être
tout y satisfait nos désirs
et tout les fait renaître.

2  N'est-ce par ici le jardin
où notre premier père
trouvait sans cesse sous sa main
de quoi se satisfaire.

3  Dans ce jardin delicieux
on y voyait deux pommes
faites pour charmer tous les Dieux
et damner tous les hommes.

4  Ne sommes-nous pas beaucoup mieux
qu'Adam dans son bocage
il n'y voyait que deux beaux yeux
j'envois bien davantage.

5   Amis en voyant tant d'appâs!
quels plaisirs, tous les notres!
Sans le peché d'Adam, hélas!
nous en verrions, bien d'autres.

6   il n'avait qu'une femme avec lui
encore c'était la sienne—
et moi, j'avais celle d'autrui
et ne vois pas la mienne

7   il buvait de l'eau tristement
avecque sa compagne
quand nous nous amusons gaîment
à sables du champagne.

8   Si l'on eut fait dans un repas
cette chère, au bon homme
le gourmand, ne nous aurait pas
damnés pour une pomme.

*Fin.*

### Réflexions sur Circonstance[?] des Hommes

dans un bois solitaire, au bord d'une onde pure,
l'autre jour en rêvant, je conduisais mes pas
de ces lieux retirés par la simple nature
j'admirais en secret les rustiques appas.
voilà dis-je aussitôt, comme tout devait être—
la beauté paraîtrait, sans secours et sans fard.—
et le cœur, ne tenant que de son premier être,
s'appliquerait toujours, sans détour et sans art.
l'amant serait fidèle, et l'amante sincère.—
dans des jeux innocents, le temps s'écoulerait;
on se plairait toujours, sans trop chercher à plaire
et l'estime surtout, jamais ne finirait,
mais hélas, où trouver un ami véritable!
de la tendre amitié, les temples sont déserts.
de son frère *l'amour* la lutte condamnable
lui ravit la moitié des cours de l'univers.

# Pierre Gibault and the Critical Period of the Illinois Country, 1768-78

## Joseph P. Donnelly

On the occasion of the celebration of the second centenary of the existence of the city of St. Louis, the historian is again faced with the question of why this frontier outpost, founded in 1764, should have survived successfully while many other similar and perhaps even more promising establishments failed to develop into flourishing cities. Though such factors as geographic location, economic prosperity of the fur trade, and the absence of close governmental control were largely responsible, perhaps a more important element was the presence in the area of a few influential men, not the least of whom was Father Pierre Gibault. It seems appropriate on some occasion during this bicentenary celebration to focus attention briefly on this "patriot priest" whose stabilizing influence was an important factor in the Illinois Country, particularly during the ten critical years, 1768–78.

The term Illinois Country employed in this discussion is given a wider sense than we find it used by such scholars as Clarence Walworth Alvord and Clarence E. Carter, who, technically and properly, limited their excellent work to that portion of the Mississippi Valley which came into the possession of Great Britain by the Treaty of Paris of 1763, that is, the territory bounded roughly by the Mississippi River, the Allegheny Mountains, perhaps Prairie du Chien to the north, and the Wabash River on the south. In Father Gibault's mind the Illinois Country, the mission to which he was assigned in 1768, included every hamlet, every Indian village, and every living soul within the confines of the great Mississippi Valley above the Ohio. A brief glance at the settlements in that area, a quick review of the character of the people dwelling there, as well as the shortest possible review of the politico-military atmosphere, would seem to have a place here.

As everyone is well aware, Great Britain rather reluctantly accepted Canada and the eastern half of the Mississippi Valley as part of the spoils of war in 1763. The hesitancy of the British is perhaps more understandable if one recalls the almost religious dedication of English businessmen to the theory of mercantilism.[1] The western stretches of Canada would still produce rich fur harvests, but what could one do with the eastern half of the Mississippi Valley? To exploit its agricultural possibilities would require a great river of immigrants who could not, even if available, be safely transplanted there until something was done to solve the Indian problem. Perhaps the most practical solution would be simply to repeat the Acadian experiment, resettling the French in Canada or even, perhaps, in Florida which the English had acquired by the Treaty of Paris. And what sort of people were these French of the Mississippi Valley to whom the English had recently fallen heir?

Philip Pittman, whose *Present State of European Settlements on the Mississippi* appeared in 1770, estimated that there were approximately two thousand white settlers dwelling in the Illinois Country.[2] Kaskaskia had a white population of six hundred which was augmented by three hundred Negro and Indian slaves. There were twenty-five families at Prairie du Rocher, forty at Fort Chartres, three at St. Phillipe and about sixty at Cahokia. Vincennes had a population of about two hundred and fifty whites besides a few Negro and Indian slaves.[3] While residents of these villages were for

---

[1] Oscar Theodore Barck and Hugh Talmadge Lefler, *Colonial America* (New York, 1958), p. 472.

[2] Captain Philip Pittman, *The Present State of the European Settlements on the Mississippi with a Geographical Description of That River, Illustrated by Plans and Draughts* (London, 1770), p. 50.

[3] Evarts B. Greene and Virginia D. Harrington, *American Population Before the Federal Census of 1790* (New York, 1932), p. 188.

the most part French or French Canadians, there was a growing influx of Anglo-Saxon traders and even a few Irish. Witness, for example, the marriage of Henry O'Hara and Bridget Bolton; or better, the nuptials of Mary Whalen of Waterford in Ireland, the daughter of Laurence Whalen and Catherine Ferrell.[4]

When British authorities, in the person of Captain Thomas Stirling, finally took possession of the Illinois Country in 1765, it was discovered that the new English subjects were accustomed to quite liberal democratic forms of government on a local level. The civil code under which they lived was, generally, an adaptation of that applicable to the *faubourgs* of Paris, a system which linked local civil government to the ecclesiastical confines of a parish.[5] Within such units the citizenry directly elected church wardens as well as some local civil officials. This unique arrangement had the advantage of making it possible for some sort of civil order to persist even in the face of vital changes of national ownership. It also gave the local pastor an unofficial but very real position of influence in the civil affairs of the local community. In a vague, general way the pastor somehow appeared to be importantly connected to the crown of France. Herein, it may be conjectured, rested the importance of Father Gibault to the great community which he served, particularly between 1768 and 1778, a decade during which the British government failed to introduce any civil authority into the portion of the Mississippi Valley which was a possession of the crown of England. The absence of civil government, unless unofficially supplied by some source, would have been disastrous to the population of England's Illinois Country, for those hardy, rugged frontier folk were much given to contention.[6]

The fate of the inhabitants of the Illinois Country west of the Mississippi at the hands of their new Spanish masters, who came into possession of the area in 1762, differed somewhat from that of their neighbors to the east. With the announcement of Spain's acquisition, a noticeable immigration from the eastern shore of the Mississippi began to occur, perhaps because Louis St. Ange de Bellerive, after surrendering Fort Chartres to the English in 1765, removed to St. Louis where he assumed control of the area in the name of the

---

[4] Records of the Parish of the Immaculate Conception at Kaskaskia, Illinois. These are on deposit in the archives of St. Louis University.

[5] Clarence Walworth Alvord, *The Illinois Country, 1673–1818* (Springfield, 1920), p. 221.

[6] *Old Cahokia*, ed. John Francis McDermott (St. Louis, 1949), p. 11.

Spanish absentee owners. The crown of Spain, long experienced in colonial administration, appears to have had no intention of introducing radical changes in its newly acquired territory.[7] The two major centers, Ste. Genevieve, with a population of six hundred, and St. Louis, whose inhabitants numbered about five hundred, were to be governed, if possible, by the local citizenry whose loyalty to Spain would be insured by an oath of fidelity. Spain's bureaucracy made certain that her royal privileges in ecclesiastical matters would not be contravened. Father Sebastian Meurin, the only priest in the Mississippi Valley between 1763 and 1768, was summarily forbidden to exercise his spiritual functions in Spanish territory because he had received his ecclesiastical jurisdiction from the French bishop of Quebec.[8] If souls were to be saved in Spain's territory, they would go to heaven through the instrumentality of Spanish episcopal authority, specifically through the bishop of Havana to whose diocese Spain had attached her new territory. It was into this troubled area that Pierre Gibault was dispatched in the summer of 1768 by the Most Reverend Joseph Olivier Briand, seventh bishop of Quebec.

Pierre Gibault, the eldest of three children, was born at Montreal on April 7, 1737, the son of a poor French Canadian who seems to have been something of a drifter, for each of his children was born in a different location. Although there is no documentary evidence for his early life, it is supposed that Gibault received his elementary training from the local pastors of the various villages in which he lived during his childhood.[9] It is thought that he was a student at the Jesuit college in Quebec before that institution was closed. Prior to his inception of ecclesiastical studies he spent some time in the Illinois Country. This we know from a letter of Briand written to the young man, then a priest, warning him: "Even though you knew the country as it was previously, I warned you that it has changed."[10] Gibault was a mature man when he decided to embrace an ecclesiastical career. He received his theological training at the seminary in Quebec during the years when the English were attacking French

[7] John Walton Caughey, *Bernardo de Gálvez in Louisiana, 1776–1783* (Berkeley, 1934), p. 53.

[8] Meurin to Briand, June 11, 1768, *Illinois Historical Collections*, XVI, 302.

[9] Ross F. Lockridge, *George Rogers Clark, Pioneer Hero of the Old Northwest* (New York, 1927), p. 189.

[10] Briand to Gibault, Apr. 26, 1769, *Illinois Historical Collections*, XVI, 537.

Canada. It is not too likely that he had more than two years of study. Three weeks before his thirty-first birthday he was ordained by Bishop Briand on March 19, 1768.[11] After serving as a curate at the cathedral in Quebec for about two months, Gibault was appointed to assume spiritual care of the whole of the Illinois Country.

Some estimate of Father Gibault's character at the outset of his career will prove of interest. Informing Father Meurin of Gibault's appointment, Bishop Briand continued: ". . . he is a young priest and I beg you to watch him and to instruct me religiously whether he merits my confidence or not. I should be sore distressed if he should go astray; he has given me beautiful and good promises and I love him. But I am not entirely without uneasiness and I believe he will not blame me for it: he knows me."[12] In his directions to the departing Gibault the bishop, kindly but quite firmly, instructed his fledgling missionary to reflect frequently on the truths of religion, to avoid carefully showing favoritism, and to shun loquacity.[13] One gathers from the above that in his bishop's eyes Gibault was a sufficiently dedicated man, but perhaps a very impetuous one who just might be a shade imprudent.

A further matter was Gibault's instructions regarding the British officials and their official control of the Illinois Country: ". . . do not allow the people to keep themselves in the hope of the visionary return of the French; incline them on the contrary to great docility towards the commander and attachment to the government."[14] Thus Gibault was expected by his bishop to conduct himself as a loyal British subject who, because of his position, would be able to influence the French to accept, wholeheartedly, their new nationality.

Armed with Briand's instructions, as well as a permit to travel to the Illinois Country, a permit issued by Guy Carleton, lieutenant-governor of Canada, Gibault left Montreal for his distant apostolate some time after June 7, 1768.[15] Accompanying him were his aged

---

[11] Cyprien Tanguay, *Dictionnaire geneologique des familles canadiennes depuis la fondation de la colonie jusqu'a nos jours* (Montreal, 1871–90), IV, 262.

[12] Briand to Meurin, Apr. 26, 1769, *Illinois Historical Collections*, XVI, 535.

[13] The original of this letter is preserved in the archives of Notre Dame University, Notre Dame, Indiana.

[14] Archives of Notre Dame University, Notre Dame, Indiana.

[15] There is a manuscript copy of this permit at the Missouri Historical Society Library. See New Madrid Archives, XI, 1431.

mother and his youngest sister, Marie-Louise, who was then just seventeen. The presence of these two relatives, though not pleasing to the bishop, was very useful to Gibault. Domestic details could be relinquished to them, leaving the young priest freer for his spiritual activities. Chided by his bishop for having brought them, Gibault defended himself: ". . . do I not have my mother and sister with me only so that I need not bother myself about household matters: otherwise I should be obliged to go boarding where I should have to be exposed to seeing and hearing many things which I neither see nor hear in my home. Besides my mother and sister have lodgings adjacent to the rectory . . . to which I am not near enough to be distracted by those who come to see them."[16]

The confused and disorganized state of society, both civil and religious, before the arrival of Gibault in the Illinois Country is attested to both by Father Meurin and General Thomas Gage. On January 6, 1769, the latter wrote describing his impressions of the inhabitants of the Illinois Country: "I find that strollers and vagabonds from Canada, Detroit, Illinois and other places have assembled there to live a lazy kind of Indian life, or have taken shelter there from justice."[17] On March 25, 1767, Father Meurin wrote to Bishop Briand, urging that priests be sent to the Illinois Country where they were desperately needed to stem the tide of irreligion and immorality which was overwhelming the populace. He complained that few people attended the religious services any longer and those who did were present, often enough, only to manifest their lack of respect for religion. All moral sense was being lost, but, what was far worse, children and slaves were remaining in ignorance of their duties to God.[18] Meurin's own declining health made it impossible for him any longer to visit the many French settlements, even if in his zeal he wished to do so. Also, governmental authorities on both sides of the river had placed obstacles in his way. The Spanish attitude toward Meurin has been noted earlier. The British commandant at Cahokia, Captain Gordon Forbes, forbade the priest to function freely until permission for his presence be procured from General Gage in New York.[19]

---

[16] Gibault to Briand, Mar., 1770, *Illinois Historical Collections*, XVI, 618–619.

[17] Gage to Hillsborough, Jan. 6, 1769, *Illinois Historical Collections*, XVI, 485.

[18] Meurin to Briand, Mar. 25, 1767, *Illinois Historical Collections*, XI, 628.

[19] Meurin to Briand, June 11, 1768, *Illinois Historical Collections*, XVI, 302.

Some of these difficulties were eliminated for Father Gibault simply because he was a British subject commissioned by Lieutenant-Governor Guy Carleton to minister to the spiritual needs of His British Majesty's subjects.[20] About a year after his arrival in the mission, Gibault reported to Briand: "I get along very well with the English. I have *carte blanche* to go everywhere. . . ."[21] Apparently this was also more or less true for him regarding the Spanish authorities, for in 1770 Father Meurin informed Briand that while he could visit Spanish territory only clandestinely, Gibault went there openly whenever it was necessary.[22] Meurin's report seems to have been in no way exaggerated, for it is known that on June 24, 1770, Gibault publicly blessed a new wooden church recently completed in St. Louis.[23]

At the beginning of his ministry Gibault made his headquarters at Kaskaskia whose inhabitants considered themselves to be a cut or two above their neighbors. Kaskaskians were a contentious lot to whom just a year before Gibault's arrival Bishop Briand had written sharply: ". . . I warn you that if you disregard these councils which I give you as a father, I shall henceforth pay no attention to your requests and look upon you as members of my diocese who do not merit my attention."[24] After two years of experience with these new parishioners, Gibault reported to Briand about the Kaskaskians: ". . . they have always been the head of the country, that is the principal village by reason of the educated classes, the men of commerce, and the better *habitans;* they have always been somewhat restless and enterprising and they have need of being held in check by someone whom they love, fear and respect."[25]

Kaskaskia may be used, perhaps, as the prime example of the influence, both civil and religious, which was wielded for the betterment of the Illinois Country by Father Gibault. This rather boastful village, numbering a thousand souls, was a kind of melting pot in Father Gibault's day. Besides the original French, the village shel-

[20] See above, n. 16.
[21] J. H. Schlarman, *From Quebec to New Orleans* (Belleville, Ill., 1929), p. 446.
[22] Schlarman, *From Quebec to New Orleans*, p. 446.
[23] John F. Rothensteiner, *History of the Archdiocese of St. Louis in Its Various Stages of Development from A.D. 1673 to A.D. 1929* (St. Louis, 1928), I, 126.
[24] Briand to Gibault, August 13, 1769, *Illinois Historical Collections*, XVI, 583.
[25] Schlarman, *From Quebec to New Orleans*, p. 446.

tered some three hundred Negro slaves, a detachment of the Eight-eenth Royal Irish Regiment, and an influx of Yankee traders, to say nothing of scores of wandering Indians. Neglecting the innumerable problems which the Royal Irish Regiment could have created, Gi-bault had his troubles with the French. At first they were grateful for his presence, but soon animosities arose over financial support of the church. These culminated in a threat from the bishop to employ the severest of ecclesiastical penalties against all who refused to bear their fair share of the support of the church. But even in the face of such rather formidable opposition, Gibault was able to build a new church and to bring some moral order into the life of Kaskaskia. It is not too unlikely, also, that he took an important part in the effort of the Kaskaskians to procure permission for the establishment of a recognized civil government in 1771. Though the town's agents, Blouin and Clazon, who presented General Gage with a memorial of grievances against the military and a plan of civil government, gained nothing for the effort, it is noteworthy that the form of government petitioned was widely liberal in character.[26]

Something of the same pattern of difficulties awaited Gibault in all of the settlements which he served in the British Illinois Country. Cahokia, where he resided off and on, was inhabited by a litigious folk who never forgot the fact that in 1763 Father Jacques François Forget du Verger, pastor of Cahokia and a member of the congrega-tion of the *Missions Étrangères*, had, in protest against the banishment of the Jesuits in that year, sold the ecclesiastical property at Cahokia and departed permanently. The settlement of Vincennes, from which the Jesuit Julien De Vernay had been expelled in 1763, be-came the charge of a pious layman named Phillibert, who described conditions there to Briand: "I dare take the liberty to write to you these lines . . . to represent to you that since the departure of the reverend Jesuit fathers . . . I have the sorrow of seeing numbers of small children growing up who are of an age to make their first communion and who are unfortunately deprived . . . of the sacra-ments . . . of many marriages contracted without the power to make the parties have recourse to the church . . . this can cause only great scandal. . . ."[27] It may be asserted, then, that during the first decade of his presence in the British Illinois Country religious

[26] Alvord, *Illinois Country*, pp. 293–295.
[27] Meurin to Briand, Mar. 23, 1767, *Illinois Historical Collections*, XI, 526.

conditions, and hence general moral and civic order, improved, thanks to the apostolate of Father Gibault.

Gibault's ministry to the people living under Spanish dominion ran a much smoother course. In great measure this may have been due to the fact that villages such as Ste. Genevieve and St. Louis were the recipients of immigrants from the eastern shore of the Mississippi who placed a higher value on their religion. Quite likely they believed that within the domain of a Catholic monarch, even though not French, life would be preferable to that in a land whose ruler was to them an Anglo-Saxon and a heretic. Neither St. Louis nor Ste. Genevieve manifested any particularly ambitious political pretentions. It is noteworthy, also, that the Indian problem on the western bank of the Mississippi was not as pressing as it was across the river. Gibault frequently visited the villages under the Spanish flag, baptizing the children, solemnizing marriages, visiting the sick, and burying the dead.

As the years rolled on and the English colonists on the Atlantic seaboard became embroiled with the mother country, Gibault was far from unaware of the issues involved. Though Bishop Briand, in 1776, issued an exhortation to his flock, urging them to oppose the American cause, there is no documentary evidence to demonstrate that Gibault supported these views of his bishop. In view of the frequency of communication between the seaboard colonies and the British Illinois Country during those stirring years, we know that news of events on the Atlantic shore were rather quickly known in the Mississippi Valley. An invasion of the insurgent colonists could well be expected if for no other reason than that British strategists could be expected to incite the Indians to launch an attack upon the rebels on their exposed western flank.[28]

Gibault's conduct at Kaskaskia, and later at Vincennes, when George Rogers Clark attacked those outposts, thereby giving us claim to the eastern portion of the Mississippi Valley, is too well known to require repetition. It is significant, however, that when the citizens of Kaskaskia came to deal with General Clark, upon the capture of Kaskaskia, it was Gibault, accompanied by five or six elderly gentlemen, who acted as spokesman for the town. Clark's own reaction to the meeting was as follows: ". . . the priest in-

---

[28] Samuel Knox Wilson, "Bishop Briand and the American Revolution," *Catholic Historical Review*, XIX (1933–34), 141–142.

formed me (after asking which was the principal) that as the inhabitants expected to be separated never perhaps to meet again they begged through him that they might be permitted to spend some time in the church to take their leave of each other (I knew they expected thair very religion was obnoxious to me) I carelessly told him that I had nothing to say to his church that he might go there if he would if he did it to inform the people not to venture out of the town."[29]

We know that, after visiting the church, Gibault, accompanied by a throng of still frightened citizens, returned for a conference with their victor. During this encounter we learn of Clark's moving appeal to the Kaskaskians to aid him in the effort to bring the blessings of liberty to the Illinois Country. After assuring himself that the invading army in no way opposed the free exercise of religion, Gibault not only won the Kaskaskians to Clark's cause, but went to Vincennes himself where his presence was probably a vital factor in effecting the surrender of the place to General Clark.[30] For these and other more striking and dangerous services to George Rogers Clark, Father Gibault has been called "the patriot priest."

The subsequent career of Father Gibault may be dismissed in a single phrase, a series of misunderstandings. Bishop Briand, Gibault's ecclesiastical superior and a staunch supporter of the British during our Revolution, severely chastised any of his clergy who sympathized with or actively supported our cause. Gibault found himself an ecclesiastical renegade, though whether he ever learned the exact extent of the censure imposed upon him is doubtful. After the Treaty of 1783 Gibault's ecclesiastical status was an ambiguous one. In those days Catholic dioceses normally did not cross international boundaries. Father Gibault was, thus, no longer a subject of the bishop of Quebec. But he was all but unknown to John Carroll of Baltimore into whose dominion the Illinois Country now fell. Gibault's relations with Carroll were not pleasant, perhaps because of simple distance. Nonetheless Gibault undoubtedly felt himself an alien in an alien land, a land which in all justice owed him much. Divorcing himself from the whole thorny matter of jurisdiction, he retired to New Madrid where, aged and broken, he lived out his days. He did not escape his share of persecution, for he was described to episcopal authorities as a somewhat disreputable character, a

[29] See Clark's *Memoir, Illinois Historical Collections*, VIII, 230.
[30] Schlarman, *From Quebec to New Orleans*, p. 511.

person of questionable worth. The accusations were false, but in those days of delayed communications months and years could pass without a solution for a problem which might crush the soul of a devoted man. Gibault died piously at New Madrid at about seven o'clock in the morning on August 16, 1802. For the exact date of his death historians are indebted to John Francis McDermott, whose researches on Gibault's library uncovered the information.[31]

Much has been made by historians of Gibault's aid to George Rogers Clark, overemphasizing the fact that a priest of French extraction rendered aid and comfort to our revolutionary cause. Though these contributions to the future of our country deserve their meed of praise, it would seem that Gibault's real contribution to the Mississippi Valley had already been made before he and Clark faced one another at Kaskaskia on July 4, 1778. For the ten years previous to that incident Father Gibault had plodded his way up and down the Mississippi River comforting, cajoling, warning, urging all to peace and order in a land troubled by the absence of authority and the uncertainty of a stable future. Wherever order existed during those unsettled times in great measure it was there because of Gibault's guiding hand.

---

[31] John Francis McDermott, "The Library of Father Gibault," *Mid-America*, VI (1935), 273–276.

# The French Mountain Men
# of the Early Far West

### Frederic E. Voelker

The fur trade of the American Far West had its beginning with the French founders of St. Louis, which was indeed established for the primary purpose of developing that trade. Its development required an impressive manpower. The local demand for men to bring to fruition the dreams and ambitions of Pierre de Laclède Liguest and young Auguste Chouteau was satisfied by men of adventurous nature who congregated in and were sent out from St. Louis, sole administrative center of the fur trade of the American West.[1] In the beginning practically all the men who manned the trade, the men who worked in the field, were of French origin or ancestry.[2]

Because the manpower of the western fur trade came from the settlements along or near the Mississippi and because there is no land barrier between the valley of the Mississippi and that of the Missouri, so that the land mass between the Alleghenies and the Rocky Moun-

---

[1] Hiram M. Chittenden, *The American Fur Trade of the Far West* (Stanford, 1954), I, 97–98, 109; Katharine Coman, *Economic Beginnings of the Far West* (New York, 1925), I, 89–90.

[2] Chittenden, *American Fur Trade*, I, 56; Coman, *Economic Beginnings*, I, 302–303.

tains constitutes one vast trough, containing what is usually considered one water system, it is fitting that a consideration of the men of French blood, who largely manned the first industrial enterprise at its westernmost segment, should find a place in this conference on "The French in the Mississippi Valley."

These men carried out the necessary work of the trade: stowing merchandise and supplies; manning the keel boats; cordelling, poling, or rowing up the Missouri to operational headquarters; seeking out and trading at the Indian villages; trapping the beaver and other fur-bearers; hunting meat animals; maintaining the equipment; carrying messages through unknown country; cooking; keeping camp; tending the horses; and performing a score of other regular and extra duties.[3]

At first this trade was largely confined to the country along the lower and middle Missouri, but after the reports brought back by Meriwether Lewis and William Clark had been evaluated by St. Louis entrepreneurs, it rapidly expanded into and across the Rocky Mountains and thence to the Pacific.[4]

During the years between 1800 and 1840 there emerged from the legions employed in the western fur trade a class of hardy individuals known as "mountain men." They were the working trappers and traders who performed the hardest work of the trade: finding trails through unknown country; discovering the beaver waters; trapping; skinning and preparing for transportation the furs they gathered; locating the Indian villages and dealing, sometimes with great difficulty, for furs taken by the natives; living by their wits off the country; remaining alert to every hazard of the wilderness, including frequent Indian hostility; and, as part of their work, thoroughly exploring the immense area west, northwest, and southwest, from the Missouri River to the Pacific Ocean.[5]

The best beaver streams were in the mountains, and by 1840, the year the fur trade, as the mountain men had known it, had entered its final decline, these men had penetrated every mountain range in that vast region. They were mountain men, they called themselves "mountain men," and they were proud of their work.[6]

---

[3] Chittenden, *American Fur Trade*, I, 52–58.

[4] Chittenden, *American Fur Trade*, I, 94–96; Coman, *Economic Beginnings*, I, 246, 289.

[5] Chittenden, *American Fur Trade*, I, 51–55; Ray A. Billington, *The Far Western Frontier* (New York, 1956), p. 44.

[6] Chittenden, *American Fur Trade*, I, xxv.

During the forty years within the scope of this paper, and most particularly in the earlier years, more men of French birth or ancestry had worked in the western fur trade than men of any other origin. Their geographical origins were various: there were men from France, the French settlements in the Louisiana Territory, the West Indies, and Canada. Here we consider only those who came to St. Louis and worked out of there. Some of them were sons and grandsons of the men who had come up the Mississippi River from New Orleans with Laclède and Auguste Chouteau, and of this group some were native St. Louisans and many more came from the Mississippi River settlements established prior to the founding of St. Louis, such as Fort Chartres, Kaskaskia, Cahokia, and Ste. Geneviève. Later they came from St. Charles and other settlements along the lower Missouri,[7] and from Florissant and Portage des Sioux, the latter two having since their founding furnished numerically respectable contingents to the ranks of the mountain men.[8]

As a rule these westward-faring French became employees, or *engagés* of the various corporations, partnerships, and proprietorships engaged in the trade. Apart from several conspicuous exceptions few of them ventured out as independent operators ("freemen" or "free trappers"), especially in the early years when the country was almost completely unknown and the temper of the Indians a matter of conjecture. These "company men" occupied various positions, ranging from *bourgeois* ("partisan" or field manager) downward to *mangeurs de lard* (literally "eaters of pork"), who were the camp keepers and handymen. In between these, in a firmly stratified social structure, were the clerks (who sometimes served as leaders of detached trapping or trading parties), traders, trappers, hunters, artisans (carpenters, blacksmiths, and boat builders), *coureurs de bois* (literally "woods messengers"), *voyageurs* (boatmen), horse tenders, packers, and cooks. Although there was some shifting of duties, as most *engagés* could turn their hands to a variety of labors,

---

[7] Sources cited in n. 2 above; Louis Houck, *A History of Missouri* (Chicago, 1908), II, 11–14. Some of the earliest French families who had members in the mountain trade were Bissonette, Dubreuil (Dubray), Gervais, Berger, Morin, Lambert, Thibault (Tebeau), Dufresne (Dufrain), Roy, Papin, and a number of others.

[8] The writer's informants, more than fifty years ago, were, for Florissant, Peter Barteau and George Weaver; and for Portage des Sioux, Auguste Pujol, Jerome Duval, and Antoine LeClair. They are all now deceased.

men seldom passed from a lower to a higher class, although real merit was recognized and promotion sometimes achieved. The real mountain men, those we here consider, invariably were of the five upper classes: the partisans, clerks, traders, trappers, and hunters.[9]

Far out in the field, after the camp or trading post had been established on a major, easily accessible watercourse, the duties of these mountain men carried them farther into the mountain wilderness, rediscovering old trails, blazing new ones, seeking passes into and across the mountains, finding profitable trapping waters, locating likely game and grazing grounds.[10] As we have noted, for forty years this work was carried forward, and when it was over, every stream, mountain range, isolated peak, natural park, tribal domain, and practically every natural phenomenon between the Missouri and the Pacific had been discovered.[11] Consequently, when, years later, military, scientific, and survey expeditions appeared in the West, the survivors among the mountain men were in great demand as guides, escorts, hunters, packers, interpreters, and intermediaries. In performing such duties they made their most important and valuable contribution to the westward expansion of the nation. So far as the national growth is concerned, all they had done before was rehearsal for the big events of the years between 1840 and 1880.[12]

All the work of the mountain men necessitated rather close relations with certain friendly Indian tribes and an avoidance of hostile ones. By meetings on the trail with Indian friends and by visits to their villages, the mountain man could usually gain valuable knowledge of the proximity of Indian enemies. Sometimes, as an added protection, he made his home in an Indian village and naturally made some close personal friends, including women.[13] Many domestic alliances were formed in this way, and many half-breed children were born thereof; not infrequently the boys themselves grew up to become mountain men. Sometimes, too, these unions lasted for life and were surprisingly happy. Thus, among the mountains, remote from civilization, self-sufficient, self-reliant, and self-supporting, in the midst of his family and red friends, the French

---

[9] Chittenden, *American Fur Trade*, I, 51–58.

[10] Chittenden, *American Fur Trade*, I, xxiv.

[11] Chittenden, *American Fur Trade*, I, xxv; George F. Ruxton, *Adventures in Mexico and the Rocky Mountains* (London, 1847), p. 242.

[12] Chittenden, *American Fur Trade*, I, xxv–xxvi; Billington, *Far Western Frontier*, p. 101.

[13] Billington, *Far Western Frontier*, p. 48.

mountain man tended to remain a mountain man, although, as we shall see, there were some conspicuous examples of the reverse.[14]

How did the French mountain man compare in character, ability, and intelligence with his Anglo-Saxon counterpart? Because of humanity's infinite variety and, at the same time, regardless of origin, its proneness, within certain limits, to run to type, I shall speak in general terms. The Frenchman displayed more tractability; was probably less independent and less critical of his superiors; had more loyalty (although there were desertions among them, too); was capable of tremendous sustained labor and able to withstand great hardships, particularly the lack of food and shelter, without grumbling; was upon the whole more philosophical about adverse conditions; had more tolerance of Indian peculiarities and was able to make friends among them more rapidly; and was probably more apt to achieve efficiency in assigned tasks. The French were more cheerful and more voluble; they sang, laughed, joked, and told stories as they worked, seeming to make a caper out of labor.[15]

The traders among them were astute in fur deals with the Indians and at the same time willing to stretch a point to retain friendly relations; they appear to have been somewhat more diplomatic and able to give and take to a greater degree than their Angle-Saxon rivals. To be short, their habits of trade were Latin, not Yankee.[16]

As in the entire stratified structure of the fur trade, the French on the lower levels were mostly illiterate, and, ascending, those on the upper levels, as a group, were quite easily the mental peers of any men in the mountains, as we shall learn.[17]

As a permanent result of their years in the mountains, the French mountain men, as well as those of other origins, have left their marks upon the western land in names that persist to this day. Mountains, streams, and other natural features named by them and for them are many, and a complete catalog would fill a volume. However, in following up some of the promises made above, I shall,

---

[14] Coman, *Economic Beginnings*, I, 370–371; Frederic E. Voelker, "The Mountain Men and Their Part in the Opening of the West," *Missouri Historical Society Bulletin*, III (July, 1947), 157.

[15] Chittenden, *American Fur Trade*, I, 56–57.

[16] Such traders were the Robidoux, Janis, St. Vrain and Richard brothers, the Papins, Sarpys, Jean B. Gervais, Joseph Bissonette, Charles Lajeunesse, and others.

[17] For instances, see below the accounts of Antoine Leroux, Étienne Provost, and Charles Larpenteur.

in a few brief biographical paragraphs, mention some of the geographical names of western America bestowed in honor of some of the best-known French mountain men, all of whom, so far as has been ascertained, died Americans.[18]

Perhaps the most noted French family actually operating in the mountain trade was that of Robidoux. The first Robidoux in St. Louis came from Canada. There were five brothers in the trade, all believed to have been born in St. Louis: Antoine, François, Joseph, Louis, and Michel. Collectively they covered just about every part of the Far West, and they were known to everybody in the mountains.[19] It has been said that Antoine was the "first trader out of Taos," New Mexico. (This means the first Indian trader based in Taos.) This was about 1822. About 1828 he built a trading post on the Gunnison River, in the Colorado wilderness, and about 1832 built Fort Robidoux, or Uinta, in Utah.[20] Later in life Joseph and Louis became town builders: Joseph laid out the city of St. Joseph, Missouri, in 1843; Louis developed the well-known Jurupa Rancho in California in the late 1840's and 1850's. His rancho became the city of Riverside, and nearby Mount Robidoux is named for him.[21]

Perhaps the most important of the French mountain men, so far as the exploration of the West is concerned, was Antoine Leroux, born in St. Louis, presumably of French Canadian ancestry, but he may have had a Spanish ancestor. For the greater part of his life he was a far-ranging free trapper whose wanderings took him from Wyoming to the Mexican border and out to the Pacific. His knowledge of western topography was enormous, and his services as a guide were much in demand in the 1850's, particularly on government surveys being conducted to determine a right-of-way for a southern railroad to California. Among his most valuable services during this and the immediately prior period were with Colonel Philip St. George Cook in 1846 during the Mexican War, with Captain Lorenzo Sitgreaves in 1851 on an expedition westward from Zuni to San Diego, with John Russell Bartlett on the Mexican bound-

---

[18] Ordinary maps of the far western states will yield scores of such names, and detailed topographic maps will give many more.

[19] *Dictionary of American Biography* (New York, 1935), XVI, 32. See also Orral Messmore Robidoux, *Memorial to the Robidoux Brothers* (Kansas City, 1924), a poorly organized, rather confused work.

[20] *Dictionary of American Biography*, XVI, 32.

[21] *Dictionary of American Biography*, XVI, 32; Robert Hornbeck, *Robidoux's Ranch in the '70s* (Riverside, 1913), pp. 81–89.

ary survey in 1852, with Captain John W. Gunnison on an 1853 railroad survey, and with Lieutenant A. W. Whipple on a similar survey in the same year. He was considered so indispensable that when he agreed to go out with Gunnison he stipulated it would be necessary for him to leave the expedition far short of its destination because of a prior commitment to guide Whipple. This is but part of his excellent record as a guide. He has been written about in more official reports than any other mountain man, and he deserves a full biography. No mountain man had a more exciting life or a more useful one.[22]

Étienne Provost was born in Canada, and he, too, ranged widely over the Far West. Apparently valid claims have been advanced for him by others that he was the discoverer of both Great Salt Lake and South Pass, but credits for these discoveries have not yet been awarded to anyone. Provost was John James Audubon's guide on the famous artist-naturalist's expedition to the upper Missouri, and is frequently mentioned in Audubon's journal. Although information about Provost is not plentiful, his name lives on in a city, valley, river, canyon, mountain peak, and several lesser natural landmarks.[23]

The three Lajeunesse brothers, Basil, Charles, and François, were all well-known mountain men. They were all born in Canada and ranked as stalwarts in the mountain trade. Basil was one of the most reliable men on John C. Frémont's first, second, and third exploring expeditions, and on the third expedition, in 1846, lost his life at the hands of the Klamath Indians. François joined Frémont's second expedition, in 1844. Charles, called "Simoneau," was the trader of the family. He operated chiefly in Wyoming, where there are a range of mountains named Seminoe (sometimes erroneously called "Seminole") and a nearby Seminoe Dam on the North Platte River, which, it is respectfully suggested, are derived from the nickname of Charles Lajeunesse.[24]

Auguste Archambault, probably one of the best liked of the later mountain men, was born in Canada, lived many years in Florissant, and died there. He went as a hunter with Frémont's third

---

[22] Grant Foreman, "Antoine Leroux, New Mexico Guide," *New Mexico Historical Review*, XVI (Oct., 1941), 367–377.

[23] *Dictionary of American Biography*, XV, 250–251; Writers' Program, W.P.A., *Utah* (New York, 1945), p. 216.

[24] Notes of my interviews with Mr. Leon Lajeunesse, August and September, 1958 (MS); John C. Frémont, *Narratives of Exploration and Adventure*, ed. Allan Nevins (New York, 1956), pp. 89, 142, 186, 189, 244, 260, 500, 502.

expedition and proved himself a mighty one. He served in Frémont's California Battalion during the war with Mexico. Archambault joined Captain Howard Stansbury's party on an exploring expedition in the valley of Great Salt Lake, which began in June, 1849, and ended in December, 1851. Again he proved his value.[25]

One of the French mountain men about whom we know little has, nevertheless, been memorialized by the bestowal of his name on not less than eight places in Wyoming. He is Jacques Laramee, whose misspelled name has been given to a city, town, river, fort, plain, mountain range, mountain peak, and county. It is known he was killed by Indians on the banks of Laramie River, that he was a trapper, and that he was probably born in Canada.[26]

The St. Vrain brothers, trappers in early manhood, became potent traders in the Southwest, Ceran as a partner of the Bent brothers, and Marcellin as an employee of the famous partnership of Bent, St. Vrain and Company. The St. Vrains were born at Spanish Lake, St. Louis County.[27]

A phenomenal individual among the French mountain men was Jacques Fournais, known as "Old Pino," probably a native of Canada. It is said that he spent sixty active years trapping in the Southwest, that he remembered incidents of the American Revolution, and that he served under Andrew Jackson at New Orleans. After a fantastically adventurous life in the Far West, Fournais retired, and died in Kansas City at the reputed age of one hundred and twenty-four.[28]

When Francis Parkman came west in 1846 on the health excursion that resulted in a classic of western life, *The Oregon Trail,* he chose as his guide Henri Chatillon, who already had spent some years as a trader, trapper, and hunter in the West and reputedly had killed more than thirty grizzly bears. As an important figure in Parkman's book, Chatillon has, right up to the present, had considerable publicity. According to all accounts, and not Parkman's alone, he was a

---

[25] Frémont, *Narratives of Exploration,* pp. 488–491; notes of interviews with Archambault's daughter, Mrs. Cora Weldon, October, 1946, and his granddaughter, Mrs. Lucy Goll, May, 1938 (MSS); Hubert H. Bancroft, *Works: California* (San Francisco, 1885), XIX, 700; Howard Stansbury, *Exploration and Survey* (Philadelphia, 1852), pp. 22, 36, 78–79, 245, 247.

[26] Notes of my interviews with Leon Lajeunesse; Writers' Program, W.P.A., *Wyoming* (New York, 1941), p. 196.

[27] *Dictionary of American Biography,* XVI, 305–306; David Lavender, *Bent's Fort* (New York, 1954), p. 52.

[28] Carrie W. Whitney, *Kansas City* (Chicago, 1908), I, 24.

man of exceptional character, amply justifying Parkman's encomium: "the brave and true-hearted Henry Chatillon." Chatillon was born in Carondelet, now a part of South St. Louis, and settled there when he retired. He built a house in Carondelet, part of which is a corner of the more pretentious DeMenil house, now in process of rescue from destruction.[29]

François De Lisle is an example of an artisan turned mountain man. He was born in Canada and started his life in the West as a carpenter during the construction of Fort Cass, Fort Union, Bent's Fort, and other trading posts. He became a trader and hunter for Bent, St. Vrain and Company, later served as guide and hunter for military expeditions in the Southwest, and in 1864 fought under Colonel Kit Carson in the battle of Adobe Walls, in Texas. De Lisle returned to St. Louis in 1877 after about fifty years in the West.[30]

The ubiquitous yet elusive Joseph Bissonette probably was born in St. Louis of parents said to have come from New Orleans. He was a trapper and trader who became something of a legend in the West. Scarcely a traveler on the Oregon Trail had not seen or heard of him, and he exerted a powerful conciliatory influence upon the Sioux Indians along the trail in the Fort Laramie neighborhood. He displayed a keen sense of responsibility toward government expeditions and emigrant parties moving westward. Well known though he was in the 1840's and 1850's, information about him is scarce.[31]

Another early mountain man was Joseph Philibert, one of the first trappers and traders in the Southwest. He usually led an independent group of trappers. When he was eighty-nine, retired and living in St. Louis, he contributed some important information on the western fur trade to the compilers of a local publication. The data have been tested and found to be entirely accurate.[32]

---

[29] Francis Parkman, *The Oregon Trail* (Boston, 1895), particularly pp. xi, 10–13; memorandum from the late Dr. William G. Swekosky, May 16, 1955 (MS).

[30] Lavender, *Bent's Fort*, pp. 285–286, 288; *Missouri Republican*, Nov. 19, 1877.

[31] Notes of interviews with Leon Lajeunesse; Jay Monaghan, *The Overland Trail* (Indianapolis, 1947), pp. 227–230, 252, 316; George E. Hyde, *Red Cloud's Folk* (Norman, Okla., 1937), pp. 64, 94–96; Frémont, *Narratives of Exploration*, pp. 139, 142, 152; many other references scattered throughout the literature of the West, 1840–90.

[32] Richard Edwards and Menra Hopewell, *Edwards's Great West and Her Commercial Metropolis, Embracing a General View of the West, and a Complete History of St. Louis, from the Landing of Ligueste, in 1764, to the Present Time* (St. Louis, 1860), pp. 298–302.

Charles Larpenteur, a late comer in the trade, has given us a good insight not only into its later days but into what had happened earlier in his two volumes, *Forty Years a Fur Trader on the Upper Missouri*. Larpenteur was born near Fontainebleau, came to St. Louis about 1830, and first went up the Missouri in 1833. He became acquainted with many of the most important figures in the trade, and for certain of its aspects his book is a prime source.[33]

There are many more French mountain men who have a place in the history of the Far West and deserve some treatment here, but the roster is formidable, and time is available for merely naming a few more: Lucien Fontenelle; Charles Sanguinette; François Valle; Auguste Clermont, known as "Old Claymore"; Hubert Papin; the Janis brothers; Jean Baptiste Champlain, companion of Ezekiel Williams, the "lost trapper"; Antoine Godin; Jean Baptiste Gervais; François and Narcisse LeClerc; the Sarpys; François Matthieu; Pierre Dorion; Pierre LeBec; George Drouillard; Honoré Picotte; the Richard brothers, each of whom had a personal history that would not only make fascinating reading but also throw more light on the history of the western fur trade. This list is no attempt at individual evaluation and no attempt at moral judgment, and any student of the early Far West could expand it by dozens more.[34]

These, the saints and the sinners, are our French mountain men. Many of them, after adventurous years in the West, came back to retire and rest in St. Louis, and die there; many lie buried in our cemeteries.

In the van of the forces moving the frontier ever westward, these French mountain men command attention. Let us, in this bicentennial year, not forget them.

---

[33] Charles Larpenteur, *Forty Years a Fur Trader on the Upper Missouri*, ed. Elliott Coues (New York, 1898). See particularly I, 1, 3, 8.

[34] Chittenden, *American Fur Trade*, in both volumes, mentions many of these men, and the fur trade documents at the Missouri Historical Society, St. Louis, account for hundreds more, many of whom, not included in this paper, were of some importance in the trade.

# Colonial Fortifications and Military Architecture in the Mississippi Valley

## Samuel Wilson, Jr.

### INTRODUCTION

In an eighteenth-century French work on world travels, the author, obviously borrowing from many sources, naturally begins his discourse on Louisiana with the great river saying that "this famous river, which has since been so well known in France under the name of Mississippi, had been given, by flattery, that of Colbert; afterwards by devotion, that of Saint Louis; but its first name has prevailed." The author then goes on to relate that "The Chevalier de la Salle left with a detachment, entered the Illinois area, took possession of the country in the name of Louis XIV, called it Louisiana in honor of this prince, and constructed a fort there; the Spaniards would have built a church; the English, a tavern."[1]

The building of forts was indeed a principal objective of France in America, forts which would maintain its domination over its vast new empire against threats from the English on the one side and the Spanish on the other. Toward the end of the seventeenth century the

---

[1] *Le Voyageur François*, ed. Abbé Delaporte (Paris, 1769), X, 6.

France of Louis XIV was the great military power of Europe. Vauban (1633–1707) was the engineering genius of the day, under whose direction the art of fortifications became an almost new science, and in the French army his corps of engineers achieved the position of highest honor. The principles of fortification developed under Vauban were still being followed until after the middle of the nineteenth century. The period of Vauban was also the period of the exploration and settlement of the Mississippi Valley, and all the forts established there by the French, from the simplest stockade to the greatest fortresses and fortified towns, reflected his influence. The general principles, of course, had been established long before, their origins going back at least to the works of the Romans.

## The Period of Discovery and Exploration

### FORT CAROLINE–1564

Perhaps the earliest graphic examples we have of French fortification construction in America are the two drawings of Fort Caroline on the Atlantic coast published by Le Moyne de Morgues.[2] This fort near the mouth of the St. John's River, Florida, was established by French Huguenots in 1564 and destroyed the following year by the Spaniards. This was a triangular timber structure with bastions and a symmetrical arrangement of buildings within.

### FORT CRÈVECOEUR–1680

La Salle, over a century later, first introduced French military construction methods into the Mississippi Valley. In a letter that he wrote on September 29, 1680, the explorer describes the building of Fort Crèvecoeur in the Illinois Country on an elevated site enclosed by ravines and ditches

on the height of which I had a parapet built capable of covering a man, the whole revetted from the foot of the knoll up to the top of the parapet with great timbers, the bottom of which was in siding between great pieces of wood which ran all around the bottom of the eminence and the top of planks held by other great cross pieces retained, with tenons and mortices, by other pieces of wood which went out from the thickness of the parapet. In front of this work I had planted all around pointed stakes twenty-five feet high, a foot in diameter, driven three feet into the

[2] Charles Germain Marie Bourel de La Roncière, *La Floride française, scène de la vie indienne, peintes en 1564 (par Jacques Le Moyne De Morgues)* (Paris, 1928), plates 9, 10.

ground. . . . I had two lodgings built for my people in two of the flanking angles to be ready in case of attack, the middle made of thick pieces of wood, musket-proof; in the third the forge, made of similar material, along the curtain that overlooks the woods; the lodging for the Recollets in the fourth angle, and had my tent and that of the Sieur Tonty placed in the middle of the place.[3]

### FORT PRUDHOMME–1682 (FEBRUARY)

Toward the end of February, 1682, on his journey to discover the mouth of the river, La Salle, encamped on the banks of the Mississippi below its junction with the Ohio, "built a small stockade fort on a high bluff,"[4] to which he gave the name of Fort Prudhomme. It was not a significant work and was probably abandoned before 1700.[5]

### FORT ST. LOUIS (ILLINOIS)–1682 (DECEMBER)

After his return from the mouth of the Mississippi, La Salle constructed a second fort on the Illinois River, giving to this one the name of St. Louis. The site was a cliff called Starved Rock, a natural citadel, a hundred and twenty-five feet above the river. In December, 1682, La Salle and Tonty began the work. "They cut away the forest that crowned the rock, built storehouses and dwellings of its remains, dragged timber up the rugged pathway, and encircled the summit with a palisade."[6] Franquelin's map of 1684 indicates Fort Crèvecoeur with the familiar symbol of a square fort with four bastions, the typical Vauban fort. The symbol for Fort St. Louis seems to indicate a lesser work.

### FORT ST. LOUIS (TEXAS)–1685

When La Salle began his last construction project, he thought he was at or near the mouth of the Mississippi. Instead it was far to the west at Matagorda Bay on what is now known as the La Vaca River that La Salle built a new Fort St. Louis using what local timber he could obtain and whatever wood he could salvage from his wrecked ships. Although there are no known drawings of La Salle's fort and

---

[3] Pierre Margry, *Découvertes et établissements des français dans l'ouest et dans le sud de l'Amérique septentrionale (1614–1754)* (Paris, 1879–82), II, 49.

[4] Francis Parkman, *La Salle and the Discovery of the Great West* (Signet Classics Edition, New York, 1963), p. 222.

[5] Marcel Giraud, *Histoire de la Louisiane française, tome 1er: Le Règne de Louis XIV, 1698–1715* (Paris, 1953), p. 8.

[6] Parkman, *La Salle*, p. 233.

but few descriptions, it may be assumed that it was of palisades crudely following the Vauban form, influenced perhaps by La Salle's recollection of Fort St. Louis of Quebec. An excellent drawing of this Canadian fortress was made in 1683 by Jean Baptiste Louis Franquelin,[7] probably the same draftsman who produced the maps of La Salle's explorations. Joutel, who accompanied La Salle on his last and fatal expedition, recorded in his journal the story of the construction of Fort St. Louis.[8] Work began about the middle of July, 1685; trees were felled and squared, timbers from the wrecked ships were brought to the site. The principal building within a small square palisade was designed by La Salle himself, "but," says Joutel, "the ignorance of the carpenters was so great that M. de La Salle was forced to become the master contractor and to mark the pieces for the design he had in mind." A second house was then built:

. . . each was put to work at his own trade and as a number of pieces of wood were found sizable enough for building a house, M. de La Salle had all the pieces cut to the length he judged proper and built a building of it, adjoining the other one that had been commenced; but the latter was larger and finer. The first one was built in the Canadian manner and the other almost the same, but as the pieces of this latter were straighter and thicker they were adjusted better. All the pieces were dovetailed at the corners, fastened with a good peg. . . . This house was the first one ready; it was roofed with the old planks . . . on which we nailed the skins of oxen.[9]

## THE ARKANSAS POST–1686

La Salle left Fort St. Louis with Joutel and some others to seek the Mississippi and died en route at the hands of an assassin.

Joutel and his companion finally reached the Arkansas River in July, 1687, making their way over land from Texas after the assassination. Here they found a fortified house that had been built there the year before by Tonty's followers. Across the river they saw a large cross such as is set up by French missionaries, and near it "was a house in the French manner. . . . It is built of heavy pieces of wood notched one into the other, dovetailed, all the way up to the height of the roof, and of fine cedar wood and roofed with bark, not a bad roofing."[10]

---

[7] Paris, Archives, Ministère des Colonies (hereafter PAMC), no. 805, order no. 347.

[8] Margry, *Découvertes et établissements*, III, 163.

[9] Margry, *Découvertes et établissements*, III, 173.

[10] Margry, *Découvertes et établissements*, III, 442; Giraud, *Histoire de la Louisiane*, p. 8.

La Salle's and Tonty's buildings were probably of the type of construction known as *pièce sur pièce*, a house built of squared timbers laid one upon the other and dovetailed at the corners. The roof was steep, in the Canadian manner, a type of house which became prevalent throughout the Mississippi Valley, modified in time by the addition of galleries and other amenities.

## THE PERIOD OF DEVELOPMENT AND SETTLEMENT

### FORT MAUREPAS–1699

France made no further effort to take advantage of La Salle's discoveries until 1698 when Lemoyne d'Iberville was ordered by the King to rediscover the mouth of the Mississippi and "to choose a good spot that can be defended with few people and at the same time prevent other nations from entrance into the river."[11] Masons, house carpenters, cabinet makers, and other craftsmen[12] were sent on the expedition, and even a good draftsman, a man named Remy (Reno), proposed by Iberville for this position[13] was sent along. This was perhaps the first time that anyone trained in the art of military engineering and fortification design had been sent to the Mississippi Valley. Iberville seems to have somewhat regretted his choice, for he later wrote:

> The Sieur Remy Reno sailed with me on the Badine in order to draw the plans and maps of the countries where I would pass. This he did not do. He is a man fifty years old who is married to an Irish woman at Saint-Martin de Rhe. I shall not judge of his competency for building a fortification, not knowing him well enough for that. I was not able to make use of him for the one at Biloxi, for in all the plans that he made me, he cut out more work for me than I would have been able to have done by three hundred men in a year. I thought of him as a more competent contractor than engineer. A work that had been decided for him to do, he conducted quite well.[14]

It was probably Remy, nevertheless, who prepared the plan of the fort constructed "on the coast of Florida," receipt of which the Minister Pontchartrain acknowledged in a letter to Iberville dated July 15, 1699.[15] This was Fort Maurepas on Biloxi Bay, site of the present town of Ocean Springs, Mississippi, a site which Iberville began to clear on April 8, 1699. In his journal he wrote:

---

[11] Margry, *Découvertes et établissements*, IV, 74.
[12] Margry, *Découvertes et établissements*, IV, 66.
[13] Margry, *Découvertes et établissements*, IV, 72.
[14] Margry, *Découvertes et établissements*, IV, 420.
[15] Minister Pontchartrain to Iberville, Paris, July 15, 1699: AM. B2, 137:77.

I put ten men to squaring logs for the bastions made of "piece sur piece," a foot and a half thick. . . . The work goes slowly. I have no men who know how to hew; most of them are a day in felling a tree, which are in truth quite large—hard walnut and oak. I have had a forge set up to repair the axes which are always breaking. . . . The 14th . . . I sent a half league from here to cut the stakes for the palisade; every day the sloop brings eighty to a hundred of them. I am having work done to build an oven and to dig the ditches for the palisades. The bastions are advancing. . . . The 19th, 20th and 21st, I have had work done squaring stakes and reducing them to three inches thick for flooring the bastions that I have had erected nine feet high, on which I have put the cannons, with a four foot parapet. . . . The 24th I had the cannons mounted on the bastions and entirely finished the fort. The 25th I set up the magazines and completed the lodgings for the garrison.[16]

A few days later, on May 3, 1699, having left Sauvole as commandant, Iberville left to return to France aboard his ship, the *Badine*.

On arriving at La Rochelle he wrote to the minister of the marine on June 29, 1699, giving his reasons for selecting the site and describing the fort: "This fort is of wood with four bastions, two are of 'piece sur piece' [timbers], a foot and a half by a foot high, decked like a ship, on which the cannon is placed, with a parapet four feet high. The two other [bastions are] of good palisades, well doubled, in which there are fourteen pieces of cannon and sufficient supplies."[17]

The journal of another vessel of the expedition, *LeMarin*, gives the additional information that: ". . . two [of the bastions] are from two to three feet thick, made of pieces of squared wood, one upon the other with embrasures for putting the cannons, and a ditch around it. The two other bastions are made of such heavy stakes that it takes four men to carry them. There are twelve pieces of cannon mounted around."[18]

This is the fort as it appears on the undated and unsigned drawing in the Ministry of the Colonies in Paris, undoubtedly the work of Remy Reno, entitled "Plan of fort de Maurepas [*sic*] on the southern coast of Florida."[19] Here the two bastions of *pièce sur pièce* are clearly shown, the other two and the curtain walls being of posts in the ground. In opposite corners of the square fort were the Royal Bastion and the Bastion of the Chapel. The other two were the Biloxi

[16] Margry, *Découvertes et établissements,* IV, 195–198.
[17] Margry, *Découvertes et établissements,* IV, 125.
[18] Margry, *Découvertes et établissements,* IV, 286.
[19] PAMC, no. 3.

Bastion and the Bastion of the Sea, the latter enclosing the powder magazine. Platforms as described by Iberville are indicated above the first two. Inside, buildings were symmetrically arranged around the Place d'Armes; outside, the "covered way" was shielded by an outer palisade or "curtain" of posts in the ground. Here was a fort, built of crude local materials but containing all the elements of Vauban's system of fortification, a fort built during Vauban's lifetime. After Iberville's departure, Sauvole kept his men busy at work on the fort: "Their lodgings being finished I have had them enclose the warehouse that had been set up; afterwards we had a hospital built (spending some days) felling trees all around that were of a prodigious size."[20]

Although Fort Maurepas was perhaps the best-designed and best-constructed fort built by the French in the Mississippi Valley up to that time, its site was poor and in a few years it was abandoned when the capital was moved to Mobile in 1702. On its site in 1910, a small rough stone slab was unearthed on which the following inscription was crudely carved:

COLONIE•

FRANCOISES

1699

PR LE MOYNE

SR DE IBVLE

L.P.  P.L.

This purported relic of Fort Maurepas is now in the Cabildo at New Orleans.

THE MISSISSIPPI FORT (DE LA BOULAYE)–1700

On his return from France, Iberville wrote to the minister on September 7, 1700, that he had further examined the mouth of the Mississippi and decided "to build a small establishment there in order to have possession of it, for fear that another nation might challenge us and occupy it."[21]

This Mississippi fort was probably not much more than a blockhouse on which Iberville began construction in February, 1700. In his journal he wrote: "On the 6th and 7th I continued the work of clearing and squaring logs with which to build the house and have been working on a powder magazine 8 feet square, raised 5 feet above

---

[20] Margry, *Découvertes et établissements,* IV, 447.

[21] Margry, *Découvertes et établissements,* IV, 372.

the ground, made of wood and covered and surrounded with 1-½ feet of mud plaster."[22] Again, he wrote: "On the bank was the edge of a wood, fifty paces deep of oaks, ash, elms, planes and poplars. . . . I have set to work to cut down these trees and square them in order that we may build a square house twenty-eight feet on each face, two stories with machicolations, with four four-pound and two eighteen-pound cannons, with a moat twelve feet across."[23]

Iberville's chaplain, in his journal, gives a few additional bits of information concerning the building of the Mississippi fort:

February 6 [1700] We are clearing land, hewing, digging, burning and forging. Sailors, Canadians, and officers, all are so active that the settlement will be completed in a short time. . . .[24]

February 8—M. d'Iberville went up the river to search for large timbers to form the main beams of the fort. . . . On his return he found a large house erected. The walls are of cane laid cross-wise between large poles. The roof is made of palms [palmettos] whose leaves are flat and arranged like a fan. All this is well tied together and firmly supported. The building, which is about twenty feet square, is intended to serve as a magazine [warehouse] until there is a better one. . . . [Feb. 9] A powder magazine has been begun and is almost completed. It is two stories high so as to be drier.[25]

This Mississippi fort, called Fort De La Boulaye on some early maps, was but a simple construction, built without trained direction—Remy Reno had returned to France with Iberville the year before and presumably did not come back to Louisiana. Although the fort was officially abandoned in 1707, its importance as the site of the first French outpost on the lower Mississippi cannot be overlooked. A few remnants of its ancient timbers were found in 1927, and the facts fully recorded in an article in the *Louisiana Historical Quarterly* for October, 1936.

MOBILE BAY AREA –1702-17

In 1702 the French moved from Fort Maurepas to the Mobile River and here established the first town in the colony which had any semblance of town planning. This was an important development, but as it is rather far from the Mississippi, it and subsequent work in the area will be but briefly mentioned. The first settlement was made somewhat above the present city of Mobile. A gridiron plan was laid

[22] Margry, *Découvertes et établissements*, IV, 403.
[23] Margry, *Découvertes et établissements*, IV, 364.
[24] Ruth Lapham Butler, *Journal of Paul Du Ru* (Chicago, 1934), p. 7.
[25] Butler, *Journal of Paul Du Ru*, pp. 8-9.

out around a citadel, a "fort of four bastions following the plan sent by the Sieur Le Vasseur."[26] Le Vasseur, a lieutenant of infantry and commandant of the Canadians, had accompanied Bienville in the selection of the site[27] and probably served as his engineer and author of the town plan.

The first site proving to be unsatisfactory due to flooding conditions, Fort Louis of Mobile was relocated about 1711. The new plan adopted was similar to the first one, a fine drawing of it by the Sieur Chevillot giving much information about the fort and the town and its buildings.[28] Eventually the palisade fort was rebuilt in brick, renamed Fort Condé, and became one of the finest French fortifications in America. No trace of it now remains except for a few bricks turned up in excavations for new construction on the site.

In 1715 instructions were given for the construction of a stone fort at Dauphin Island at the entrance to Mobile Bay, a Sieur Bajot being appointed as engineer to direct the works.[29] The plan proposed was a pentagon,[30] evidently a favorite form for the military, a fortified town with radial streets. Nothing came of the interesting plan and only a small four-bastioned palisade was built on the island.

## THE BEGINNINGS OF NEW ORLEANS–1718

With the establishment of John Law's Mississippi Company development of France's Colony of Louisiana received a new stimulus. Now for the first time trained engineers were sent to carry out the planning of new towns and the building of new fortifications. The first of these was the Sieur Périer, appointed engineer-in-chief of Louisiana who was given instructions on April 14, 1718, to go to the colony for the prime purpose of establishing the new town of New Orleans.[31] He was told to "begin by marking the enclosure of a fort which could subsequently become a citadel. It needs at first simply to be enclosed with stakes in the manner of the country, and inside this fort place the warehouses of the Company and the lodgings of the Directors General, Staff, officers and soldiers who compose the garrison of New Orleans. After this the said Sieur Perrier shall mark the enclosure of the town and the alignment of the streets, with

---

[26] Paris, Archives Nationales (hereafter PAN), C–13–A–2, p. 468.
[27] PAN, C–13–C–2, p. 36.
[28] Peter J. Hamilton, *Colonial Mobile* (2nd ed., Boston, 1910), p. 86.
[29] PAN, C–13–A–3, p. 683.
[30] PAMC, no. 131.
[31] Margry, *Découvertes et établissements*, V, 599.

suitable lots for each inhabitant within the enclosure." A fine undated and unsigned plan in the Bibliothèque Nationale in Paris
entitled "Plan of New Orleans"[32] may well be one prepared by
Perrier in accordance with his instructions, for it shows an enclosed
town with a pentagonal fortress or citadel. In this plan the Vauban
influence is apparent; the citadel is taken directly from a plate in
*Elemens de fortification*.[33] No attempt was made to execute this
plan, for Perrier died en route to Louisiana and Le Blond de la Tour
was appointed to replace him. New instructions were issued to him
on November 8, 1719,[34] as engineer-in-chief as well as to the Sieurs
De Pauger and de Boispinel as engineers-in-second and to Franquet
de Chaville, also engineer.

Le Blond de la Tour[35] began his military career about 1697, was
sent to Portugal as a draftsman during the War of the Spanish
Succession, and was appointed engineer in 1703, when the corps was
still under the leadership of Vauban. He served in Spain from 1704 to
1708, being taken prisoner at Alcantara in 1705 and exchanged in
1706. In the campaign of 1707–9 in Spain, he participated in the
sieges of Lerida and Tortosa, which were directed by the Duc
d'Orléans who, on the death of Louis XIV in 1715 became Regent of
France and for whom New Orleans was named. It was probably as a
result of this service and a personal acquaintance with the regent that
he was appointed engineer-in-chief of Louisiana. De Pauger and de
Boispinel also had long careers in the Corps of Engineers and de
Chaville had served under de la Tour since 1715.[36] All were flattered
by their appointment by no less a personage than the regent.[37] It
should be noted too that de la Tour was also appointed as director of
the Louisiana concessions of the Marquis d'Asfeld, Vauban's successor as director-general of fortifications of France.

NEW BILOXI–1720

Le Blond de la Tour arrived at Old Biloxi (near the site of old Fort
Maurepas) on December 17, 1720.[38] Three days later he made a

---

[32] Baron Marc De Villiers du Terrage, *Histoire de la fondation de la
Nouvelle Orleans* (Paris, 1917), p. 54.
[33] M. Le Blond, *Elemens de fortification* (5th ed., Paris, 1764), plate XX.
[34] Margry, *Découvertes et établissements*, V, 610.
[35] *Dictionary of American Biography* (New York, 1943), XI, 19.
[36] PAN, C–13–A–7, p. 223.
[37] PAN, C–13–A–6, p. 37.
[38] PAN, C–13–A–6, p. 121.

report to the council which then decided to have him begin work on a new establishment across the bay at New Biloxi.[39] On January 8, 1721,[40] he presented four plans, elaborately drawn and rendered, for this new fort and town. Each plan was for a fortified town in the Vauban manner, not unlike Vauban's plan for Fort Louis du Rhin.[41] The streets were laid out in gridiron pattern around a Place d'Armes, the same plan form to be later adopted for New Orleans. The plans differed only in the size of the proposed town and the elaborateness of the fortifications. The council approved plan number 3[42] which was a bit larger than number 4 but smaller than the other two. This was a rectangular fort of four bastions, open to the sea and with all the most elaborate moats and outer works. The plan included a small port enclosed by jetties which was hopefully designed to be kept scoured out by the waters of a small stream that was to supply the moat and then flow out to sea through the port.

Work was immediately begun on this new Fort Louis under the direction of de Boispinel, but by the end of the year little progress had been made.[43] On December 9, 1721, de la Tour wrote that de Boispinel began "by felling the trees and clearing the land, building some huts to lodge himself and the workmen, constructing forges for the tool makers and blacksmiths, sheds for the carpenters, a chapel and lodging for the chaplain, a frame hospital to contain sixty to eighty sick plus the hospital attendants."[44] His plan for a more permanent hospital is basically the same as that shown on plate 31 of *La Science des ingenieurs*,[45] but on a smaller scale. Food and supplies were scarce and because of the summer heat "it has been impossible to work except up to nine o'clock in the morning, and to return to work at three o'clock, and the nights impossible to rest because of the gnats and mosquitoes." In 1722 orders were finally received from France to abandon this useless project and to transfer the capital to

---

[39] PAN, C–13–A–6, p. 143; translation in *Mississippi Provincial Archives,* ed. and trans. Dunbar Rowland and Albert Godfrey Saunders (Jackson, Miss., 1932), III, 298.

[40] PAN, C–13–A–6, pp. 121–124.

[41] Vauban, *Plans des villes et places importantes qui sont dans la carte de l'Alsace, avec leurs fortifications* (Paris?, 1697).

[42] Baron Marc De Villiers du Terrage, *Les Dernières années de la Louisiane française* (Paris, 1904), p. 12 (illustration).

[43] PAN, C–13–A–6, pp. 121–124.

[44] PAN, C–13–A–6, pp. 130–133.

[45] Bernard Forest de Belidor, *La Science des ingenieurs* (Paris, 1729), bk. IV, plate 31, p. 76.

New Orleans.[46] Le Blond de la Tour began to believe that he had been deliberately misled by the council and Bienville into wasting his efforts so as to be discredited before the court.

## DEVELOPMENT OF NEW ORLEANS

On March 29, 1721, De Pauger arrived at New Orleans[47] to lay out the town in accordance with a plan that had been designed by de la Tour and himself at Biloxi. Bienville in founding the city in 1718 had apparently decided upon the direction of the streets and the alignment of the first houses, as indicated on a plan of 1723[48] that shows the clearings made prior to De Pauger's arrival and those made by him. A plan marked "March 1721"[49] may be the rough sketch De Pauger brought with him to begin the project. In his letter of December 9, 1721, de la Tour wrote that he had sent De Pauger to New Orleans "in order to make the establishment of this city according to the project that I made for it. . . . He has begun by making the clearing and laying out the streets and giving some designs for the houses that face the river where they are beginning to build. Formerly there were only poor huts as in almost all the other posts. He has had a fine and large warehouse constructed there for storing the Company's effects."[50] On April 14, 1721, soon after his arrival in New Orleans, De Pauger wrote to de la Tour sending him the plan of the city and pointing out "the changes I have been obliged to make because of the situation of the terrain. As it is higher on the bank of the river, I have brought the town square and the sites marked for the houses of the principal inhabitants closer to it, so as to profit not only from the proximity of the landing place, but also from the air of the breezes that come from it."[51] The plan sent by De Pauger may be the one recently found in the Library of Congress with the list of persons to whom lots had been distributed. A copy of this plan with such a list was transmitted by de la Tour with his letter to the court of April 28, 1722.

This plan with "the lots of the town, especially those facing the river . . . marked by alphabetical letters"[52] shows the gridiron plan

[46] PAN, C–13–A–6, p. 321.

[47] Margry, *Découvertes et établissements*, V, 634.

[48] PAMC, no. 68; illustrated in Samuel Wilson, Jr., *The Capuchin School* (New Orleans, 1961), p. 15.

[49] PAMC, no. 66.

[50] PAN, C–13–A–6, pp. 130–133.

[51] Paris, Cartes et Plans, vol. 67, no. 5, no. 3 portfolio 135, piece 13.

[52] PAN, C–13–A–6, p. 314.

with its central Place d'Armes, the plan that has survived to this day, a New Orleans heritage from its French colonial founders. The plan also shows an enclosing fortification of a simplified Vauban type, and subsequent plans that were periodically prepared to show the growth of the town indicate the same fortifications. But they only existed on paper; the French found it easier and cheaper to keep the Indians friendly with gifts, and English and Spanish forces seemed far away. Lassus' perspective of New Orleans in 1726[53] and Gonichon's plan of May, 1728,[54] show the town as it really existed.

THE WORKS OF BARON AND BROUTIN

Military engineers, besides designing fortresses and fortified towns, were also called upon to design many of the buildings within them. Some of the first buildings in New Orleans are shown on de la Tour's drawing of January 3, 1723.[55] They include the house for the directors of the Company of the Indies as well as barracks for the troops and workmen and a small military hospital. All these buildings were of colombage, or timber frame construction covered over on the outside with wide boards, a sort of ship-lap siding. De Pauger's parish church, designed in 1724,[56] was of similar construction, with curious timber props or buttresses at the sides to resist the frequent hurricane winds. These were omitted when the building was erected, and instead the walls were filled in with brick (*briqueté entre poteaux*) to give them the necessary rigidity.

De Boispinel and Le Blond de la Tour both died in 1723, the former while working at rebuilding the fort at Mobile; de Chaville returned to France in 1724; De Pauger died in 1726. Louisiana was again without a trained architect or military engineer. For a time Ignace François Broutin, a captain who had come in 1720 with de la Tour in command of the troops of the d'Asfeld concession[57] and who had served under the engineers, took over the task temporarily. However, when Étienne de Périer succeeded Bienville as governor in 1728, he gave the position of engineer-in-chief to Pierre Baron who had been sent to Louisiana by the Royal Academy of Sciences to do research in natural history and astronomy.[58]

---

[53] PAMC, no. 71; Wilson, *Capuchin School*, p. 8.
[54] London, British Museum, King's Collection.
[55] PAMC, no. 67; Wilson, *Capuchin School*, pp. 10–11.
[56] PAMC, no. 70; Wilson, *Capuchin School*, p. 16.
[57] Louisiana State Museum Library, "Passengers. 1718–1724," p. 279.
[58] PAN, C–13–B–1, Aug. 6, 1730.

It was during this period that the massacre of the French by the Natchez Indians occurred in 1729. The resultant panic in New Orleans caused Baron to attempt to fortify the town. A plan dated April 10, 1730,[59] showing a moat and canal with an indication of outer works of palisades is probably Baron's project. How little of it was carried out is shown by Gonichon's plan of New Orleans of 1731.[60] Before the moat had been dug much more than half-way around, the Natchez had been attacked and destroyed, and the inhabitants soon lost interest in the fortification project that required the time and labor of their slaves which they thought could be put to better use.

Baron did present a project for new barracks and probably made the drawings, dated March 30, 1729,[61] for an elaborate brick building to be erected on the edge of the town just within the proposed ramparts, a location entirely in keeping with Vauban's principles. Before the project could be carried out, Baron was dismissed and Bienville returned as governor in place of Périer. Broutin then became engineer-in-chief, a position he held until his death in 1751. He prepared new designs for the barracks, designs that could have been literally lifted from the plates of *La Science des ingenieurs*.[62]

On September 15, 1733, the Count Maurepas, minister and secretary of state, gave his approval to the project and ordered the construction of the barracks "to be placed at one of the extremities of the town."[63] Bienville and his staff, however, had other ideas, "and having reflected that the town not being surrounded by walls, [decided] it would be much more suitable to place it at the center."[64] To justify this change in location from the traditional one, Bienville wrote that "the idea came to me to make a sort of fort in the middle of the town by dividing these barracks in two on the two sides of the Public Square, by means of which, with the church that is located at the extremity of the Square, we could close up the inhabitants and their possessions by barricading the streets which abut upon it . . . besides . . . it would make a decoration for the town."[65]

This last aesthetic consideration was perhaps the dominant one,

---

[59] PAMC, no. 85.
[60] PAMC, no. 89.
[61] PAMC, nos. 77, 78, 79.
[62] Belidor, *La Science des ingenieurs*, bk. IV, plate 29, p. 72; PAMC, no. 29.
[63] PAN, C–13–A–18, p. 176.
[64] PAN, C–13–A–18, p. 176.
[65] PAN, C–13–A–19.

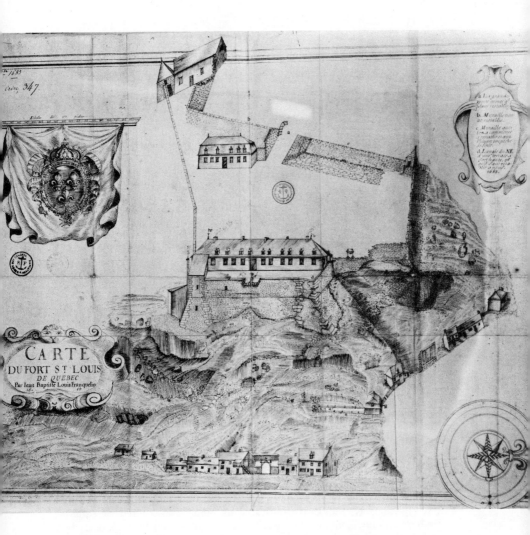

1. Fort Louis of Quebec, by Jean Baptiste Louis Franquelin, October 25, 1683, the principal French fortification in North America as it appeared at about the time La Salle left it on his explorations on the Mississippi. (*Paris, Ministère des Colonies, No. 347.*)

a. The great gate, ruined, that must be rebuilt. b. Wall newly rebuilt. c. Wall that they had begun to rebuild and that winter prevented finishing. d. N.E. angle of a very high terrace that must be rebuilt anew. 1683.

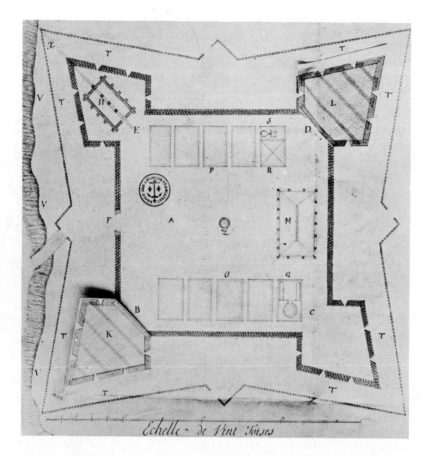

2. "Plan of Fort Maurepas on the Southern Coast of Florida." The fort established by Pierre Lemoyne d'Iberville in 1699 on the shore of Biloxi Bay. Bastions K and L are indicated as being constructed of squared timbers laid horizontally (*pièce sur pièce*) and decked over, as described in Iberville's journal. The remainder of the fort is of palisades. This unsigned drawing was probably made by Iberville's draftsman, Remy Reno. (*Paris, Ministère des Colonies, No. 3.*)

A. Place d'Armes. B. Royal Bastion. C. Biloxy Bastion. D. Bastion of the Chapel. E. Bastion of the Sea. F. Royal gate. G. Chapel. H. Lodging of the governor. I. Lodging of the major. K. Platform above the Royal Bastion. L. Platform above the Bastion of the Chapel. M. General warehouse. N. Powder magazine. O. Lodging of the Canadians and filibusters. P. Lodging of the soldiers. Q. Oven. R. Magazine for the arms. S. Forge. T. Covered way. V. Curtain. X. Canal. Y. Cellar. Z. Well.

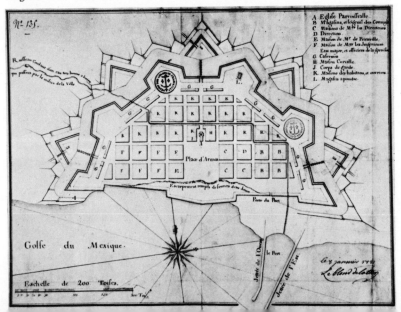

3. Proposed Fort Louis at Dauphin Island, 1715. An unusual pentagonal fortified town intended to protect the entrance to Mobile Bay. The drawing is probably by the engineer, Bajot, and was never executed in this form. (*Paris, Ministère des Colonies, No. 131.*)

1. Government house. 2. Lieutenant of the king. 3. Major. 4. Aide major. 5. Clerk. 6. King's warehouse and warehouse keeper. 8. Hospital. 9. Chapel and Missionary. 10. Chaplain. 11. Surgeon. 12. Engineer. 13. 3 Cannoneers. 14. Gunsmith, marshal, cooper, and wheelwright. 15. Barracks. 16. Company's warehouse. 17, 18, 19, 20, 21, and 22. Lots to be distributed.

4. "Plan of the Works Proposed for the New Establishment of New Biloxy" by Le Blond de la Tour, January 8, 1721, probably the largest of the four suggested plans presented to the Superior Council on that date. A smaller scheme was adopted but was abandoned before completion. (*Paris, Ministère des Colonies, No. 125.*)

A. Parish church. B. Warehouses and lodgings of the clerks. C. Houses for the directors. D. Management (office). E. House of M. de Bienville. F. House for the engineers, general staff, and officers of the garrison. G. Barracks. H. Rectory. J. Guardhouse. K. Houses for the inhabitants and workmen. L. Powder magazine.

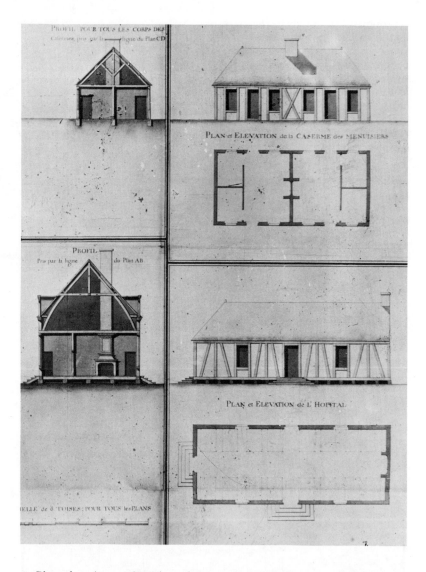

5. Plan, elevation, and section of the workmen's barracks and the military hospital, typical of the first timber framed buildings constructed in New Orleans. Detail of Le Blond de la Tour's drawing dated January 3, 1723, entitled "Plans, Sections, and Elevations of the Buildings and Barracks Built for the Company Since the 1st August 1722 Until the 3 January of the Present Year, 1723." (*Paris, Ministère des Colonies, No. 67.*)

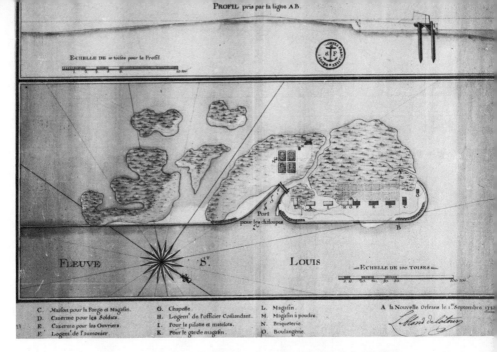

PROFIL pris par la ligne A.B.

ECHELLE DE 10 toises pour le Profil

FLEUVE S<sup>T</sup>. LOUIS

ECHELLE DE 100 TOISES

Port pour les chaloupes

A la Nouvelle Orleans le 1<sup>er</sup> Septembre 1723

| C. | Maison pour la Forge et Magasin. | G. | Chapelle. | L. | Magasin. |
| D. | Caserne pour les Soldats. | H. | Logem<sup>t</sup> de l'officier Comandant. | M. | Magasin à poudre. |
| E. | Caserne pour les Ouvriers. | I. | Pour le pilote et matelots. | N. | Briqueterie. |
| F. | Logem<sup>t</sup> de l'aumonier. | K. | Pour le garde magasin. | O. | Boulangerie. |

6. "Plan of the Works Proposed to Be Built at the Island of La Balise, with the Necessary Lodgings; the Buildings Marked in Red Are Built." Drawing signed by Le Blond de la Tour, dated at New Orleans, September 1, 1723. (*Paris, Ministère des Colonies, No. 105.*)

A–B. Line of the section. C. House for the forge and warehouse. D. Barracks for the soldiers. E. Barracks for the workmen. F. Chaplain's lodging. G. Chapel. H. Lodging for the commanding officer. I. For the pilot and sailors. K. For the warehouse keeper. L. Warehouse. M. Powder magazine. N. Brickyard. O. Bakery.

7. Section, showing construction, signal lantern and fog signal gun at La Balise. Detail of a drawing signed by Le Blond de la Tour, dated at Fort Louis (Biloxi) April 23, 1722, entitled "Plan, Section, and Elevation of the Battery to Be Built at the Mouth of the St. Louis River, on the Two Small Islands That Are Located at the Extremities of the Two Proposed Jetties, and That Form a Breakwater, on One of Which There Will Be a Flag During the Day and a Signal Light at Night." (*Paris, Ministère des Colonies, No. 28.*)

PROFIL
Pris par la ligne du Plan A.B.

Laisse de la haute Mer.

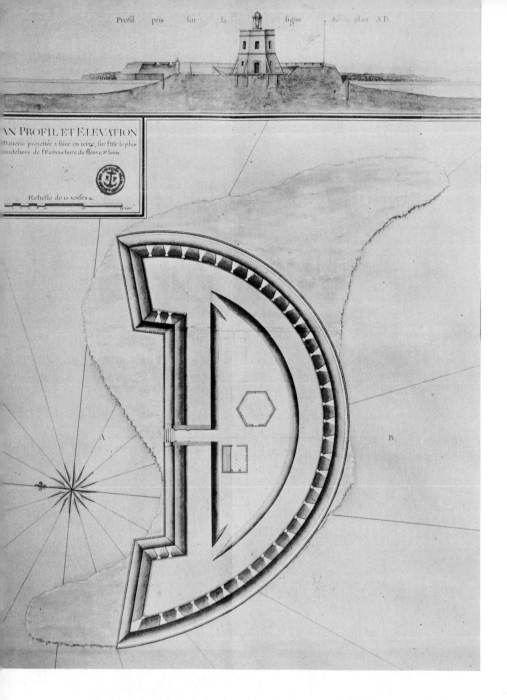

8. "Plan, Section, and Elevation of the Battery Proposed to Be Built of Earth, on the Outermost Island at the Mouth of the St. Louis River." Drawing signed by De Pauger dated May 29, 1724, showing the small fort and lighthouse opposite La Balise at the mouth of the Mississippi. (*Paris, Ministère des Colonies, No. 34.*)

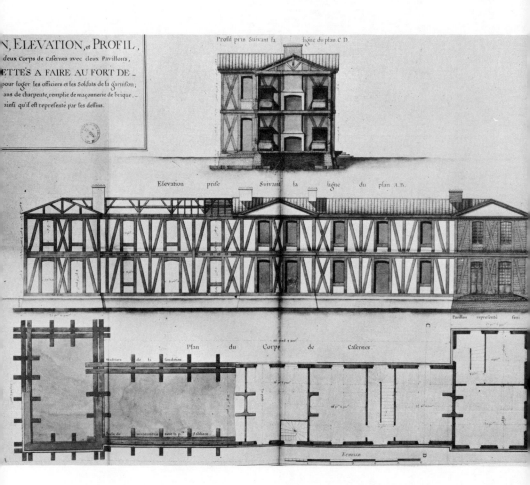

9. "Plan, Elevation, and Section of One of the Two Barracks Buildings with Two Pavilions, Proposed to Be Built at the Fort of La Balise, for Lodging the Officers and Soldiers of the Garrison; Built with a Timber Frame, Filled In with Brick Masonry, As It Is Represented by the Drawings." Dated July, 1731. Note the large timber footings shown at the left in the plan; on these timbers brick foundations were constructed as shown in the section. (*Paris, Ministère des Colonies, No. 110.*)

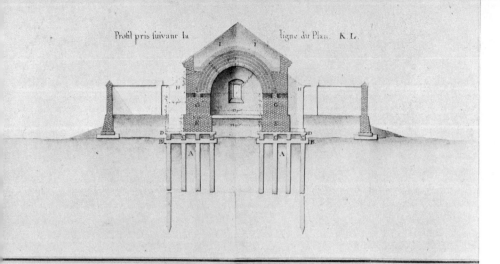

PLAN D'UN MAGAZIN A POUDRE PROIETE a FAIRE au POSTE de LA BALISE

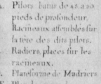

a. Pilots batus de 45 a 50
pieds de profondeur,
Racineaux assemblés fur
la tête des dits pilots.
Radiers, places fur les
racineaux.
. Plateforme de Madriers
F. Plan des murs de maçon-
nerie.
G. Sur le profil, marquent
l'épaisseur des murs des
costés au dessous de la
retraite et ainsy qu'au dessus
Contreforts.
Terrasse fur la Voute
couverte de tuile plate.

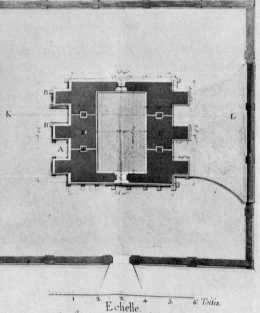

Echelle.
1 2 3 4 5 6: Toises.
a la Nouvelle orleans ce vingt quatrième fevrier 1734.

10. "Plan of a Powder Magazine Proposed to Be Built at the Post of La Balise." Drawing signed by Deverges, dated at New Orleans February 24, 1734. (Paris, *Archives Nationales*.)

A. Piles driven 45 to 50 feet in depth. B. Sleepers fit together on the heads of the piles. C. Cross-beams placed on the sleepers. D. Platform of planks. E–F. Plan of the masonry walls. E–G. On the section, marks the thickness of the side walls below the offset as well as above it. H. Buttresses. I. Terrace above the vault covered with flat tile.

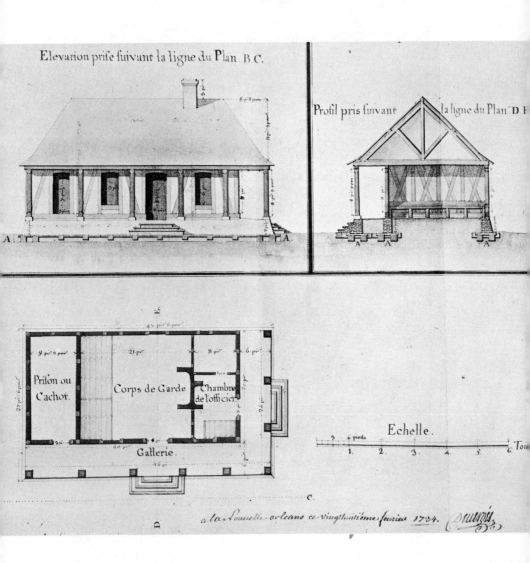

11. "Plan, Section, and Elevation of a Guardhouse and Prison, Proposed to Be Built at the Post of La Balise." Drawing signed by Deverges, dated at New Orleans February 28, 1734. One of the earliest drawings by a military engineer in Louisiana showing a gallery. (*Paris, Archives Nationales.*)

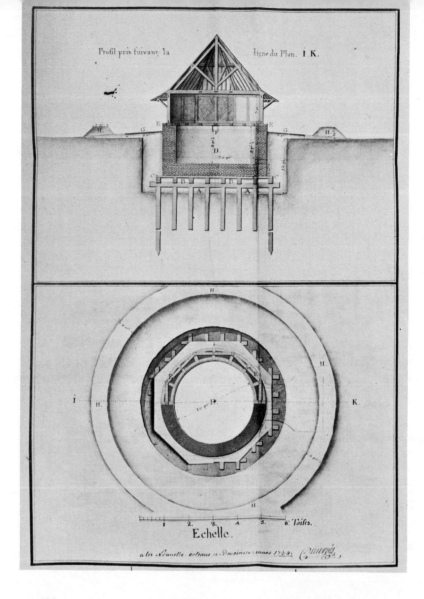

12. "Plan and Section of a Cistern Proposed to Be Built at the Post of La Balise to Conserve the Rainwaters from the Roof Drains of Several Lodgings for the Subsistence of the Garrison During Four Months of the Year when the Water from the Lower Saint Louis River Is Salty." Drawing dated New Orleans, March 2, 1734, and signed by Deverges. (*Paris, Archives Nationales.*)

A. Foundation on piles driven as far as possible. B. Grillage fit together on the heads of the piles. C. Platform of planks. D. Plan and section of the basin of the cistern. E. Plan and section of the platform and walls of the housing over the basin. F. Space for the overflow of excess waters. G. Brick paving. H. Water barrier to keep out the seawater while they are working to build this project.

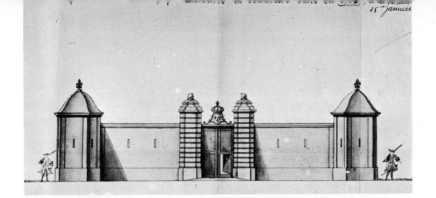

13. "Elevation (from the Entrance Side) of the Enclosure of the Powder Magazine, Built in 1732." Drawing dated New Orleans, January 15, 1733, and signed by Broutin. The powder magazine, with its monumental fence, was destroyed in the conflagration of December 8, 1794. (*Paris, Archives Nationales.*)

14. "Plan, Section, and Elevation of a Hall for the Sick Proposed to Be Built in 1733." Drawing dated May 1, 1733, and signed by Broutin. This brick structure was erected adjacent to the three-story half-timbered Ursuline Convent that appears to the left in the plan and elevation. (*Paris, Archives Nationales.*)

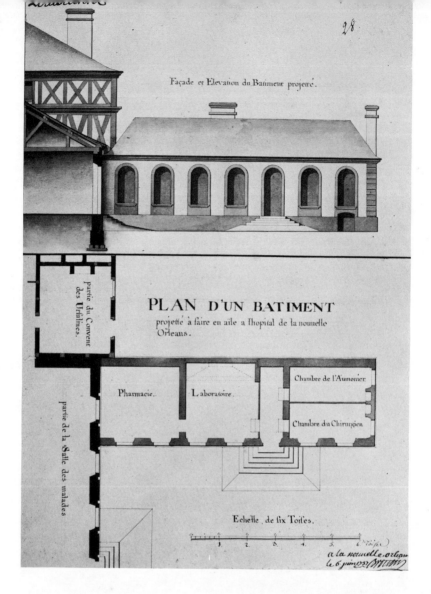

Façade et Elevation du Batiment projetté.

partie du Convent des Ursulines.

**PLAN D'UN BATIMENT**

projetté à faire en aîle a l'hopital de la nouuelle
Orleans.

partie de la Salle des malades

Pharmacie.     Laboratoire.     Chambre de l'Aumonier.

Chambre du Chirurgien

Echelle de fix Toifes.

1.   2.   3.   4.   5.   6. Toifes.

a la nouuelle orleans
le 6 juin 1737 Broutin

15. "Plan of a Building Proposed to Be Built as a Wing of the Hospital of
New Orleans." Drawing dated New Orleans January 6, 1737, and signed
by Broutin. This hospital wing containing a pharmacy and laboratory, as
well as rooms for the surgeon and the chaplain, was also adjacent to the
half-timbered Ursuline Convent that appears to the left. This drawing
made three years after the completion of the convent indicates that the
timbers of this "brick between posts" structure were left exposed, a
practice that caused rapid deterioration of the building. In later buildings
of this type, the frame was covered over either with boards or cement
plaster. (*Paris, Ministère des Colonies, No. 28.*)

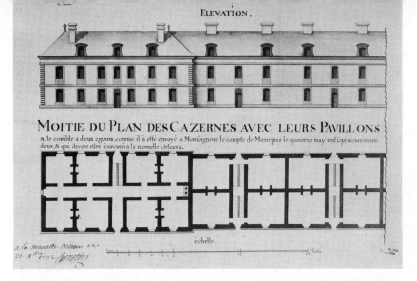

MOITIE DU PLAN DES CAZERNES AVEC LEURS PAVILLONS
& le comble a deux egouts, comme il à efté envoyé a Monseigneur le compte de Maurepas le quatorze may mil sept cents trente deux, & qui devoit eftre executé a la nouuelle Orleans.

échelle.

16. "Half of the Plan of the Barracks with Their Hip-Roofed Pavilions As Sent to Monseigneur the Compte de Maurepas, the Fourteenth of May, Seventeen Thirty-Two, and Which Is Due to Be Executed at New Orleans." Drawing dated at New Orleans, October 26, 1732, and signed by Broutin. One of the earlier designs for the barracks similar to plate 29, book IV of Belidor's *La Science des ingenieurs*. The second building for the Ursuline Convent was designed in this same style by Broutin in 1745 and is the only building still standing in New Orleans definitely known to date from the French colonial period. (*Paris, Ministère des Colonies, No. 29.*)

17. "Plan of One of the Two Barracks Buildings to Be Executed at New Orleans on the Two Sides of the Place d'Armes, One of Which Has Been Commenced. The Part in Yellow Is Only Proposed." The right wing beyond the heavy vertical line in the elevation was not built. Drawing dated New Orleans, October 26, 1734, and signed by Broutin. (*Paris, Archives Nationales.*)

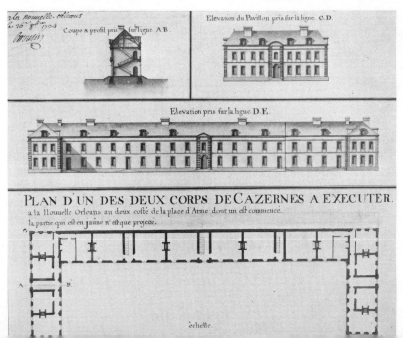

Coupe & profil pris fur ligne A B.

Elevation du Pavillon pris fur la ligne. C.D.

Elevation pris fur la ligne D.E.

PLAN D'UN DES DEUX CORPS DE CAZERNES A EXECUTER.
a la Nouuelle Orleans au deux cofté de la place d'Arme dont un eft commencé.
la partie qui eft en jaune n' eft que projetée.

échelle.

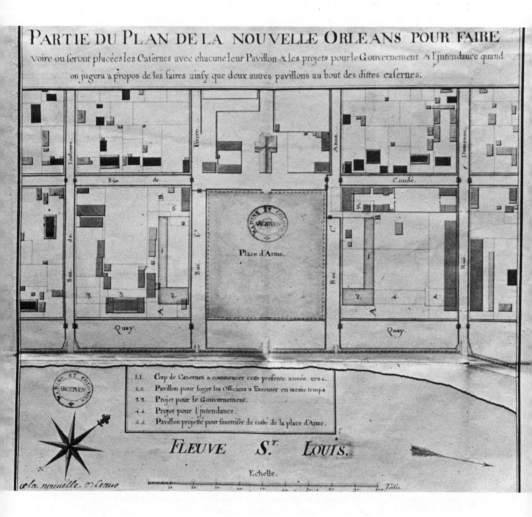

PARTIE DU PLAN DE LA NOUVELLE ORLEANS POUR FAIRE

voire ou feront placées les Cafernes avec chacune leur Pavillon & les projets pour le Gouvernement & l'Intendance quand
on jugera a propos de les faire ainfy que deux autres pavillons au bout des dittes cafernes.

Place d'Arme.

FLEUVE S.T LOUIS.

Echelle.

1.1. Corp de Cazernes a commencer cette prefente année. 1734.
2.2. Pavillon pour loger les Officiers a Executer en meme temps
3.3. Projet pour le Gouvernement.
4.4. Projet pour l'Intendance.
5.5. Pavillon projetté pour fimetrifer du cotté de la place d'Arme.

18. "Part of the Plan of New Orleans Showing Where the Barracks Are
to Be Placed, Each with Its Pavilion, and the Projects for the Government
House and the Intendance When It Will Be Judged Proper to Build
Them, as Well as Two Other Pavilions at the End of the Said Barracks."
Drawing signed by Broutin and dated New Orleans, July 25, 1734. (*Paris,
Archives Nationales.*)

1.1. Barracks buildings to be commenced this present year 1734. 2.2. Pavilion
for lodging the officers to be executed at the same time. 3.3. Project for the
Government House. 4.4. Project for the Intendance. 5.5. Proposed pavilion for
the symmetry of the sides of the Place d'Armes.

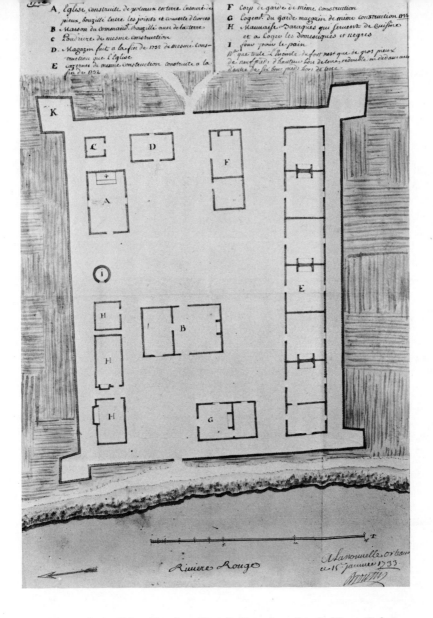

19. "Plan of the Natchitoches Fort." Drawing dated New Orleans, January 15, 1733, and signed by Broutin. (Paris, *Archives Nationales*.)

A. The church constructed of posts in the ground, enclosed with stakes, mud filled (*bouzillé*) between the joints, and roofed with bark. B. House of the commandant, the frame filled in with earth. C. Powder magazine of the same construction. D. Warehouse built at the end of 1732 of the same construction as the church. E. Barracks of the same construction, constructed at the end of 1732. F. Guardhouse of the same construction. G. Lodging for the warehouse keeper of the same construction, 1732. H. Wretched huts which serve as kitchen and to lodge the servants and Negroes. I. Oven for bread. Note that the entire enclosure of the fort is only of heavy stakes, nine feet high above ground, doubled on the inside with others six good feet above ground.

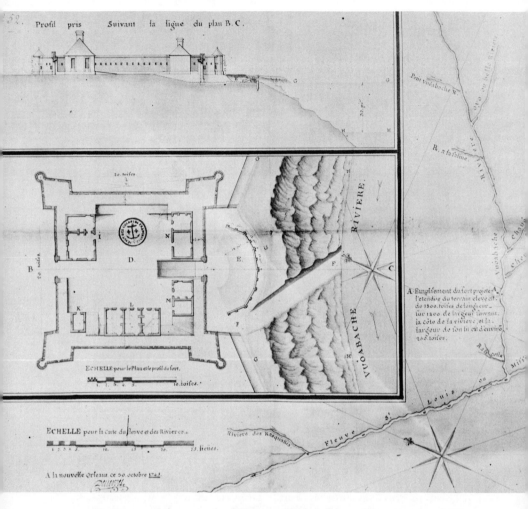

20. Proposed fort on the Wabash (Ohio) River. Drawing dated New Orleans, October 30, 1745, and signed by Deverges. (*Paris, Ministère des Colonies, No. 52.*)

A. Site of the proposed fort. The extent of elevated land is 1300 toises (7800 feet) long by 1200 toises (7200 feet) wide following the bank of the river, and the width of its bed is around 250 toises (1500 feet). D. Parade. E. Battery of cannons. F. Landing ramp. G. Line of the highest waters of the river. H. Line of the lowest waters. I. Lodging of the commandant. K. Powder magazine. L. Barracks. M. Guardhouse and prison. N. Warehouse for provisions, with a bedroom.

for two splendid brick barracks were built and must have given the square the monumental character envisioned by its original designers and retained in the Pontalba Buildings which for over a century have occupied the barracks site. Unfortunately, though the barracks cost a great sum of money and took many years to complete—they were not both finished by 1739—they were soon found to be badly constructed and by 1750 were showing dangerous signs of deterioration. New barracks were proposed, but before anything was done war with England was declared in 1756 and funds could not be provided for such a project. However, in order to conserve the materials in the old barracks and prevent a sudden collapse on the troops quartered there, both buildings were demolished, and by 1759 the sides of the Place d'Armes were bare.

Louisiana's military engineers were often responsible for the design and construction of buildings not of a military nature. De Pauger designed the parish church in 1724 and Broutin designed the Ursuline Convent in 1727, a design later altered by Baron and completed by Broutin in 1734.[66] This convent was to house the nuns who were to care for the sick in the adjacent military hospital, a building of brick construction designed by Broutin in 1733 and attached to one end of his half-timbered convent building. In 1737 he added a wing to the rear of this hospital to house the pharmacy and the chaplain. The kitchen was in a parallel wing.

In 1745 when the convent was found to be in precarious condition due to the rotting of its timber frame, Broutin prepared plans for a new convent in the same Louis XV style he had used for the barracks. This is the only building known to have survived from the French colonial period, and from it some idea of the character of Broutin's barracks can be obtained. It is possible that the interior stairway may have been reused from the earlier convent.

In 1732 Broutin rebuilt a wall around the New Orleans powder magazine, replacing the old wood palisade with a monumental enclosure of plastered brick; soon after he rebuilt the magazine also. The same year, 1732, Broutin went up to Natchitoches, made a survey of the fort there, and constructed in it a crude barracks, a warehouse and a house for the warehouse keeper.[67] Based on this plan

---

[66] Samuel Wilson, Jr., "An Architectural History of the Royal Hospital and the Ursuline Convent of New Orleans," *Louisiana Historical Quarterly*, XXIX (July, 1946), 559–569.

[67] PAN, C–13–A–17, p. 34.

and other research, the town of Natchitoches hoped to reconstruct this Fort St. Jean Baptiste to commemorate the two hundred and fiftieth anniversary of its founding in 1715.

Also in 1732 Alexandre De Batz was sent to Natchez where Broutin had once been commandant to make a similar survey of Fort Rosalie there.[68] This was the fort where the Indians had massacred the French in 1729. A similar massacre had occurred at Fort St. Claude on the Yazoo which had been built in 1722 for the d'Asfeld-LeBlanc Concession, another typical four-bastioned palisade fort.[69]

BERNARD DEVERGES AND THE END OF THE FRENCH REGIME

Broutin died in 1751 and was succeeded as engineer-in-chief by Bernard Deverges who had come to Louisiana as Le Blond de la Tour's draftsman in 1720. Under his direction an enormous new military hospital was constructed adjacent to and below the old one. By the time it was completed, however, the barracks had failed and the new hospital buildings were pressed into service to house the troops. The buildings continued in use as barracks during the Spanish period and were so used by the Americans after 1803. The old barracks were demolished in the 1830's when the Jackson Barracks were constructed below the city.

Deverges had served many years at the mouth of the Mississippi constructing Fort La Balise from designs first proposed by Le Blond de la Tour and developed by De Pauger. An interesting series of drawings by these different engineers and their assistants show the development of this important post which Deverges proudly considered as the position of honor and the key to the colony.[70]

As danger of war with England increased, Governor Vaudreuil appointed Deverges to take on the task of strengthening the colony's fortifications, relieving the then ailing Broutin.[71] He designed new forts to be built at English Turn, forts indicating some departure from the Vauban style and having a curious baroque character. He made numerous studies for these forts, and one of them was finally completed in 1747.[72] He also designed forts at Plaquemines Bend

[68] PAN, C–13–A–15, p. 152.
[69] Jean François Benjamin Dumont de Montigny, *Mémoires historiques sur la Louisiane* (Paris, 1753), II, 163.
[70] PAN, C–13–A–27, p. 150.
[71] PAN, C–13–A–32, p. 74.
[72] Library of Congress, Map Division: "Plan of the North Fort at English Turn, April 12, 1749"; reproduced in Samuel Wilson, Jr., "Louisiana Drawings

where Forts Jackson and St. Philip were later constructed. In 1745 he had prepared plans and estimates for a fort on the Wabash. This was to be a masonry structure planned "to prevent the savages, our enemies, and the Europeans who are in this continent from communicating with the St. Louis [Mississippi] River."[73]

Deverges designed new buildings for Fort Tombecbec in Alabama in 1751 and 1759, and the fort at Mobile was strengthened under the supervision of François Saucier, a surveyor and draftsman who had been in the colony since 1730 and who was assigned to the engineers about 1735.[74] After working for a time in Alabama, Saucier was sent to build a new fort at Kaskaskia for which he sent an estimate in 1753. Instead it was decided to rebuild Fort Chartres, and it was while working on the project that Saucier died on February 26, 1757. He was succeeded at Fort Chartres by Alexandre De Batz who died there soon after, in 1759, his position being taken by the Sieur Dufossat.[75]

Fort Chartres had always been one of France's chief strong points in the Mississippi Valley. An inventory made when it was transferred to the king by the Company of the Indies on June 1, 1732, describes it as being about one hundred and fifty feet square, "of four bastions, constructed of stakes, falling into ruin, sustained only by a prop upon which the said stakes are leaning."[76] A few buildings of colombage or stakes in the ground were inside the fort; there was probably not much left when Saucier began the work of rebuilding it in masonry. Captain Philip Pittman, a British officer, described it about 1764 "as the most commodious and best built fort in North America."[77]

The French had counted largely upon Fort Chartres to protect New Orleans from attack by way of the river. However, when word reached New Orleans in December, 1759, that Quebec had fallen to the English in September, Governor Kerlerec called a special council of war at which it was decided that the city should be immediately fortified by a moat and palisades. Kerlerec, on March 30, 1760, wrote

---

by Alexandre De Batz," *Journal of the Society of Architectural Historians,* XXII (May, 1963), 86.

[73] PAMC, no. 53.

[74] PAN, C–13–A–20, p. 66.

[75] Wilson, "Louisiana Drawings by Alexandre De Batz," p. 89.

[76] PAN, C–13–B–1.

[77] Captain Philip Pittman, *The Present State of the European Settlements on the Mississippi* (Cleveland, 1906), p. 89.

that "this operation would have been accomplished a long time ago if I had not been restrained by the consideration of expense . . . but it is to-day a question of putting ourselves in position to make a more vigorous defense, [and] in case of a reduction to the last extremity, might be able to procure a capitulation more honorable to the Arms of the King and more advantageous for his subjects' possessions."[78]

Accordingly Deverges prepared plans for the moat "and a palisade with its bastions, platforms and curtains"[79] which he estimated to cost five hundred thousand livres but feared it might cost up to a million. Work was begun immediately even though work on the Royal Hospital (that became the barracks) had not yet been finished. The design and construction of these fortifications brought to a head the antagonism between Governor Kerlerec and the Intendant Rochemore which had been growing since the latter's arrival in the colony about 1758. French colonial policy at this time seemed to be to appoint a governor and an intendant who would be as opposed to each other as possible so that one could watch and report on the other. This was certainly the case with Kerlerec and Rochemore.

On December 6, 1758,[80] Kerlerec reported on an association that had been formed since Rochemore's arrival for undertaking all the king's works, a group composed of Destrehan, the royal treasurer, Grondel, a Swiss captain, and Villars du Breuil, most important building contractor in the colony, "and a fourth who is only named in a whisper," undoubtedly Rochemore himself. All contracts apparently went to du Breuil to the exclusion of other contractors or the taking of bids, everything, Kerlerec says "by an underhand society and contracts made (as is ordinarily said) under the chimney." Among contracts let by Deverges on Rochemore's orders without prior approval from France was one for the construction of a kitchen for the new hospital.

Kerlerec implied that the intendant was everywhere proposing new and unnecessary projects in order to increase the contracts of his secret associates "and that the visionary list of [projects proposed by] these gentlemen would amount to four million at least, and their aim was to proceed immediately even with the [new] barracks, to propose to you a Government House, an Intendance, a powder magazine, the enclosure of this town, and to work, while waiting, on

[78] PAN, C–13–A–42, p. 7.
[79] PAN, C–13–A–42, p. 93.
[80] PAN, C–13–A–40, p. 128.

the completion of the works on the King's hospital."[81] Rochemore's letter of January 3, 1759,[82] to the minister, did indeed propose all these projects, and in his letter of March 6, of the same year, he turned the attack on the governor and the engineer, Deverges. He pointed out that in many of the posts, the commandants and officers were contractors for the king's works with the approval of Deverges, and that they (Kerlerec and Deverges) "have demolished the major part of the buildings of New Orleans belonging to the King, and they have sold the materials at vile prices."[83] In his letter of June 23, 1760, he expressed his amazement, on his arrival, at finding a 336-foot-long hospital being constructed to serve a garrison that never exceeded six hundred men while this hospital could serve a garrison ten times that size. He also reported progress on the hospital kitchen estimated at 130,000 livres, construction of a new battery to defend Mobile Bay, a new palisade at Fort Tombecbec, a new fort at Pointe Coupée nearly completed, extensive repairs at Fort Rosalie at Natchez, a new Arkansas fort completed, good progress at Fort Chartres which he described as "very advanced." Continuing, he said that "last autumn it had been pushed up to its sentry boxes on the flanked angles of the bastions, to its doors and to its platforms." He also reported the commencement of a small fort at Kaskaskia of *pièce sur pièce* and the reconstruction of Fort Ascension on the Cherokee River.[84]

The last bitter battle between Kerlerec and Rochemore began over the plans for the New Orleans fortifications. Rochemore objected to the location proposed for the gates in the palisade across the river front of the town. He explained his wishes in the matter in a letter to Deverges on August 11, 1760,[85] to which the engineer replied with disdain on the following day.[86] Obviously furious at Deverges' letter, Rochemore sent copies of this correspondence to the minister with a letter on August 24, 1760. The basis of his displeasure seems to have been that, by Kerlerec's orders, Deverges refused "to build in the palisade, opposite my lodging, a small false gate, like the one he has built in it opposite the Government House, which would have been of great utility to Mde. de Rochemore and

---

[81] PAN, C–13–A–40, p. 158.
[82] PAN, C–13–A–41, p. 155.
[83] PAN, C–13–A–41, p. 185.
[84] PAN, C–13–A–42, p. 118.
[85] PAN, C–13–A–42, p. 137.
[86] PAN, C–13–A–42, p. 134.

to me for going walking on the levee, and to my servants for drawing, at the river bank, water necessary for consumption in my house."[87]

As a result of this foolish controversy, Kerlerec was able to have Rochemore as well as Grondel recalled to France.[88] His own recall followed soon after. Intendant and governor were both thrown into the Bastille and the records of the trial that ensued take up an entire volume (C–13–A–44) in the Paris archives. Thus ignominiously ended France's efforts to fortify and hold Louisiana. All of the colony east of the Mississippi except New Orleans was seized by a victorious England while the rest was ceded by secret treaty in 1762 to Spain. It was one of Louisiana's last Spanish governors, Carondelet, who demolished Deverges' New Orleans fortifications and replaced them with new ones designed by Guillemard in 1791.

---

[87] PAN, C–13–A–42, p. 131.
[88] PAN, C–13–A–41, p. 430.

# Some French Engineers in Spanish Louisiana

## Jack D. L. Holmes

The Royal Engineer Corps of Spain was one of the best of its type in eighteenth-century Europe. Considerable time and effort, if not complete financial support, were devoted to the several engineering schools in Madrid, Barcelona, and North Africa. The indomitable director, Lieutenant-General Francisco Sabatini, took vigorous measures to improve the quality of instruction of his Department of Civil Architecture and the Royal Engineer Corps from 1789 until his death in 1798.[1]

Although General Sabatini took special interest in the unique defensive problems of Louisiana and West Florida in 1794, he was not able to change the direction of its numerous and varied works.[2] The terrain and strategic demands of the Mississippi Valley offered little

---

[1] Sabatini was named commander of the Engineer Corps on January 14, 1789 (statement of the Corps, Archivo General de Simancas, Guerra Moderna [hereafter AGS, GM], leg. 3794). When he died in 1798 he was replaced by José de Urrutia (Manuel Gayoso de Lemos to Conde de Santa Clara, no. 167, New Orleans, July 19, 1798, Archivo General de Indias, Papeles Procedentes de la Isla de Cuba [hereafter AGI, PC], leg. 1501-B).

[2] Sabatini examined a report by Pedro Garrido y Durán on a "Plan of Defense for Louisiana," dated Madrid, July 12, 1794, in Archivo del Servicio

challenge to engineers trained in the construction of complex programs of fortification, designed for permanence, located in urban or populated frontier regions, and built with vast funds. The typical fort encountered in Louisiana was a "campaign fort," built of wood and banked with earth to resist artillery. The shape was roughly square with four "arrows" located at each of the corners for the placement of artillery. Such a fort, usually measuring no more than 2400 feet in circumference, would cost ideally $11,367, including its various outer defenses and trenches.[3]

Louisiana's military needs called for ingenuity, flexibility, economy, and, above all, harmony between the various engineers and between them and their superior military chiefs. Unfortunately, a careful scrutiny of Spanish military history in Louisiana reveals an almost criminal lack of capable engineers to fulfill the myriad tasks that faced them. It is not surprising that governors in Louisiana frequently turned to foreigners for assistance in engineering matters. Apparently ready to answer the clarion call were numerous French and Creole officers who had training or skill in the construction of fortifications of a type needed in Louisiana.

Among the most notable and distinguished who could be called military engineers and who were also born in France or of parents of French extraction may be distinguished four distinct types: the foreign officer, experienced in military engineering, who reconnoitered the Mississippi Valley, such as Victor Collot; the regular Spanish army staff officer with talents in engineering; the Royal Engineer Corps officer; and the "free-lance" engineer who offered his services on a soldier-of-fortune basis. The latter types were best typified in Gilberto Guillemard, Juan María Perchet, and Nicolás de Finiels.

## GILBERTO GUILLEMARD

Gilberto Guillemard was born in Longwy, in the Diocese of Trèves, September 27, 1746, the son of Arnoult and Elizabeth Marechal

Histórico Militar (Madrid, hereafter ASHM), leg. 5–1–7–6. Sabatini's own report on Louisiana defenses was prepared on August 15, 1794, in ASHM, 5–1–7–1. A condensed version with notes and illustrations is in Leoncio Cabrero Fernández, "Francisco Sabatini y la fortificación de la Luisiana," *Trabajos y Conferencias* (Seminario de Estudios Americanistas, Facultad de Filosofía y Letras de la Universidad de Madrid), II (1958), 142–148.

[3] Julián Álvarez, Estimate . . . , New Orleans, Feb. 27, 1779, AGI, PC, leg. 2351, with plan in AGI, Planos, Luisiana y Floridas, no. 78.

Guillemard.[4] He came to New Orleans as a youth and joined the New Orleans militia, organized by Alejandro O'Reilly, on January 1, 1770. As a cadet in the third company of this unit, young Gilberto lived at No. 7 St. Philippe Street in New Orleans.[5]

After five years service as a cadet, on June 1, 1775, he was promoted to sublieutenant, and just prior to the entry of Spain into the war against England, earned a post as adjutant of militia. When Bernardo de Gálvez led his raw troops against the British posts in 1779, Guillemard saw considerable service. He was one of the first to enter Fort Bute at Manchac and took part in the siege and capture of Baton Rouge. At Mobile the following year he was ambushed by an advanced guard of British troops. Returning the fire, Guillemard's gallant little band caused the death of five of the enemy, including the commanding officer of the guard. Bernardo de Gálvez took an immediate liking to the brave adjutant and transferred him to his personal staff as garrison adjutant. During the siege and capture of Pensacola, Guillemard performed the functions of voluntary engineer. He captured a post from the British with only thirty men, but an exploding bombshell left him slightly crippled.[6]

As a result of his bravery and excellent service, he was brevetted captain with full salary as of August 23, 1781. In 1784, when the safety and security of lower Louisiana plantations were endangered by a large band of escaped slaves called "cimarrons," Colonel Francisco Bouligny appointed Guillemard and four other leaders to command an expeditionary force of regular troops, militia, and free Negroes. The expedition was a success, and Guillemard's command captured over three hundred of the "savage Negroes and their leaders."[7]

Guillemard was promoted major on February 7, 1788, and to lieutenant-colonel on January 1, 1795.[8] In 1787 he was married to

[4] Baptismal records of Guillemard, copy enclosed with his request for permission to marry (*Expediente matrimonial*), 1787, Archivo General Militar de Segovia (hereafter AGMS).

[5] Guillemard's service sheet, June 30, 1795, AGI, PC, leg. 1443; Grand-Pré's report on the four companies of the New Orleans militia, New Orleans, Feb. 12, 1770, AGI, PC, leg. 198.

[6] Service sheet; *Diario de las operaciones contra la plaza de Panzacola, 1781* (2nd ed., Madrid, 1959), p. 83.

[7] Service sheet; *Actas* (Minutes) of the New Orleans Cabildo (5 vols., W.P.A. typescripts, New Orleans Public Library Archives), June 11, 1784, II, 217–219.

[8] Service sheet.

Marie Felicité Barbeau Boisdoré.[9] One of his sons, Arnaldo, entered the Spanish service as a cadet on May 10, 1799, and, as his father did before him, rose rapidly in the ranks through his talents and ability.[10]

In 1796, while acting as adjutant-major of the New Orleans garrison, he was named cartographer and surveyor of the Spanish boundary commission, destined to meet with the American commissioner Andrew Ellicott to draw the thirty-first parallel separating American from Spanish territory in accordance with the Treaty of San Lorenzo.[11] Expressing his confidence in Guillemard, Governor-General Carondelet, wrote, "I chose Guillemard because he is well trained in mathematics and fortifications; furthermore, he is a man of wealth and honesty—qualities which are uncommon in the Americas. . . . I have every reason to believe he will do an excellent job."[12]

News of an impending attack on Spanish Louisiana from Canada via the Great Lakes in 1797 frightened the Spanish governors, however, and Guillemard did not join Ellicott. He and another engineer, Juan María Perchet, were sent to the Spanish military post of Nogales, located at the Walnut Hills near the confluence of the Yazoo and Mississippi rivers where Vicksburg stands today. He was ordered to inspect the works and make necessary improvements so that Nogales could repulse any attack directed against it from above. It was a difficult task, for carelessness and lack of funds had caused the fort's stockade to crumble in the constant rains. By the end of the summer, however, Nogales was in a reasonable state of defense.[13]

---

[9] Marriage records, AGMS.

[10] Account of the Louisiana Regiment, Pensacola, Dec. 31, 1809, AGI, PC, leg. 161-B; José Masot to Nicolás de Finiels, Pensacola, June 23, 1817, AGI, PC, leg. 80; Arnaldo Guillemard to de Finiels, Observation Post on the Perdido River, June 26, 1817, AGI, PC, leg. 221-A; Casa-Calvo to Carlos Howard, New Orleans, Oct. 29, 1804, AGI, PC, leg. 70-B. A possible relative, Manon Guillemard, was born in New Orleans in 1768 and died there on November 21, 1855 (obituary notice, *L'Abeille de la Nouvelle Orleans,* Nov. 21, 1855, p. 1).

[11] Carondelet to Luis de Las Casas, no. 162, confidential, New Orleans, Sept. 13, 1796, AGI, PC, leg. 1447; Carondelet to Las Casas, New Orleans, Sept. 19, 1796, AGI, PC, leg. 1444; Juan Ventura Morales to Pedro Varela y Ulloa, no. 108, New Orleans, Mar. 31, 1797, Archivo Histórico Nacional, Sección de Estado (hereafter AHN, EST), leg. 3902.

[12] Carondelet to Gayoso, New Orleans, Apr. 26, 1797, AGI, transcript in Mississippi Provincial Archives, Spanish Dominion (Jackson, Miss.), VI, 425–428.

[13] Carondelet to Gayoso, New Orleans, Apr. 24, 1797, Mississippi Provincial Archives, VI, 359–366. Gayoso had the difficult job of explaining

Nogales and Natchez were both evacuated by the Spaniards in 1798, and Guillemard petitioned for the command of the Texas post of San Antonio. In supporting his request, Governor-General Manuel Gayoso de Lemos wrote, "This official is one of the most deserving of many who have served their King; his voluntary services, always exposing himself to danger, the marks of his recognized bravery acquired in the campaigns of this Province during his twenty-eight years' service . . . and the innumerable commissions of merit which he has performed force me to do justice to his particular merit. . . ."[14]

Guillemard did not get the post, however, and by 1805 he was still living in New Orleans, where he earned the further esteem of Gayoso's successor, the Marqués de Casa-Calvo. Like so many Spanish officers, Guillemard sacrificed his fortune in the service of the king, having proven through his long and distinguished career that a Frenchman could make a very good Spaniard.[15]

His engineering abilities were employed in 1787 when he designed fortifications for the harbor and the San Carlos Battery at Pensacola.[16] In 1792 he drew up beautiful plans for the proposed fortifications at New Orleans.[17] His touch is evidenced in the archi-

---

to Ellicott that the reason why Guillemard was not coming to Natchez was because the Americans employed a mulatto geometer on the boundary commission! (Carondelet to Gayoso, New Orleans, Mar. 24, 1797, in Mississippi Provincial Archives, VI, 407–413). On Guillemard's mission at Nogales, see also, Gayoso to Beauregard, Natchez, May 8, 1797, AGI, PC, leg. 43; reports of Guillemard and Perchet, Nogales, May 21, 1797, AGI, PC, leg. 43; Guillemard to Carondelet, Nogales, May 22, 1797, AGI, PC, leg. 35, with draft of Carondelet's answer of May 28, 1797. Guillemard's report is actually included with his drawing of the dilapidated fort at Monte Vigia in AGI, Planos, Luisiana y Floridas, no. 182.

[14] Gayoso to Santa Clara, no. 116, New Orleans, Apr. 17, 1798, AGI, PC, leg. 1501-A.

[15] *New Orleans in 1805* (reprint ed., New Orleans, 1936), shows Guillemard lived at No. 4 Rue d'Orléans. He had not been paid since September, 1804, and was penniless when he finally left the province (Casa-Calvo to Vicente Folch, New Orleans, Aug. 3, 1805, Casa-Calvo to Howard, New Orleans, Oct. 29, 1804, AGI, PC, leg. 70-B; Guillemard to Casa-Calvo, New Orleans, July 18, 1805, AGI, PC, leg. 142-A.

[16] Esteban Miró to Marqués de Sonora (José de Gálvez), no. 261, New Orleans, June 10, 1787, Biblioteca Nacional (Madrid), vol. 19,509, fol. 157; account of Guillemard, New Orleans, June 10, 1787, AGI, Audiencia de Santo Domingo (hereafter cited as SD), leg. 2543; "Plan of the Projected Fort St. Charles and battery of San Antonio for the defense of the entrance of St. Mary of Galvez Bay in Pensacola," New Orleans, May 10, 1787, AGI, Planos, Luisiana y Floridas, no. 113.

[17] Carondelet to Conde de Aranda, no. 1, New Orleans, Nov. 6, 1792, AHN, EST, leg. 3898; Guillemard, "Plan of the Fortifications of New Orleans

tecture of New Orleans' most beautiful colonial buildings—the Cabildo, the Presbytère, the St. Louis Cathedral, the Petit Théâtre du Vieux Carré, and the Charity Hospital of St. Charles.[18] He drew plans for a powder magazine, a rice warehouse, and a fish market for New Orleans.[19] In 1793 he drew plans of Fuerte Carlota de la Mobila.[20] His ability as an appraiser was demonstrated at Natchez in 1790, where he estimated the cost of constructing the church and hospital, and at Cole's Creek (Villa Gayoso), where he listed expenses for building several structures in the town then forming.[21] In New Orleans he was often called upon to appraise houses and real estate because of his long experience in estimating values of civil and military structures in Louisiana.[22]

## JUAN MARÍA PERCHET

Joan María Narcis Perchet was born on December 2, 1769, in the Catalonian city of Gerona, Spain, the son of Joan (Catalán for Juan) Perchet, a commissary of war in the Royal Armies, and Maria Vance.[23] On December 1, 1785, he entered the royal army as a cadet

---

in Louisiana," New Orleans, Nov. 8, 1792, approved by Carondelet, Biblioteca Nacional (Madrid), maps, M-I 328.

[18] Samuel Wilson, Jr., *A Guide to Architecture of New Orleans, 1699–1959* (New Orleans, 1960), pp. 12, 13, 17; Robert Glenk, *Handbook, Louisiana State Museum, New Orleans* (New Orleans, 1934), p. 243.

[19] Guillemard, "Powder Magazine . . . ," AGI, PC, leg. 652, Planos, Luisiana y Floridas, no. 143; "Plan and Elevation of a Warehouse for the Storage of Rice. . . ." enclosed in Carondelet to Las Casas, New Orleans, May 31, 1796, AGI, SD, leg. 2643, Planos, Luisiana y Floridas, no. 175; "Resultat des changements a faire a la Nelle. Hale au poisson . . . ," New Orleans, Feb. 22, 1799, AGI, PC, leg. 219, Planos, Luisiana y Floridas, nos. 207–208.

[20] "Plan of Fort Carlota de la Mobila," May 6, 1793, AGS, GM, leg. 7240, Planos, VII-75.

[21] Gayoso to Miró, New Orleans, two letters dated March 29, 1790, both in AGI, PC, leg. 41; Gayoso to Miró, no. 160, Natchez, July 27, 1791, AGI, PC, leg. 41, indicates Guillemard tended to underestimate the cost of buildings on occasion.

[22] Petition of Bartolomé Bosque, New Orleans, Mar. 2, 1805, AGI, PC, leg. 142-A. Guillemard had also drawn a 1787 map showing western American settlements (AHN, Mapas, and printed in Miguel Gómez del Campillo, *Relaciones diplomáticas entre España y los Estados Unidos* . . . (Madrid, 1944–45), I, 78. A brief sketch of Guillemard is in *Documentos inéditos para la historia de la Luisiana, 1792–1810*, ed. Jack D. L. Holmes (Madrid, 1963), pp. 334–335 n.

[23] Baptismal record, copy in Perchet's *Expediente matrimonial*, 1803, AGMS. His father died in Puerto de Santa María on September 14, 1800, and his mother followed on September 19. A brother, Antonio, was captain of infantry and first lieutenant in the Jaén Regiment (documents in Perchet's *Expediente matrimonial*, 1803, AGMS).

and thereafter received advancement in military rank as well as in the Royal Engineer Corps. He was appointed a lieutenant and engineer extraordinary on December 2, 1794. His training had been taken at the Royal Engineering School of Ceuta on the coast of Africa. After service in the Galician Regiment and assignment to that northwestern province, he embarked for America with the task of aiding the governor-general of Louisiana in fortifications during 1794.[24]

Carondelet, the governor-general of Louisiana, put Perchet to work immediately on sketches and plans for the works at New Orleans. By 1794 Guillemard's original projected defenses for the city were well under construction. The "Vieux Carré" was enclosed on three sides by stout walls, which were broken at regular intervals by artillery emplacements and five strong redoubts. In the northern corner of the city was the redoubt of St. John; to the south lay St. Louis. San Carlos was on the eastern point and opposite it lay the Burgundy redoubt. Midway between Burgundy and St. John was the central redoubt of St. Ferdinand. Perchet drew several plans of the city and wrote a full report on the city's fortifications in the summer of 1794.[25]

On December 8, 1794, New Orleans suffered its most disastrous fire since 1788. Much of the city was destroyed, and Carondelet sought to discover the causes of the fire by assigning Perchet and the commander of engineers in Louisiana, Joaquín de la Torre, to inspect buildings for fire hazards, particularly from poorly functioning chimneys.[26] Perchet drew several sketches and plans of the portions of the city damaged in the 1794 fire.[27]

The Plaquemine Turn of the Mississippi River below New Orleans was considered an essential point of defense for the city, and Perchet next undertook a military reconnaissance of that post and its new fort, San Phelipe de Placaminas.[28] He was then ordered to

---

[24] Perchet's service sheet, AGS, GM, leg. 3794; Josef de Urrutia, account of the officers of the Royal Engineers Corps, Madrid, Jan. 1, 1800, AGS, GM, leg. 3794.

[25] Perchet to Carondelet, New Orleans, May 28, 1794, AGI, PC, leg. 28, with accompanying map in AGI, Planos, Luisiana y Floridas, no. 154; military inspection of the city by Perchet, New Orleans, Aug. 7, 1794, and his estimate of costs, Aug. 10, 1794, ASHM, 5–1–7–8; his detailed plan of New Orleans in 1794, ASHM, K–b–4–41.

[26] Inspection, New Orleans, Dec. 19, 1794, AGI, PC, leg. 30.

[27] Carondelet received various sketches from Perchet on the fire. Two are in AGS, Planos, XVI–132, and ASHM, M–b–11–19.

[28] Perchet to Carondelet, New Orleans, Jan. 10, 1795, ASHM, 5–1–7–8. The accompanying plans are in ASHM, M–b–11–21, with date of January 11, 1795.

inspect and draw plans of the fortifications at Galveztown, Baton Rouge, Natchez, and Nogales with particular attention to immediately necessary repairs.[29] At Natchez Perchet found the fort almost destroyed by the heavy rains of the preceding season, and he recommended a "crash program" to save the fort from utter ruin.[30] Before he could continue his inspection of other posts, however, he was called to accompany the Natchez governor, Manuel Gayoso de Lemos, on an expedition which resulted in the founding of Fort San Fernando de las Barrancas at the Chickasaw Bluffs where Memphis today stands.[31]

Perchet had little prior experience to prepare him for the difficult engineering problems he encountered on this frontier. Moreover, he was plagued by the "too-many-cooks-spoiling-the-soup" concept—Gayoso insisted on his form of stockade; de la Torre and Carondelet wrote conflicting orders; and Perchet became little more than a draftsman following the directions of others. Fever attacked Perchet and almost killed him. Gayoso suspected him of Jacobin sympathies when he saw a medal showing the taking of the Bastille and when, at the dinner table, the governor was forced to quiet Perchet's antireligious statements. In October Perchet's work was done; he had drawn several plans of the post at San Fernando and went down the river to recover his health in New Orleans, having earned the enmity of Gayoso.[32]

---

[29] Carondelet to Francisco de Rendón, New Orleans, Jan. 19, 1795; de la Torre to Carondelet, New Orleans, Jan. 22, 1795, AGI, PC, leg. 31; Carondelet to Gayoso, New Orleans, Feb. 1, 1795, AGI, PC, leg. 22.

[30] Perchet to Carondelet, Natchez, Mar. 11, 1795, AGI, PC, leg. 31.

[31] Gayoso's diary of the galeot *La Vigilante*, 1795, AGI, PC, leg. 2364, printed in *Documentos de la Luisiana*, ed. Holmes, p. 197. The story of Spanish-American rivalry over the founding of this post is told in Jack D. L. Holmes, "The Spanish-American Struggle for Chickasaw Bluffs, 1780–1795," *Publications* of the East Tennessee Historical Society, no. 34 (1962), 26–57.

[32] Carondelet to Gayoso, New Orleans, June 30, July 2, Nov. 20, and Dec. 10, 1795, AGI, PC, leg. 22; Perchet to Gayoso, New Madrid, Sept. 8, 1795, AGI, PC, leg. 48; Gayoso to Carondelet, no. 9, confidential, San Fernando de las Barrancas, June 13, 1795, AGI, PC, leg. 2364; Gayoso to Perchet, Apostadero de la Esperanza, May 22, 1795, and New Madrid, Sept. 7, 1795, Oct. 5, 1795, and Perchet to Gayoso, San Fernando de las Barrancas, Oct. 10, 1795, all in AGI, PC, leg. 48; Perchet to Carondelet, San Fernando, July 12, Aug. 11, Oct. 9, 1795, AGI, PC, leg. 32; Gayoso to Carondelet, San Fernando, June 18, Aug. 13, 1795, AGI, PC, leg. 43; Gayoso to Carondelet, New Madrid, Dec. 3, 1795, AGI, PC, leg. 43; Gayoso to Carondelet, New Madrid, Sept. 12, 1795, AGI, PC, leg. 32; Folch to Carondelet, San Fernando de las Barrancas, Oct. 9, 1795, and no. 5, Oct. 22, 1795, AGI, PC, leg. 52. Perchet's map of the Chickasaw Cession, June 20, 1795, exists in various copies, the best

Once again Perchet returned to the Plaquemine Turn to inspect the works and appraise their value to settle the estate of Colonel Gilberto de St. Maxent, who had undertaken their construction. He also inspected the fort at the entrance to the Mississippi called La Balise.[33] From May to December, 1796, he resumed his assignment of inspecting the fortifications at Baton Rouge, Galveztown, and the Arkansas. His extensive reports were of particular value when the Council of War met in New Orleans during 1798.[34]

When Gayoso became governor-general of Louisiana in 1797 to succeed the Baron de Carondelet, Perchet was recalled from Nogales where he had been helping with fortifications under the direction of Guillemard.[35] Gayoso ordered Perchet to follow the instructions of the Council of War in preparing Baton Rouge for a stout defense against possible invasion from the United States. Perchet's old illness returned, but he finished the job after considerable delay. With his report, he included a number of military reflections which opposed those of Gayoso and the Council of War. Such insubordination the governor-general considered inexcusable, and he once again dismissed Perchet from the field with considerable heat.[36]

of which is in the AHN, Mapas. It is also included in *Documentos de la Luisiana*, ed. Holmes, appendix.

[33] De la Torre to Carondelet, New Orleans, Dec. 6, 1795, AGI, PC, leg. 32.

[34] Carondelet to Perchet, New Orleans, May 18, 1796, AGI, PC, leg. 1444; Carondelet to Gayoso, New Orleans, Oct. 12, 1796, AGI, PC, leg. 23; Perchet to Carondelet, New Orleans, Jan. 19, 1796, AGI, PC, leg. 33; Pay sheet of Pedro Buigas (whose boat Perchet used in his inspections), AGI, PC, leg. 538-B; Perchet's report on military inspection of Baton Rouge, Baton Rouge, Dec. 19, 1796, copy enclosed in Gayoso to Santa Clara, no. 191, New Orleans, Sept. 26, 1798, AGI, PC, leg. 1501-B; Perchet's reflections on Post of Galvez-Town, Iberville, and Amite Rivers, Galvez-Town, Dec. 29, 1796, AGI, PC, leg. 2354; Perchet's complete report on Galveztown, New Orleans, Mar. 6, 1797, approved by the Council of War, New Orleans, Feb. 7, 1798, copies enclosed in Juan Morales to Pedro Varela y Ulloa, no. 132, New Orleans, June 30, 1797, AGS, GM, leg. 7245. An undated, anonymous map of the Baton Rouge district, *c.* 1798–1800, possibly drawn by Perchet to illustrate his report, is in ASHM, K–b–4–66.

[35] Perchet to Gayoso, Nogales, Aug. 3, 1797, AGI, PC, leg. 48, with accompanying sketch in AGI, Planos, Luisiana y Floridas, no. 185; Gayoso to Beauregard, Natchez, May 11, 1797, and report of Perchet and Guillemard, Nogales, May 21, 1797, AGI, PC, leg. 43. Perchet assisted with the evacuation of Nogales (Gayoso to Perchet, New Orleans, Jan. 10, 1798, AGI, PC, leg. 154-A). Later he was ordered to supply the boundary commission with necessary surveying equipment (Gayoso's memorandum on Dunbar to Gayoso, [Feb.–Mar., 1798?], AGI, PC, leg. 215-B).

[36] Gayoso to Perchet, New Orleans, July 19, 1798, Sept. 6, 17, 1798, Gayoso to de la Torre, New Orleans, Sept. 19, 1798, Perchet to Gayoso, Baton

Perchet returned to active duty in 1800 at New Orleans, where he once again wrote a report on the necessary repairs and their costs to improve New Orleans' crumbling fortifications.[37] He served at La Balise later the same year.[38] On June 24, 1802, Perchet was promoted to captain,[39] and in 1803 he was granted permission to marry Juana María Ramona Sinforoza, an orphan girl he had been courting since 1796.[40]

Perchet's hydraulic knowledge was put to good use near Pensacola, where he built a dam in 1803.[41] He drew plans of the fort at San Marcos de Apalachee,[42] before leaving Louisiana for Texas the following year.[43]

On his service record, Sabatini had written that Perchet had average talent, application, and knowledge of theory, but lacked

Rouge, Sept. 6, 1798, Perchet's military reflections on Baton Rouge, Sept. 5, 1798, Perchet to Gayoso, Baton Rouge, Sept. 10, 1798, all copies enclosed in Gayoso to Santa Clara, no. 191, Sept. 26, 1798.

[37] Perchet's report, New Orleans, July 31, 1800, ASHM, 1–1–7–3, Perchet also drew plans of a city block in New Orleans occupied by the Ursuline Convent, Royal Hospital, and government property, dated January 30, 1800, AGI, SD, leg. 2673, plan in Planos, Luisiana y Floridas, no. 215.

[38] Pay sheet of Perchet, AGI, PC, leg. 538-B.

[39] A captain earned one thousand dollars a year, representing an increase of two hundred dollars over his former rank's pay scale (pay sheet of Perchet, AGI, PC, leg. 538-B). A copy of his captain's commission is enclosed in his *Expediente matrimonial*, AGMS.

[40] Permission granted October 25, 1803, in Perchet's *Expediente matrimonial*, AGMS. In 1796 the Baron de Pontalba had written his wife, "I announce to you the marriage, absolutely decided, of Perche, the officer of engineers, with the orphan girl who resides at Madame Armesto's. He has asked her permission" (Pontalba to [Jeanne Françoise Lebretton des Charmeaux] his wife, New Orleans, Mar. 22, 1796, in "Pontalba's Journal" [unpublished typescript copies and translations by the W.P.A., Louisiana State University Archives], p. 42). Perchet renounced a prior marriage contract with María de la Esperanza Miñana of Spain (statement, New Orleans, Jan. 23, 1797, Notarial Records, New Orleans Court House, Pedesclaux, XXIX, fol. 32).

[41] Anonymous voyage journal to the Creek Nation from Pensacola in the year 1803, AGI, PC, leg. 2372.

[42] Perchet was at San Marcos from October 21, 1801, to December 15, 1803 (pay sheet, AGI, PC, leg. 538-B). Two extant plans are dated New Orleans, August 20, 1794, ASHM, printed in Servicio Histórico Militar (Madrid) and Servicio Geográfico del Ejército (Madrid), *Cartografía de Ultramar*, Carpeta II (Estados Unidos y Canadá) (Madrid, 1953), plates, p. 84, and an 1802 map and plan in ASHM, K–b–4–79. A different plan of the latter, dated January 20, 1802, is in AGI, PC, leg. 1553, Planos, Luisiana y Floridas, no. 223.

[43] State of the Engineer Corps in 1805 by Mariscal de Campo Antonio Sampér, AGS, GM, leg. 3794.

experience.[44] In his ten years of service in Louisiana Perchet earned valuable, if costly, experience, and his numerous plans, executed with great precision and skill, attest to his ability.

## GEORGES HENRI VICTOR COLLOT

Of all the travelers whose journals down the Mississippi during the 1790's have been preserved, none reaches the extent of General Victor Collot's. Francis Baily, Andrew Ellicott, Samuel S. Forman, André Michaux, and Colonel John Pope have left us various pictures of life in Spanish Louisiana at that time, but their narratives pale in comparison with the scintillating prose of Collot. Moreover, Collot represented that type of enlightened humanist whose observations extended to virtually every activity in which men engaged—agriculture, health, anthropology, history, commerce, geography, meteorology, politics, and, above all, military affairs.

Born about 1751 in France, General Collot had served under Rochambeau in the American Revolution. By 1792 he had earned a major-general's commission and had seen duty as chief of staff of the French Army of the North.[45] His next appointment was not characterized by success. In his own words, "I was governor at Guadaloupe in 1793 and 1794, without money, without marine, without soldiers, and without laws."[46] It was not surprising, therefore, that the British soon captured that French island and made General Collot a prisoner. He was sent to the United States where a merchant filed a complaint against him for alleged confiscation of his property at Guadaloupe. Having put up his bail and promised to remain in the United States pending the settlement of the suit, Collot grew restless with inactivity.[47]

The French minister to the United States, Adet, persuaded the French general to undertake an exploration and military reconnaissance of the Ohio and Mississippi rivers along the vast Spanish-American frontier. Collot eagerly accepted and, armed with Spanish

---

[44] Service sheet, AGS, GM, leg. 3794.

[45] Samuel Cole Williams, *Early Travels in the Tennessee Country, 1540–1800* (Johnson City, Tenn., 1928), p. 345; *The Spanish Regime in Missouri*, ed. Louis Houck (Chicago, 1909), II, 133.

[46] Georges Henri Victor Collot, *A Journey in North America* (Paris, 1826; reprint edition, ed. J. Christian Bay, Florence, 1924), I, 21.

[47] Williams, *Early Travels*, p. 345.

passports, he left Philadelphia on March 21, 1796. He was accompanied by his assistant, Adjutant-General Joseph Warin, a skilled draftsman whose engineering skill matched that of Collot himself.

Their inspection included Pittsburgh and the Monongahela River, where Collot made a number of important military calculations. He equally took an interest in the type of boats, soil, price of land, ornithology, weather, the people, and distances between the various points. By the middle of June, he was well down the Ohio River, having begun its survey on the sixth.[48]

Collot continued past Kentucky and the American settlements farther down river. At Fort Massac, just below the confluence of the Cumberland and Tennessee with the Ohio, Collot's party received a rude jolt: Captain Zebulon Pike, the American commander, had received a suggestion, ostensibly from Governor Arthur St. Clair, to arrest Collot and his party. Collot was able to persuade Pike not to do so and continued on his journey, though not without a growing uneasiness. By the time Collot reached lower Louisiana he was to find himself pursued by American, Canadian, and Spanish authorities.[49]

After inspecting Cape Girardeau and the Illinois Country, the travelers reached St. Louis, which fascinated the French general. Prosperous merchants, he claimed, were impeded by a poor Spanish government and lesser military protection: "It might easily be presumed from the situation in which we found the forts, and the weakness of the garrison . . . that Spain had the intention of abandoning Upper Louisiana."[50] Collot obtained from a confidant in Tennessee news of an imminent invasion of Louisiana by a strong British force in Canada via the Great Lakes in 1797. Indeed, Collot

---

[48] Collot, *Journey in North America,* I, 45–96.

[49] Collot, *Journey in North America,* I, 193–194; II, 3–4. The Spanish consul at Frankfort, Kentucky, wrote Carondelet that Collot was suspicious and that the Chevalier Casa Irujo at Philadelphia distrusted his motives in undertaking the Louisiana expedition (Antonio Argote Villalobos to Carondelet, Frankfort, June 2, 1796, AGI, PC, leg. 34). Carondelet then wrote Gayoso to provide Collot with a "guide" to keep them under surveillance at all times (Carondelet to Gayoso, New Orleans, July 26, 1796, AGI, PC, leg. 23).

[50] Collot, *Journey in North America,* I, 248. Collot's military observations on St. Louis and his suggested plans for fortifying it are in *Journey in North America,* I, 257–264, and Collot to Irujo, Philadelphia, Mar. 1, 1797, copy enclosed in Irujo to Príncipe de la Paz, no. 37, Philadelphia, Mar. 5, 1797, AHN, EST, leg. 3896 *bis.* A plan is in AHN, Plans, which is similar to Collot's in the atlas of *Journey in North America,* plate 27.

was one of the first to break what was later known as "The Blount Conspiracy" to the Spanish officials.[51]

After predicting a glowing commercial future for St. Louis and determining several alternative plans for insuring its defenses,[52] Collot and his party left in the middle of September. He failed to report his departure to its commandant, Zenon Trudeau, because news had drifted in that the Spaniards intended to arrest and detain Collot. Spaniards were in no mood to hear that the retrocession of Louisiana to France was a *fait accompli,* and rumors had it that Collot's purpose was somehow involved in this action. Although Governor Gayoso attempted to stop Governor-General Carondelet's orders, he was unsuccessful, and Collot's party was arrested on October 27 by none other than the lieutenant-colonel and major of the New Orleans garrison, Gilberto Guillemard, at Étienne Boré's sugar plantation two leagues north of New Orleans.[53]

Collot was conducted under close guard to the Fort San Carlos guardhouse in New Orleans, and his papers were carefully examined by Carondelet in an effort to find evidence against the Frenchman. Collot's diaries—he kept one for Carondelet to see full of praise for the Spanish governor-general—notebooks, sketches, and plans were quite revealing. Every Spanish fort from Cape Girardeau to Nogales was drawn by Warin and accompanied by military observations of Collot. San Fernando de las Barrancas, New Madrid, Nogales, and Natchez were all included. Coming as they did from a foreign observer, Collot's military comments were indeed important.[54] Carondelet determined to get rid of Collot as tactfully as possible

---

[51] Irujo to Carondelet, Philadelphia, Mar. 13, 1797, AGI, PC, leg. 2365; Collot remarks, in *Journey in North America*, II, 12, that he learned of the attack from Louis Lorimier. Collot also discussed the English threat with Gayoso (*Journey in North America*, II, 64–68).

[52] See above, n. 50.

[53] Carondelet to Gayoso, New Orleans, Oct. 14, 30, 1796, AGI, PC, leg. 23.

[54] Collot in *Journey in North America*, II, 114–128, gives his side of the arrest. Spanish documents relating to the event are Carondelet to Gayoso, Oct. 14, 30, 1796, instructions to the guard at San Carlos redoubt, New Orleans, Oct. 26, 1796, Carondelet to Gayoso, New Orleans, Nov. 6, 1796, AGI, PC, leg. 23. An interesting account which employs private papers of Gilberto Guillemard's descendants as well as Collot's journal is Heloise H. Cruzat, "General Collot's Arrest in New Orleans," *Louisiana Historical Quarterly,* I (1918), 303–320. Also on Collot, see Guiseppi Caraci, "Il generale francese Giorgino Enrico Vittorio Collot et suo viggio nell' America Settentrionale, 1796," *Atti d' XXII Congresi Internationale digli Americanisti* (Rome), II (1928), 619–648.

without offending the French Republic, with whom Spain was then allied. He was sent to La Balise to await a ship, which finally left in December. Warin succumbed to the 1796 yellow-fever epidemic in New Orleans, as did several of Collot's companions.[55]

Collot soon forgot the insults and even the loss of a number of his papers thrown overboard when a British ship intercepted the Spanish craft carrying them.[56] What must they have contained! The extant materials cover virtually every aspect of Spanish Louisiana from the price of goods to the number of Indians and habits of the inhabitants. From Philadelphia Collot wrote to Carondelet's successor, Gayoso, sending him a pocket telescope and asking for some good cigars in return. He also discussed means for the defense of St. Louis with the Spanish minister, Casa Irujo, and suggested sending the final subject of our brief study, Nicolás de Finiels, to supervise the fortifications.[57] Collot left a study of American history and contemporary politics which was remarkably accurate and significant.

## NICOLÁS DE FINIELS

When Collot reported on the weakness of St. Louis defenses and an impending attack from Canada on Louisiana, the Spanish minister at Philadelphia listened to his suggestions, particularly that a French engineer named Nicolás de Finiels be sent to St. Louis to supervise the construction of Collot's proposed fortifications. Finiels, as he was called by the Spaniards, had come to America with the French expeditionary force during the Revolution and helped America win its independence, after which he evidently joined the American engineer service as a captain.[58]

---

[55] Carondelet to Gayoso, Nov. 6, 1796; Pontalba to his wife, "Pontalba's Journal," Nov. 2, 3, 1796, pp. 289–291.

[56] Declaration of Juan Cortés, New York, Oct. 5, 1797, copy translated in Collot, *Journey in North America*, II, 284.

[57] Collot to Gayoso, Philadelphia, Dec. 3, 1798, AGI, PC, leg. 215-A. Collot had clearly stirred up the Creoles of lower Louisiana, and Gayoso was in doubt as to how to act in similar crises when he asked the captain-general for orders (Gayoso to Santa-Clara, no. 17, confidential, New Orleans, July 30, 1798, AGI, PC, leg. 1502-B). Separate reports on Collot's journey should also be consulted, for example, Elías Beauregard to Gayoso, confidential, Nogales, Oct. 10, 1796, AGI, PC, leg. 2364; Manuel García to Gayoso, San Fernando de las Barrancas, Sept. 24, 1796, AGI, PC, leg. 48.

[58] Marqués de Casa-Calvo to Príncipe de la Paz, New Orleans, Aug. 22, 1805, AHN, EST, leg. 5549; Casa-Irujo to Carondelet, Philadelphia, Mar. 13, 1797, AGI, PC, leg. 2365.

Armed with an unorthodox appointment from Irujo and an advance of one thousand dollars, Finiels left Philadelphia on April 2, 1797, and, after a long and difficult voyage arrived at St. Louis on June 3. He carried dispatches and newspapers regarding the defenses of the province, but all of these failed to impress the military commander of upper Louisiana, Lieutenant-Colonel Carlos Howard.[59] Howard wanted Carondelet's authorization for employing Finiels on the top secret fortifications. He wrote that the Frenchman was more specialized in artillery than in campaign forts. Frustrated and reduced to menial tasks, Finiels watched with jealousy Carondelet's appointee at St. Louis, the Dutchman, Louis van den Bemden, take charge of those works Finiels felt he should direct.[60]

Finiels inspected the course of the Missouri River and environs of St. Louis and drew an excellent map of the area.[61] Unfortunately, his salary of one hundred dollars per month, which was to begin on June 3, was ordered stopped in May, 1798, and he was ordered out of upper Louisiana.[62] The new governor-general, Gayoso, had need of a skilled, thorough, and cooperative engineer, however, and he assigned him to draw fortifications of lower Louisiana while he attempted to have Finiels' salary reinstated. The captain-general at Havana was not at all convinced by Gayoso's arguments on Finiels' behalf, particularly as war between Spain and France loomed as a distinct possibility.[63]

Finiels drew several excellent plans and maps of lower Louisiana

---

[59] Receipt for one thousand dollars from Irujo, Mar. 22, 1797, AHN, EST, leg. 3897; appointment of Finiels by Irujo, Philadelphia, Mar. 20, 1797, Bancroft Library, Louisiana Collection, translated in A. P. Nasatir, "Anglo-Spanish Rivalry in the Iowa Country, 1797–1798," *Iowa Journal of History and Politics*, XXVIII (July, 1930), 366, n.; Carondelet to Morales, confidential, copy, New Orleans, Apr. 21, 1797, enclosed in Morales to Pedro Varela y Ulloa, no. 10, confidential, New Orleans, May 10, 1797, AHN, EST, leg. 3902; Collot to Irujo, and Irujo to Collot, Philadelphia, Mar. 1, 1797, copies enclosed in Casa-Irujo to Príncipe de la Paz, no. 37, Philadelphia, Mar. 1, 1797, AHN, EST, leg. 3896 *bis.*; Howard to Carlos deHault deLassus, St. Louis, June 4, 1797, AGI, PC, leg. 131-A; Howard to Carondelet, St. Louis, June 7, 1797, in Nasatir, "Anglo-Spanish Rivalry," pp. 366–369.

[60] Finiels to Gayoso, St. Louis, Jan. 14, 1798, AGI, PC, leg. 215-A.

[61] The original is in the Archives du Service Hydrographique de la Marine (Paris). A copy is in *Before Lewis and Clark*, ed. A. P. Nasatir (St. Louis, 1952), I, opp. 94.

[62] Finiels' pay sheet, AGI, PC, leg. 538-B.

[63] Gayoso to Conde de Santa-Clara, no. 176, New Orleans, July 30, 1798, and no. 191, New Orleans, Sept. 26, 1798; draft of Santa Clara to Gayoso, Havana, Nov. 14, 1798, AGI, PC, leg. 1501-B.

before Gayoso died in 1799, and the governor-general's death failed to dislodge Finiels from government position. The Marqués de Casa-Calvo, in particular, utilized the Frenchman's services, and the royal order of June 19, 1799, reinstated Finiels' salary.[64]

When Casa-Calvo undertook his 1805 exploration of southwestern Louisiana and eastern Texas, Finiels was selected because of his knowledge of astronomy, geography, and cartography. He also had a practical twist in repairing a theodolite and measuring chain for the expedition.[65] Finiels' excellent maps of the reconnaissance accompanied his impassioned 1810 report to Luis de Onís pleading with Spain to hold not only Florida, but to recover Louisiana.[66]

Following the evacuation of Louisiana by Spanish officers in 1805 and 1806, Finiels was attached to the garrison at Pensacola. By 1815 he was appointed special engineer with an annual salary of twelve hundred dollars.[67] Later, as engineer-in-chief of West Florida with the rank of lieutenant-colonel, Finiels directed the fortifications at Mobile, San Carlos de Barrancas, and nearby Pensacola. His numerous plans of these posts rank with the finest ever done in Spanish Louisiana.[68]

Nicolás de Finiels was evidently married twice. His second wife was Mariana Rivier, a native of Pensacola. Four of his sons also joined the Spanish army and served in Havana and in Spanish regiments.[69]

---

[64] Plans of New Orleans by Finiels, *c.* 1798, ASHM, Planos, K–b–4–64, K–b–9–46; plans of Baton Rouge, 1798, ASHM, Planos, K–b–9–45, K–b–4–66 (probably by Finiels); Gayoso to Santa Clara, no. 191, Sept. 26, 1798; Cayetano Soler to Mariano Luis de Urquijo, Aranjuez, June 19, 1799, AHN, EST, leg. 5549.

[65] Casa-Calvo to Príncipe de la Paz, New Orleans, Aug. 22, 1805, in AHN, EST, leg. 5549. On this expedition and Finiels' role, see Jack D. L. Holmes, "Nicolás deFiniels and the 1805 Exploration of the Southwest," unpublished paper read at the Southwestern Social Science Association, San Antonio, April 13, 1963, and scheduled for publication in the *Southwestern Historical Quarterly*.

[66] Finiels to Luis de Onís, Pensacola, Apr. 23, 1810, ASHM, 5–1–10–4, and printed in *Documentos de la Luisiana*, ed. Holmes, pp. 369–420.

[67] Benigno García Calderón, Account of the Regiment, Pensacola, Sept. 1, 1815, AGI, PC, leg. 147-A.

[68] Plan of the Post of San Carlos de Barrancas, 1813, AGI, PC, leg. 1794, Planos, Luisiana y Floridas, No. 243; plans of San Carlos de Barrancas, 1813–18, in ASHM, K–b–4–69, K–b–4–80, K–b–4–68, K–b–9–37, K–b–4–76, K–b–4–72, K–b–4–74, K–b–4–67 (?), K–b–4–71.

[69] Finiels arrived in St. Louis in 1797 with his wife and mother-in-law and evidently left them there (Howard to Carondelet, June 7, 1797 in Nasatir, "Anglo-Spanish Rivalry," pp. 366–369). His second wife was probably the

Always in financial difficulties, in 1804 Finiels was dunned by several New Orleans merchants for a back debt of $516, although during that same year he attempted to collect over twelve thousand dollars deposited in Campeche.[70] By 1813 conditions were so bad for Finiels that he pleaded for four daily rations of bread for his hungry family.[71]

While at Pensacola he served on the Security and Vigilance Committee, and when Andrew Jackson captured that post in 1818, the French engineer was one of those wounded trying to defend it.[72] Throughout his career this courageous and capable Frenchman sacrificed much for the Spanish crown he served so well. For his excellent services he received little enough, and this was typical of all military officers who gave their lives in hacking civilization out of the rough frontier wilderness. Whether French or Spanish, the military engineers of Louisiana agreed with Collot, *"it is the situation of the frontiers which makes the safety of Empires."*[73]

## APPENDIX

### OTHER FRENCH AND CREOLE ENGINEERS IN SPANISH LOUISIANA

*Louis Bertucat.* Born in France in 1739, he served as lieutenant of the Spanish Army from May 27, 1776, and was commissioned army captain on November 22, 1786. A student of mathematics, and civil and military architecture at the Royal Engineering School in Paris, he served in Italy before joining the Spanish Engineers' Corps in 1763. He received additional instruction at the Royal School of San Fernando in Madrid. During his three years of active service as

---

mother of all four children: Juan Bautista Emilio, Juan Gabriel, Vicente Teodoro, and Pedro Arturo de Finiels. The first three were born in Pensacola; Pedro, in New Orleans (service sheets of the sons, 1824–29; service affiliation records of Juan Bautista, AGMS).

[70] W. C. C. Claiborne to Casa-Calvo, New Orleans, Aug. 7, 1804, AGI, PC, leg. 70-A; petition of N. Definiels, New Orleans, Dec. 6, 1804, AGI, PC, leg. 140.

[71] Finiels to Mauricio de Zúñiga, Pensacola, Jan. 18, 1813, AGI, PC, leg. 79.

[72] Statement of Carlos Reggio, Pensacola, June 6, 1818, AGI, PC, leg. 2356, Pensacola surrendered on May 28, but the United States officially disavowed Jackson's actions and returned the conquered posts and forts to Spain (Luis de Onís to the Captain General of Cuba, Philadelphia, July 28, 1818, AGI, PC, leg. 2356). Finiels was transferred to Havana where he evidently remained (petition of Finiels, Havana, Aug. 23, 1820, AGMS).

[73] Collot, *Journey in North America*, II, 272.

an engineer in Havana and six months in the Internal Provinces of Mexico, he demonstrated inventive genius by providing presidio troops with armor plate of his design worth two thousand dollars. After two years with the American Army of Operations during the American Revolution, he served two years in Louisiana in charge of defenses at Natchez and La Balise. He was twice military and civil commander of the post at San Marcos de Apalachee between 1787 and 1790. He saw action against the American adventurer William Augustus Bowles and was cited for bravery and engineering skill by his superiors. While directing the works at San Phelipe de Placaminas in May, 1793, he earned additional merit, but was killed during the hurricane of August 18, along with his faithful Negro assistant Joaquín.[74]

*Pierre Borel.* A lieutenant of Louisiana militia, he was killed while serving as an engineer in the attack on Mobile in 1780. His widow received an annual pension of $380.[75]

*Jacobo Dubreuil.* He was born in New Orleans about 1744. A cadet in the French army in 1753, he joined the Spanish service as lieutenant in 1769 and rose to the rank of brevet lieutenant-colonel prior to his death on January 11, 1804. He was employed as a voluntary engineer in the construction of Fort San Luis de Illinois, where he served from 1767 to 1769, and during the siege of Baton Rouge saw considerable action. As commander of the reinforcements sent to Illinois in 1781, he was attacked by the Colbert-led Chickasaws but succeeded in repelling them. As commander of Fort Carlos III at Arkansas in 1783, he again faced these invaders and succeeded in holding them off. He also served as commander of the fort at San Marcos de Apalachee and as interim commander of the third battalion of the Louisiana Infantry Regiment. He was married to Inés Otero, a Spanish beauty from Puerto Real near Cádiz. Their children included Buenaventura, a lieutenant in the Cuban Regiment, Francisco Antonio, a sublieutenant in the Louisiana Regiment who

---

[74] Service sheets of Bertucat, 1792, 1793, AGS, GM, leg. 7291, VIII, 25; AGI, PC, leg. 161-A; pay sheet, AGI, PC, leg. 538-B; will, Pensacola, July 1, 1790, AGI, PC, leg. 169; his plans of San Marcos with data, July 18, 1787, Aug. 18, 1790, June 26, 1791, Dec. 31, 1791, AGI, PC, legs. 1393, 1440-A, 178, with the plans in Planos, Luisiana y Floridas, nos. 115, 135, 139, 141. Plan of barracks at San Phelipe, AGI, Planos, no. 151, and letter of Carondelet to Bertucat, New Orleans, May 8, 1793.

[75] Bernardo de Gálvez to José de Gálvez, no. 449, New Orleans, July 19, 1781, AGI, PC, leg. 223-B.

saw service on the Mississippi Galley Squadron, and Jacobo, who rose to captain in the Spanish army.[76]

*Guido Soniat Dufossat.* An engineer in charge of drawing the fortifications for the fort at St. Louis in 1767, he accompanied the first Spanish expedition there under Pedro Joseph Piernas. Prior to his death on June 22, 1794, he was a retired captain of the Regular Louisiana Regiment attached to the New Orleans garrison. He married Francesca Claudina Dreux.[77]

*Pedro (Pierre) Joseph Favrot.* Born in New Orleans in 1749, a descendant of a distinguished French family, Favrot lived in France until 1777 when his father died. He returned to Louisiana as a captain in the second battalion of the Louisiana Infantry Regiment in 1778 and commanded Baton Rouge and was interim commander of Mobile between 1783 and 1787. He was in charge of the troops at Natchez in 1792. While commander of fortifications at San Phelipe de Placaminas and Fort Bourbon in 1796, he wrote a *Textbook in Arithmetic by Questions and Answers and a Summary of the Sciences.* He retired from the army prior to 1808.[78]

*Pedro (Pierre) Foucher y Carriere-le-Garin.* A captain in the Louisiana Regiment, born in New Orleans on December 31, 1755, he was appointed first commandant of the New Madrid post with instructions to build its fort. He was placed in charge of San Esteban de Tombecbee and Placaminas fortifications in 1792. He married Francisca Isabel Boré y Detrehan.[79]

*Bartolomé Lafon.* Engineer, architect, and cartographer of New Orleans with offices at No. 7 South Royal Street, he surveyed

---

[76] Pedro Joseph Piernas to Antonio Ulloa, San Luis, June 5, 1767, AGI, PC, leg. 2357; petition of Dubreuil, Pensacola, Mar. 15, 1796, AGI, PC, leg. 33; statement of regiment, AGI, PC, leg. 140; service sheet, June 30, 1797, AGS, GM, leg. 7292, X, 18; service records of Ventura, Francisco Antonio, and Jacobo Dubreuil, AGI, PC, leg. 161-B; *Expedientes matrimoniales* of Ventura and Jacobo Dubreuil (Jr.), AGMS.

[77] Piernas to Ulloa, June 5, 1767; pay sheets of Dufosat, AGI, PC, leg. 538-A.

[78] Service sheet, AGS, GM, leg. 7292, X, 17; regimental strength sheet, AGI, PC, leg. 161-B; *Favrot Papers* (W.P.A. records, New Orleans, Tulane University Archives, 1941–63); Helen Parkhurst, "Don Pedro Favrot, a Creole Pepys," *Louisiana Historical Quarterly*, XXVIII (July, 1945), 679–734.

[79] Foucher's *Expediente matrimonial*, 1793, AGMS; service sheet, AGI, PC, leg. 161-A; AGS, GM, leg. 7292, I, 34; petition of Foucher, New Orleans, Mar. 31, 1797, AHN, EST, leg. 3900; statement of Foucher, New Orleans, Feb. 12, 1795, AHN, EST, leg. 3900; Morales' attest, Feb. 23, 1795, AHN, EST, leg. 3900.

Orleans Territory and the lower Mississippi in 1804–5. Lafon repaired the corporal's guard building which was damaged in the 1794 fire.[80]

*Alexandro de Latill.* Director of New Orleans fortifications without military rank, he earned thirty dollars monthly from 1784 until his death on February 4, 1791.[81]

*A. Lacarriere Latour.* He was a major and principal engineer of the Seventh Military District of the United States Army in New Orleans and observer at the Battle of New Orleans.[82]

*Gilberto Antonio de St. Maxent.* He was born in Lorraine on April 4, 1727, and died in New Orleans, August 8, 1794. He gave distinguished service in the Mississippi, Mobile, and Pensacola campaigns with the rank of brevet colonel. He offered to build various structures at Villa Gayoso (Cole's Creek) and Natchez and contracted to build La Balise and San Phelipe de Placaminas. Married to Isabel de la Roche, their sons Antonio, Celestino, and Francisco Maximiliano were also in the army.[83]

[80] Lafon, *Carte generale du territoire d'Orléans,* original in Library of Congress, and reproduced in *Louisiana Under the Rule of Spain, France, and the United States* . . . , ed. James A. Robertson (Cleveland, 1911), II, opp. 82; Carondelet to Rendón, draft, New Orleans, May 9, 1795, AGI, PC, leg. 31; advertisements for Lafon's atlas and maps of the Mississippi River and Orleans Territory with descriptions are in the *Moniteur de la Louisiane,* Nov. 13, 1805, Feb. 1, 1806.

[81] Martín Navarro's order, New Orleans, Aug. 18, 1784, Biblioteca Nacional (Madrid), MSS, vol. 19,248, fols. 62–76; pay sheet of Latill, AGI, PC, leg. 538-A.

[82] Latour's "Historical Memoir of the War" of 1812 in Louisiana and West Florida is in the *Louisiana Historical Quarterly,* II (Apr., 1919), 143–153; Jane Lucas deGrummon, "Latour, Tousard, Lafon, Laclotte, Nolte and Napoleon," unpublished paper read at the Louisiana Historical Association, Baton Rouge, April 19, 1963.

[83] Service sheet, AGI, PC, leg. 161-A; pay sheets, AGI, PC, leg. 538-A, B; petition of family line purity, AGI, SD, leg. 2588; de la Torre to Carondelet, New Orleans, Dec. 6, 1795, AGI, PC, leg. 32; Gayoso to Miró, New Orleans, two letters dated March 29, 1790, AGI, PC, leg. 41.

# French Reactions to the Louisiana Revolution of 1768

Pierre H. Boulle

We are meeting today to celebrate the bicentennial of St. Louis. A little over a year ago, we could have met to celebrate another bicentennial, that of the cession of Louisiana to Spain. It is perhaps fitting that no celebration took place then, for no one wishes to be reminded of a failure, and the Louisiana cession can be seen not only as the recognition by the French of their failure to colonize Louisiana, but also as the beginning of another failure—that of Spain to profit from and hold onto a territory the wealth of which needs no longer to be proven.

Of all the cities in the old Louisiana Territory, St. Louis perhaps epitomizes best, by its growth in the last two hundred years, the fulfillment of Louisiana's promise. It has struck some people as ironic therefore that St. Louis was settled so soon after Louisiana was ceded to the Spanish, and as a direct result of the last French grant in that territory. The masters of hindsight are wont to blame France for not having held onto Louisiana a little longer, instead of washing her hands of what in appearance only was an unsound colonial policy.

Nineteenth-century historians were shocked by what appeared

to them to be such a lack of foresight and such a light-hearted abandonment of national interest. Blinded by their hatred of absolutism, they could only explain this by blaming it on a hapless and corrupt monarch, ". . . who never had either the tenderness of a woman's heart, the pride of a king, or the courage of a man."[1]

It is no longer fashionable to hold such a view, and people have generally accepted that France might have had sound reasons for getting rid of Louisiana. The colony, it is argued, was never profitable, and its unpopularity since the days of the Mississippi Bubble gave it little chance of ever showing its economic worth. Therefore, at a time when repeated colonial disasters had made it imperative that France reorganize its colonial policy along more profitable lines, it was natural that Choiseul, the French foreign minister, should concentrate all his efforts on the wealthiest French colonies, the West Indies, and abandon all territories which showed no promise of immediate profit. Having managed to hoodwink the British into leaving the French West Indies untouched, Choiseul saw his masterplan threatened by the reluctance of France's Spanish ally to agree to peace. No better role could therefore be given to Louisiana in the French scheme than to serve as a final means of inducing Spain to ratify the Treaty of Paris.

This interpretation has led many students of American history to assume that France regarded the cession of 1762 as a permanent withdrawal from the North American continent and as a recognition of the fact that this withdrawal marked the end of the Anglo-French colonial rivalry.[2] The retrocession of Louisiana to France in 1800 is therefore seen by these historians not as the continuation of the eighteenth-century French colonial policy, but as a rather un-

---

[1] Charles Gayarré, *History of Louisiana; The French Domination* (2nd ed., New York, 1867), II, 94. The famous Louisiana historian is one of the best representatives of this opinion. He ends his work (II, 359) with these words: "It was not when a poor colony, and when given away like a farm by a friend to another, royal though they were, it was not when miserably clad with the tattered livery of her colonial bondage, that she could foresee her glorious dismemberment into sovereignties, the last of which occupies so proud a position in the eye of the world. This miracle was to be the consequence of the apparition of a banner, which was not in existence at the time, the harbinger of the regeneration of nations, and which was to form so important an era in the history of the rights of mankind."

[2] The permanence of the change is the only thing noted by general texts. See John D. Hicks, *The Federal Union* (2nd ed., Cambridge, Mass., 1952), p. 101, and Oliver Perry Chitwood, *A History of Colonial America* (2nd ed., New York, 1948), p. 404.

successful departure from the normal European policy of Napoleon, ". . . temporarily dazzled by a scheme of Talleyrand's for the revival of the French Empire in America."[3]

Although I am aware that this view is not generally held by specialists,[4] I think it is a fair enough representation of the picture of historical opinion that has percolated up to the level of the non-specialist. Even though the documents bearing on the Louisiana cession have been studied fully in works too numerous to list here and even though the careful reader can reach the correct conclusions, although they are never stated in a single work, the legend remains. Since this is a case in which legend continues to overshadow fact, it is important, I think, to find a new way to evaluate the opinion in which France held Louisiana in the 1760's. The Revolution of 1768 appears ideally suited to that purpose, for it presented the French with a brief opportunity to reconsider their decision of 1762 to abandon Louisiana.

It is not my role here to describe in detail what happened in Louisiana in 1768; the story is too well known to bear repeating.[5] Let me simply remind you of the outline. Although Louisiana was ceded to the Spanish in November, 1762, the news of the cession, kept secret for a time, was not known in Louisiana until September, 1764. Even then, it took until March, 1766, for the first Spanish officials, headed by Don Antonio de Ulloa to reach Louisiana. For three and a half years the colony had been left very much on its own, with little official news from France and no directives at all. No Spanish merchant vessels ever came to supply the colony, and Louisiana would have been wholly abandoned had it not been for French merchants who continued to trade with New Orleans even after it became known that the colony was no longer French.

As the Spanish delayed, hope grew among the Louisianans, very

---

[3] Hicks, *The Federal Union*, p. 261.

[4] Arthur S. Aiton, "The Diplomacy of the Louisiana Cession," *American Historical Review*, XXXVI (July, 1931), 719, speaks of the plans which the French and the Spanish were readying for ". . . their war of retaliation against England." See also Walter L. Dorn, *Competition for Empire, 1740–1763*, in *The Rise of Modern Europe*, ed. William L. Langer, IX (New York, London, 1940), 378, where it is stated that Choiseul ". . . could not regard this peace as a permanent settlement. . . ."

[5] The most satisfactory account of the period 1762–69 in Louisiana can be found in Baron Marc de Villiers du Terrage, *Les dernières années de la Louisiane française* (Paris, 1904), pp. 138–326. That work quotes extensively from original documents, some of which can be found printed nowhere else.

reluctant Spanish subjects, that the cession would never take effect. The arrival of Ulloa was therefore not entirely welcome. To make matters worse, he arrived with only a token force with which he could not hope to assume responsibility for the colony. Unable to take over from the French, he was obliged to delay the official transfer of power and meanwhile to rule through Aubry, the French commandant, who still signed the official acts. Ulloa thus found himself in a situation which would have tried the most diplomatic of administrators.

Unfortunately, the Spanish crown had chosen in Ulloa a governor with few diplomatic qualities. He was haughty and un-bending, and Aubry noted, "He has done everything to alienate the hearts of the country, especially the members of the Council; by unwise speeches, he has made people fear Spanish rule. . . ."[6] Unable to exercise authority directly and faced with a generally antagonistic population made anxious by the news that the French crown had stopped paying any of its debts contracted in the colony since 1763, Ulloa nevertheless insisted on a rigorous application to Louisiana of the Spanish mercantilistic colonial policy. Soon after his arrival, he had issued under Aubry's signature an ordinance which permitted French vessels to disembark goods only when they had a Spanish passport countersigned upon their arrival by Ulloa himself.[7] Although the ordinance does not seem to have been applied, it worried Louisiana merchants by giving them a foretaste of what they could expect from the Spanish. Early in October, 1768, a new decree reached Louisiana. In it the King of Spain placed Louisiana within the Spanish sphere of exclusive commerce. No ships, the decree stated, were to be allowed in Louisiana unless they were built in Spain, had a Spanish captain and a crew two-thirds Spanish, and came from certain Spanish ports listed in the decree.[8] Since no such vessel had ever come to Louisiana, the decree, if enforced, would spell complete isolation for the colony.

For whatever reason (whether they feared for their commerce or whether they were genuine French patriots who considered that Spanish rule, as experienced under Ulloa, was intolerable) the leaders of the colony, backed by the French *commissaire ordonnateur*, on

---

[6] Aubry to ———, Feb. 29, 1769, quoted in Villiers du Terrage, *Les dernières années*, p. 229.

[7] Ordinance of September 6, 1766, Archives, Chambre de Commerce de Marseille (hereafter ACCM), H26.

[8] Decree of March 23, 1768. The terms of this decree are given in Villiers du Terrage, *Les dernières années*, pp. 249–250.

October 29, 1768, had Ulloa declared a "usurper" by the Superior Council of the colony, and led the people in forcibly removing him from New Orleans. On November 1, they cut adrift the vessel in which he had taken refuge. As Ulloa and his retinue sailed down the Mississippi on their way to Havana, the Louisianans gave back his authority to a reluctant Aubry.

The brief and bloodless revolution was over. While Aubry governed as he could, the Superior Council now busied itself with a justification of the revolt and the future of the colony. Throughout November, it drafted letters and petitions to the King of France and his ministers which two deputies were to carry to France.[9] In these documents, the revolutionaries appealed to Louis XV to repeal the cession of 1762 and resume his rule over his faithful subjects. They were careful to point out that Ulloa had never officially taken possession of the colony and that, therefore, the cession could still be rescinded. They further noted that the title to Louisiana was of no advantage to the Spanish, whose other colonies would be better protected by a buffer area in French hands between themselves and the British. They finally warned that continued Spanish occupation would open the colony to a British invasion if the delays in taking possession of her new colony and the weakness of the force which had accompanied Ulloa were indications of Spain's future plans for Louisiana.

It was the British danger, in fact, that struck well-informed Frenchmen first upon hearing of the revolution. Only four days after he had informed Choiseul of the events in Louisiana,[10] the Marquis

---

[9] The two deputies were named Le Sassier and Saintelette. They carried with them the following documents, which can be found in ACCM, H26, and in Archives Nationales, Fonds des Colonies (hereafter AN, Col.), C[13A] 49, fol. 195: Aubry's ordinance of 1766 and the Spanish decree of 1768; the Superior Council's decree of October 29, 1768; two letters from the Superior Council, one to the Duc de Praslin, French minister of marine, dated November 22, and the other to the chambers of commerce of La Rochelle, Bordeaux, Nantes, Marseilles, and Rouen, dated November 25, 1768; the "Très humbles representations qu'adressent au Roi . . . les gens tenant son Conseil supérieur à la Nouvelle-Orleans," dated November 12, 1768; and the colony's justification, printed in New Orleans under the title, "Memoire des habitans et negocians de la Louisianne, sur l'évenement du 29. octobre 1768." This last document is translated in full in Alcée Fortier, *A History of Louisiana* (New York, 1904), I, 177–204.

[10] Ossun to Choiseul, Feb. 2, 1769, Archives, Ministère des Affaires Etrangères (hereafter AE), Correspondance Politique (hereafter Corr. Pol.), Espagne 556, fol. 95. Choiseul in his answer of February 21, noted that Ossun had been the first to announce the revolt (AE, Corr. Pol., Espagne 556, fol. 175).

d'Ossun, French ambassador to Spain, sent him a second letter in which he warned, ". . . the position of that colony, which is contiguous to the English possessions, seems to require that effective measures be taken without delay to bring her back under Spanish rule."[11] The Comte de Châtelet, French ambassador to England, when he heard the news in London, noted that the British wanted Louisiana for themselves and were overjoyed with the opportunity which the revolt gave them. He added that, although the British realized that the revolutionaries preferred to return to their French allegiance, it was assumed that they would rather become Englishmen than be subjected once more to Spanish rule.[12]

But if the revolution endangered the existing French policy of containing the British, it also offered opportunities upon which the French soon began to speculate.

The Comte d'Estaing was one of the few soldiers who came out of the Seven Years' War with an unblemished record and certainly the only successful French naval officer during that period. Taken prisoner by the English on his return to France after a daring campaign in the Indian Ocean, he had been specially selected by Choiseul for exchange. Once back in France, he had been commissioned viceroy of Brazil, which he was supposed to conquer in an expedition the preparations for which were almost complete when the British and the French agreed on peace in 1762. After the war, he had been named governor of St. Domingue, France's most important West Indian island, at a time when France attempted to reform its colonial policy and put only proven military men at the head of its overseas possessions. He had been given extraordinary powers in that office and had been extremely successful in completing his mission. He was back at Versailles in 1769, in close contact with the minister.[13] The Comte de Châtelet was the French ambassador to England. No two men outside the ministry were better able to know

[11] Ossun to Choiseul, Feb. 6, 1769, AE, Corr. Pol., Espagne 556, fol. 103v.
[12] Châtelet to Choiseul, Feb. 24, 1769, AE, Corr. Pol., Angleterre 485, fol. 485. Londoners were not that far wrong, for there are indications that, once the leaders of the revolt lost hope of French help, they sought British support in Mobile (Villiers du Terrage, *Les dernières années*, p. 286). The Comte d'Estaing also warned against this danger, in the memoir I shall speak of presently.
[13] For Estaing's campaign in the Indian Ocean, see AN, Col., C²07, fols. 4–13. For the Brazil expedition, see AN, Col., B115, fols. 418–446v. For the governorship of St. Domingue, see letter of king to Estaing Jan. ?, 1764, AN, Col., A9, année 1764, no. 1.

what Choiseul was thinking in respect to Great Britain. It is therefore interesting to note that, soon after news of the revolution reached Europe, and within a week of each other, both these men came up with plans to establish Louisiana as a republic.[14] The two plans are so similar that I need only study one of them here.

"The singular event . . . which occurred in Louisiana will become," Estaing said in his memoir, "if it is taken advantage of, the fortunate germ of the diminution of the British Empire." Taking this as the primary goal of French foreign policy after the Seven Years' War, he proposed that Louisiana be given semi-independence, guaranteed by both Spain and France. Under his plan, Louisiana would rule itself in matters of domestic policy, but France and Spain, through *commissaires* which they would appoint to reside in New Orleans, would advise "the little Republic," as he called it, and keep in their control all external affairs. Estaing thus proposed a Franco-Spanish co-protectorate of Louisiana. This, he claimed, would present only advantages to the two powers concerned. Such a republic would rid the Spanish of the burden of a reluctant and unwanted colony, which could be held only at great cost, while still fulfilling the goal for which they had accepted it in 1762, that of serving as a buffer between the British and Mexico. It would also avoid for France the necessity of assuming an economic responsibility it could ill afford.

More important, it would be the ideal means of sowing further dissension between the British and their American colonies, already at loggerheads, by showing ". . . to colonials who wish to be free, neighbors freer than they. . . ."[15] The plan was cunningly

---

[14] "Memoire donné par M.ʳ D'Estaing," Mar. 10, 1769, AN, Col., C¹¹ᴬ125, fols. 575–577; Châtelet to Choiseul, Mar. 17, 1769, AE, Corr. Pol., Angleterre 486, fol. 93. Châtelet, in his letter of February 24, had already intimated the influence the Louisiana Revolution could have on the British colonies in America. It is worth noting again how closely these two men guessed what the Louisianans would do, for the possibility of a republic was discussed in 1769 by some of the leaders of the revolt against Spain (Villiers du Terrage, *Les dernières années*, pp. 284–285).

[15] It did not take much of a prophet to predict the American Revolution in 1769. By that time, the Stamp Act had been promulgated, repealed, and replaced by the Townshend Acts, and Boston was already in a turmoil over taxation. But the French had been hoping for a rebellion in America ever since they had lost Canada. Thiton de Silegny (or Silegne) expressed that hope in his "Moiens praticables pour concilier la france et L'Ang.ʳᵉ sur les Limites respectives dans l'amerique septentrionale" (Sept. 26, 1761, AE, Mémoires et Documents, Amérique 21, fol. 94). As early as 1748, the economist Turgot had

conceived: "To give willingly what the English Parliament refuses; to copy the form of Louisiana's government from that of the freest English colony, New York for instance; to take from the regime of each what it holds dearest, what is wisest; to go beyond that and make it free; to then maintain its privileges, so worthy of the envy of these new men of England and America and so capable of making them drunk with enthusiasm. To do so is, I repeat, to arm English America against the English; it is to risk only what we neglected." By continuing the commercial privileges which New Orleans enjoyed with Spain and France and increasing them by declaring that port open to all comers, the two crowns would not only benefit their commerce but also present the downtrodden New Englanders with an enviable example at their doorstep. The very gesture of ". . . two Potentates who forgive, protect, and deign together to speak the so-powerful word, Liberty . . ." would have the flash of grandeur capable of destroying ". . . the popular prejudice [which] . . . has made [the British colonials] see as despots . . ." the monarchs of France and Spain. Encouraged to look at these as potential allies, the British Americans would soon break away from their mother country.

There could be no fear, Estaing continued, that the movement would spread to French and Spanish territories. The loyalty of Spanish colonials was too well known for anyone to fear that they would take such a step. As for the French West Indies, Estaing, with the authority of an ex-governor of St. Domingue, noted that no one seeks self-rule ". . . in places . . . which one fears to inhabit, to which greed alone attracts, from which reason, good taste and diseases chase people, and which must seek elsewhere all articles of first necessity."

No grave danger could therefore hamper the adventure, and to risk it would be ". . . to hasten . . . the great work of Spanish and French policy: the dismemberment of [British] America. . . . What occurred in Louisiana," he concluded, "seems one of the happiest circumstances . . . for the conservation of the Spanish and French colonies."

I have spent this much time on Estaing and Châtelet's project,

---

stated that America, because it was capable of supporting itself, would one day sever its ties with Europe (Anne Robert Jacques Turgot, "Recherches sur les causes des progrès et de la decadence des sciences et des arts," *Œuvres de Turgot et documents le concernant,* ed. Gustave Schelle [Paris, 1913–33], I, 141). In his memoir of 1769, Estaing used this argument to urge that Louisiana be allowed its independence.

not only because I consider it one of the most imaginative, but also because, through it, we get a glimpse of what must have been the official aim of French foreign policy—the destruction of the British colonial empire. These two men, we must remember, were unusually well informed, and they must have suited their project to what they knew to be Choiseul's goal.

The idea of a republican Louisiana must have seeped down to the lower echelons of French society, at least in the army. As late as December, 1769, several months after the Spanish regained a firm hold on Louisiana, it was discussed in a letter written by a Captain Proterat to Choiseul.[16] Far less realistically conceived, the plan shows that the author was well outside the spheres of French policy-making. He assumed that the difficulties encountered by the British in their colonies had been engineered by French agents with French money and saw Louisiana as a splendid opportunity for the creation of a second front. He therefore proposed that, while France appear to leave the Louisianans to their own devices, it secretly arm, train, and finance them. Very soon, he claimed, with the help of the friendly Indian nations of the Illinois, these troops would be able to take the British from the rear. Since his plan excluded the Spanish, it is assumed that he would then have had the Louisianans, the Canadians, and the British colonials, now brothers-in-arms under the French flag, move west and conquer the rest of the continent for France!

Meanwhile, another proposal had been presented to the French Ministry. The Marquis de Capellis, a naval officer, saw in the Revolution of 1768 an opportunity to call attention once more to a pet project of his own—the unification of the island of Santo Domingo under the French.[17] Now that there was an opportunity to recapture Louisiana, he proposed that the colony be taken and then given right back to the Spanish in exchange for their portion of the West Indian island.[18]

Needless to say, some of the plans presented above were im-

---

[16] Captain Proterat to Choiseul, Dec. 11, 1769, AE, Mémoires et Documents, Amérique 11, fol. 436. Proterat was captain in the Orleans Cavalry Regiment.

[17] Capellis had already presented that idea in his "Memoire relatif a la Paix," June, 1761, AN, Section Outre-mer, Direction du Dépôt des fortifications des Colonies, Mémoires généraux, no. 223, pp. 22–26.

[18] Memoir of Marquis de Capellis on the advantages for France to possess the whole of Santo Domingo, Mar., 1769, sent April 5, 1769 (*Calendar of Manuscripts in Paris Archives and Libraries Relating to the History of the Mississippi Valley to 1803*, ed. Nancy Maria Miller Surrey [Washington, 1928], II, 1528–29).

practical, but it is obvious that the Revolution of 1768 had once more opened wide the Louisiana question. There was an opportunity for French gains, and Choiseul seems to have wavered for a while. Despite the fact that he had been informed of the revolution early in February and that he presumably had the detailed account of Aubry by the beginning of March,[19] he still claimed at the beginning of April that lack of information obliged him to reserve judgment on what to do about Louisiana.[20] During that period, he wrote several letters to the Spanish court assuring it of French support, but he was always careful to make that support conditional.[21] By the end of March, however, he had at least begun to see that Louisiana must be left to the Spanish. When he wrote to Châtelet to thank him for his memoir, he stated that he had at first found the project worthy of consideration but had been drawn back by the extreme difficulty of putting it into execution.[22]

What finally convinced Choiseul was the determination of the Spanish, who feverishly prepared the large expedition with which O'Reilly, an Irish officer then in the service of Spain, was to reconquer Louisiana.[23] There is no doubt that Choiseul considered France's alliance with Spain the key to his anti-British plans.[24] When

---

[19] The letter Aubry had sent with Ulloa was forwarded to Paris by Grimaldi, the Spanish prime minister on February 23 (Grimaldi to Fuentès, Spanish ambassador to France, AN, Col., C¹³ᴬ49, fol. 7). Fuentès must have delivered that letter, and yet Choiseul claimed until July not to have received details of the Louisiana Revolution from the Spanish (Choiseul to Ossun, July 11, 1769, AE, Corr. Pol., Espagne 557, fol. 145).

[20] Choiseul to Ossun, Apr. 4, 1769, AE, Corr. Pol., Espagne 556, fol. 327. His letter of May 2 to Ossun can still be construed as equivocal, although the commitment to Spain is then much more direct than it had been (AE, Corr. Pol., Espagne 556, fol. 434).

[21] Choiseul to Ossun, Feb. 21 and Mar. 21, 1769, AE, Corr. Pol., Espagne 556, fols. 175, 284.

[22] Choiseul to Châtelet, Mar. 24, 1769, AE, Corr. Pol., Angleterre 486, fol. 203.

[23] Choiseul was well informed of these preparations by Ossun (Ossun to Choiseul, Feb. 2 and 6, Mar. 6, Apr. 17 [where O'Reilly is first mentioned, although not yet definitely in connection with Louisiana], and July 8, 1769, AE, Corr. Pol., Espagne 556, fols. 95, 103v, 232, 382v, and Espagne 557, fol. 128).

[24] The Duc de Praslin, Choiseul's cousin, served as an aide to that minister with whom he shared the work of the three ministries which Choiseul had reserved for himself—war, marine, and foreign affairs. Between 1761 and 1770, Praslin headed whatever ministry was considered least important by Choiseul, thus leaving the latter free to concentrate on the crucial problems. To show how important the Spanish alliance was to Choiseul, one needs only to note that, even when Praslin was minister of foreign affairs (1761–66), Choiseul kept for himself the correspondence with Spain.

it became clear that to tamper with Louisiana would antagonize the Spanish, Choiseul had to back down in order not to wreck the careful work of cementing the Family Compact he had been carrying on for almost eight years. Even if he had been willing to chance colonial rivalry with Spain, he could ill afford to lose Spanish support in the crucial papal election of 1769, which came in the middle of the controversy over the Jesuits.[25] Despite his obvious sympathies for Louisiana and its rebels, Choiseul had to place the affairs of that colony at the bottom of the list of matters of concern in Franco-Spanish relations.[26] Therefore, when a letter was requested of the French asking Aubry and Foucault, the French top officials in Louisiana, to help O'Reilly at his arrival, Choiseul had Praslin write one in the strongest terms.[27] He only expressed one fear: "I doubt that M. O'Reilly will succeed in his operation, and I fear that most of the colony will go to the English, for the fermentation of the colonists' emotions is great, and it would have been best to wait a while for them to calm down. . . ."[28]

When the Louisiana deputies finally reached Paris in April, they therefore found Choiseul's mind made up against their plea. He refused to let them see the king and received them only reluctantly and as private individuals.[29] The deputies had had more success with another segment of the French population—the chambers of com-

---

[25] In the period between the death of Clement XIII, who favored the Jesuits (January 2, 1769), and the election of Clement XIV, who finally suppressed the order (May 18, 1769), most of the correspondence between France and Spain dealt with the papal election. This is the period during which the decisions were taken in regard to Louisiana (AE, Corr. Pol., Espagne 556).

[26] "Je vous envoie en original une lettre touchante d'un des deputés de la Colonie de la Louisianne," Choiseul to Fuentès, Aug. 27, 1769, AE, Corr. Pol., Espagne 555, fol. 173.

[27] Praslin to Aubry and Foucault, Aug. 12, 1769, AN, Col., B132, fol. 460. However, it had taken a whole month to draft that letter. The Spanish, therefore, while expressing their satisfaction that the letter was written ". . . dans les termes que nous desirions," rightfully expressed doubts that it would arrive in time to do any good (Grimaldi to Fuentès, Aug. 28, 1769, AE, Corr. Pol., Espagne 557, fol. 348).

[28] Choiseul to Ossun, July 11, 1769, AE, Corr. Pol., Espagne 557, fol. 145. The Spanish and Ossun himself took this as an effort to have Louisiana treated kindly (Ossun to Choiseul, July 24, 1769, AE, Corr. Pol., Espagne 557, fol. 182). Choiseul immediately backed down (Choiseul to Ossun, Aug. 7, 1769, AE, Corr. Pol., Espagne 557, fol. 226). In a postscript to Praslin's letter of August 12, meant for Grimaldi, Choiseul tried once more to advise clemency, recommending that only as a last resort, ". . . le proces soit fait aux Revoltes" (AN, Col., B132, fol. 461).

[29] Villiers du Terrage, Les dernières années, p. 270.

merce. Although they ultimately failed with these also, the reaction of these interest groups is worth noting.

The Louisiana deputies carried with them letters from the colony's Superior Council to the chambers of commerce of Bordeaux, La Rochelle, Nantes, Marseilles, and Rouen, the ports which had continued to send their ships to New Orleans after the Peace of Paris; in the case of La Rochelle, that commerce had been increased several times to make up for trade lost to the British in Canada. These letters told of the events of October, 1768, gave as their causes the patriotism of the inhabitants of that colony and their desire to avoid Spanish efforts to close off their "natural" trade lines with the West Indies and with France, and requested that the chambers of commerce grant the colonial deputies aid and support in their petition to the crown.[30]

French chambers of commerce were meant by the crown to function as economic sounding boards in the provinces, and they were encouraged to make the government aware of what the special interests they represented thought about any economic matter. But revolution and the ownership of a colony were political matters. La Rochelle therefore felt that "we can only consider [the events of New Orleans] . . . through the commercial angle. . . ." It was, it continued, ". . . such a delicate subject . . ." that only united action could be risked. It therefore proposed that each chamber advise its permanent deputy in Paris, who sat in the Bureau of Commerce and thus served as an economic adviser to the crown, to express, if asked by the government, the importance of Louisiana for French commerce.[31] Marseilles readily took La Rochelle's advice. It was still smarting from one of the most violent rebuffs given it by the minister Praslin who reproached it with having overstepped the bounds of its appointed role.[32] On April 27, therefore, it instructed its Paris deputy, Philibert Simian, to conduct himself in respect to Louisiana very much as La Rochelle had proposed. "It seemed to them that the Chamber [thus] could not compromise itself since its deputy in Paris would simply say what he thought of an affair on which his advice had been sought."[33]

[30] Syndics of the Louisiana planters and merchants to Chamber of Commerce of Marseilles, Nov. 25, 1768, ACCM, H26.

[31] Chamber of Commerce of La Rochelle to Chamber of Commerce of Marseilles, Apr. 9, 1769, ACCM, H26.

[32] Praslin to Chamber of Commerce of Marseilles, Nov. 28, 1768, ACCM, A22.

[33] Deliberations of the chamber's bureau, Apr. 27, 1769, ACCM, B16.

The deputies of the various chambers of commerce were no more eager than the chambers themselves to become embroiled in a situation which could only place them in a false position. "I read your letter to my colleagues . . ." Simian wrote to Marseilles, and they ". . . thought as you did . . . that this object was of a kind needing the use of the greatest circumspection, and that Commerce could help the people of Louisiana only if it was asked its advice. Matter for advice will not then be lacking. . . ."[34] The French ministry, of course, did not ask the deputies their advice, and the matter was dropped at that point.

On this matter of commercial privileges, Choiseul, however, made another effort to sway the Spanish. In June he seems to have offered the services of French merchants to help supply Louisiana; he repeated that offer in July.[35] Perhaps Choiseul felt that such a break of the Spanish *exclusif* could be made cheaply; it is more likely, however, that the proposal was caused by his fear that too stringent a rule over Louisiana would merely throw the colonials into the arms of the British. But his proposals met with Spanish determination to do things themselves,[36] and Choiseul once more gave in. In respect to the supplies which the Spanish court expected to get in Havana for Louisiana, he said piously but no doubt thinking of the past Spanish record, ". . . I very sincerely hope that they will be sufficient to accomplish the object in question."[37]

The matter of Louisiana was closed as far as the French government was concerned. In New Orleans, the affair closed with the trial of eleven of the chiefs of the revolution. Five of the accused were condemned to death, and the others were given various prison sentences.[38] The death sentences were carried out on October 25, 1769,

---

[34] Simian to Chamber of Commerce of Marseilles, May 13, 1769, ACCM, B198. I know only the reaction of Marseilles and of La Rochelle. The unanimous reaction of the deputies of commerce in Paris indicates that those of Bordeaux, Nantes, and Rouen had been given the same advice La Rochelle and Marseilles gave to their deputies.

[35] The first proposal was made in a letter to Grimaldi, June 19, 1769, known only through the answer it received (Ossun to Choiseul, July 8, 1769, AE, Corr. Pol., Espagne 557, fol. 128). The second proposal is found in Choiseul to Ossun, July 4, 1769, AE, Corr. Pol., Espagne 557, fol. 113v.

[36] Ossun to Choiseul, July 8 and 17, 1769, AE, Corr. Pol., Espagne 557, fols. 128, 165.

[37] Choiseul to Ossun, July 31, 1769, AE, Corr. Pol., Espagne 557, fol. 210. See also Choiseul to Ossun, July 17, 1769, AE, Corr. Pol., Espagne 557, fol. 156.

[38] In actuality, six death sentences were pronounced, but one of them was against Joseph Roué de Villeré, who had already died.

only a few days before the first anniversary of the revolution. Not even O'Reilly's overzealous handling of the repression seems to have stirred the French.[39] Choiseul no doubt felt that there was no point in risking the alliance by protesting an act which could not be undone. Whatever antagonism he felt for the Spanish because of O'Reilly's harshness was possibly soothed by his knowledge that the ease with which that officer had reconquered Louisiana had put an end to the British threat in that colony.[40]

From then on, the French government's only efforts consisted of attempts to have the Spanish reduce the sentences of those who had escaped the firing squad.[41] It is ironic that its most successful efforts were made in behalf of Foucault, the *commissaire ordonnateur*, who had instigated the people of Louisiana to revolt, and, as the guiltiest, least deserved mercy.[42]

One of the most striking conclusions that can be developed from this brief survey of French opinion in 1769 is that absolutely no one proposed that France take back Louisiana. Even the chambers of commerce did not consider this a worthy goal. As long as French commerce retained the right to trade there, they cared little who held title to the colony. What France feared most was that it might become British. This, by the way, indicates why the cession of Louisiana in 1762 was kept secret for over a year. It was not, as some people have thought, out of fear of what the French might say, but of what the British might do if it became known that Louisiana had ceased to be French before the Spanish were able to defend it effectively. Mostly, the anti-British attitude of influential officials indicates that, so far as the French were concerned, the Anglo-French rivalry was not over, and that the Peace of Paris was regarded

---

[39] The lack of reaction of the French opinion to these executions might have been due to ignorance. It is only in 1775, on the occasion of the defeat of a Spanish expedition against Algiers, led by O'Reilly, that Voltaire, usually well informed and generally sympathetic toward Louisiana, although not necessarily approving of the revolution there, mentioned ". . . l'indigne mort des officiers du roi de France dans la Nouvelle Orléans. . . ." He further noted that the executions of 1769 were still generally unknown in France (*Précis du siècle de Louis XV*, chap. XXXV, in François Marie Arouet de Voltaire, *Œuvres complètes*, ed. Louis Moland (Paris, 1877–85), XV, 375.

[40] Grimaldi inferred from Choiseul's silence that the French minister approved of O'Reilly's repressive measures (Grimaldi to Fuentès, Jan. 24, 1770, quoted in Villiers du Terrage, *Les dernières années*, p. 316).

[41] See, for instance, Praslin to Choiseul, Apr. 28, 1770, AN, Col., B137, fol. 156.

[42] Praslin to Choiseul, July 12, 1770, AN, Col., B137, fol. 201v.

in no way as a permanent settlement.[43] It is only in this light that Choiseul's careful handling of Spain makes sense. The Spanish alliance was essential to his plan for future retaliation against Great Britain, and he was willing to sacrifice any secondary consideration, including the fate of Louisiana, to the welfare of the Family Compact.

It is striking also to note the attention with which some segments of the French population watched the growth of discontent in the Thirteen Colonies. The memoirs to which the Revolution of 1768 gave rise show that this interest existed especially in the military and in the ranks of the crown officials. It was prevalent in the army as well as in the navy, and cut across class lines. These were the men who would fight as French volunteers in the American Revolution— Estaing among them. We hear too often that the French fought for the Americans because they had been imbued with the ideals of Montesquieu, Voltaire, and Rousseau. This is perhaps true, but we must not forget another motive, at least as important—revenge against the British for the humiliating Seven Years' War. That the French in the American War were equipped with an armament which defeated the British, especially on the sea, was due to the ceaseless efforts of Choiseul in the years he spent in office after the end of the Seven Years' War. That the French gained no territorial advantages on the North American continent at the end of the War of Independence may be due to the fact that neither Choiseul nor the king who had given him support for nine years were then in power. Those who had replaced them, Vergennes and Louis XVI, were men who saw the loss of Canada as a *fait accompli* from the beginning of their rule. Had Choiseul still been at his post, the French would no doubt have tried to recapture for themselves some part of the North American continent. Someone who values the good relations which have developed between France and the United States since 1778 might therefore consider it fortunate that Choiseul was replaced in 1770.

---

[43] A letter, written before the news of the Louisiana Revolution had reached Europe, spells out very clearly how well-informed Frenchmen viewed the future. In it, Ossun entreated Choiseul, who had been threatening to resign his cabinet post, to consider ". . . 1° que nous avons un procès aussi considerable que decisif à vuider avec L'Angleterre, dans lequel il s'agît, pour les deux couronnes, de perdre ou de gagner à jamais le premier rang en Europe du coté de l'influence et de la consideration. 2° Que cette guerre decisive ne peut pas être fort éloignée. 3° Que c'est vous qui en avés menagé et disposé les moyens, et qui êtes, sous les ordres de Sa Majesté, l'ame de ce grand projet" (Jan. 23, 1769, AE, Corr. Pol., Espagne 556, fol. 55).

# French Naturalists
# in the Mississippi Valley

## Joseph Ewan

Auguste Comte (1798–1857) said "no one can be really master of any science unless he studies its special history, which again is bound up with the general history of humanity." The American historian Arthur M. Schlesinger, Sr., praised Edward Eggleston, author of *Transit of Civilization,* for writing instead of "drum and trumpet history" the "history of culture, the real history of men and women." The record of exploration, not always happy, has sung of persistence in the face of discouragement, a fraternity of spirit, and absorbing devotion to knowledge. The naturalist: what is it that induces the naturalist to give up a life of comfort, security, and leisure to roam through alien countries in search of plants, animals, and other objects of Nature? The contemporary Dutch botanist H. J. Lam[1] suggests the reason is a longing for individual freedom, a need to follow a primitive indomitable call of the wild, to be confronted with grandeur of unspoiled nature, to satisfy insatiable curiosity, and

---

[1] C. G. G. J. Van Steenis, *Flora Malesiana* (Leiden, 1950), I, vii.

to approach Nature with the eyes of an artist, a pioneer, and a conqueror.

"During the fifty years after LaSalle's journey down the Mississippi the eastern half of the valley was in an uneasy ferment which was kept up by the yeasts of rival European policies emanating from many points on its circumference." The historian Brebner of Columbia University continues, "the historian can record the ferment and can even identify some of the agents in it, but he faces a baffling situation when he tries to build up an explicit sequence of the exploration of the region. . . . Dozens of anonymous men were busy in the Indian trade. . . . Some lived most of their lives in Indian villages or in lonely cabins far beyond the outskirts of settlement . . . some vigorous, precise reconnaissances to unify fragmentary knowledge of established military and commercial alliances. They were more than mere fur traders."[2]

Who were they? Some came on their own initiative, some were sponsored by the government or came and returned to their blackboards at a university, others were members of the military, physicians seeking a change of climate, clergy-priests, artists, adventurers, woodsmen, voyageurs, and that singular variety of adventurers called Utopians.

Father Charlevoix[3] came down the Mississippi in 1721 ostensibly to examine Jesuit missions but really as an emissary of the King of France engaged in verifying trails to the West. Letters addressed to his patroness, the Duchess de Lesdiguièrres, one of the last of a noble line, were in fact a ruse and never were sent to the lady to whom they were addressed. Charlevoix visited New Orleans only four years after its founding so that his six-volume *Histoire*, published in 1743, with its references to cypress, wax-myrtle, pitcher-plant, *Ilex vomitoria*, the "apalachine" or cassine, the black drink of the southeastern tribes[4]—all hold our interst. Wax-bearing plants in particular interested Charlevoix as a possible export of Louisiana.

Thomas Carlyle wrote Ralph Waldo Emerson on July 8, 1851,

---

[2] J. B. Brebner, *Explorers of North America 1492–1806* (London, 1933), p. 307.

[3] Gilbert Chinard, "André and François-André Michaux and Their Predecessors. An Essay on Early Botanical Exchanges Between America and Europe," *Proceedings of the American Philosophical Society*, CI (1957), 344–361. Charlevoix appears on pp. 346–347.

[4] A. H. G. Alston and R. E. Schultes, "Studies of Early Specimens and Reports of Ilex vomitoria," *Rhodora*, LIII (1951), 273–280.

"I lately read a small old brown French duodecimo, which I mean to send you by the first chance there is. The writer is a Captaine Bossu: the production, a Journal of his experiences in 'La Louisiana,' 'Oyo,' and those regions, which looks very genuine, and has a strange interest to me, like some fractional Odyssey or letter. Only a hundred years ago, and the Missississippi has changed as never valley did, older and stranger, looked at from *its* present date than Balbec or Ninevah! Say what we will, Jonathan is doing miracles (of a sort) under the sun in these times now passing."[5] Bossu's writings must have impressed Carlyle, for a month later he again wrote Emerson of the "Book of a poor Naval Mississippi Frenchman . . . I read it as a kind of defaced *Romance;* very thin and lean, but all *True,* and very marvelous as such." The first edition of Bossu's *Voyage* appeared in 1768 followed by two other so-called editions, twelve printings in all, of which three were unknown to Sabin and of one "edition" no copy has been located.[6]

In the era of Bougainville, who closely followed in the wake of Captain Cook around the world, André Michaux came to this country under the patronage of the King of France to seek out new trees for their beauty and use. After all, the continent is better suited to introductions from North America than England! None of the French naturalists accomplished so much as Michaux and his son François-André[7] in discovering and reporting on our native plants. The social historian prizes Michaux' account of the Illinois bottoms and the frontier communities which he visited all the way from Charleston across the Appalachians to Cahokia. I follow Susan Mc-Kelvey's careful reasoning that leads to the conclusion that the elder Michaux did not cross the river and set foot in Missouri.[8] He wrote with such attention to detail he would surely have mentioned the

[5] W. H. Venable, "Some Early Travellers and Annalists of the Ohio Valley," *Ohio Archaeological and Historical Quarterly,* I (1888), 230.

[6] For a critical estimate of a recent English translation, see my review, *Science,* CXXXIX (1963), 478–479.

[7] For biographical references to the Michaux and to many other persons mentioned in this paper, see Joseph Ewan, "L'Activité des premiers explorateurs français dans le S.E. des États-Unis" in Centre National de la Recherche Scientifique, *Les Botanistes Français en Amérique du Nord avant 1850* (Paris, 1957), pp. 17–40. Michaux appears on p. 37. For an English translation of a paper in this symposium, see Chinard, "André and François-André Michaux," pp. 344–361.

[8] Susan Delano McKelvey, *Botanical Exploration of the Trans-Mississippi West 1790–1850* (Jamaica Plain, Mass., 1955), pp. 107–108.

*The French in the Mississippi Valley*

fact. Incidentally, Asa Gray twice mentioned that Michaux reached the Mississippi "as far south as Natchez,"[9] but this error was based on a memorandum of the names of several towns Michaux noted down in his journal just as a traveler might plan an itinerary but not intend it as a record of accomplishment. I raise this tittle of intelligence because it bears on the source of the type specimen of the American alligator presented to the Paris Museum of Natural History by the elder Michaux. It carries the label "killed on the borders of the Mississippi." Francis Harper has reviewed the evidence and concludes that the specimen was a trade skin since Michaux tramped the "borders of the Mississippi" only above the range of what Daudin described as *Crocodilus mississippiensis*.[10]

The discoveries of Michaux appeared in 1803 in his two-volume *Flora* which described 596 genera old and new and 1740 species, and was the first comprehensive account of North American vascular plants. Seventeen of the genera and over three hundred of the species which Michaux proposed as new are admitted as valid today—a notable record![11] His classic work on the American oaks, illustrated with black and white engravings by the talented Redouté, was a scholarly memoir with references to more than ten authors for each species treated. It is to be remembered, too, that his son François-André established a fund with the American Philosophical Society for the study of forestry.[12]

André Michaux' failure to win a place on the Lewis and Clark exploring party to the western sea, which had been planned as early as 1792, determined Adet, the French ambassador to the United States, to send an officer, Georges Henri Victor Collot, to investigate the country lying to the west of the Allegheny Mountains. Collot made the trip down the Ohio and Mississippi rivers in 1796 and thirty

---

[9] Asa Gray, "Remarks Concerning the Flora of North America," *American Journal Science*, ser. 3., XXIV (1882), 323, and Asa Gray, *Botanical Gazette*, VII (1882), 139.

[10] Francis Harper, "Some Works of Bartram, Daudin, Latreille, and Sonnini, and Their Bearing upon North American Herpetological Nomenclature," *American Midland Naturalist*, XXIII (1940), 718.

[11] F. Brendel, "Historical Sketch of the Science of Botany in North America from 1635 to 1840," *American Naturalist*, XIII (1879), 761.

[12] J. R. Schramm, "Influence—Past and Present—of François-André Michaux on Forestry and Forest Research in America," *Proceedings of the American Philosophical Society*, CI (1957), 336–343.

years later his *Voyage* was published.[13] It contains sparse notes on the forest trees, herbs, and grasses but is of such a nature as to suggest that his informant, surely Henri Peyroux,[14] had fuller information which was not used by Collot.

Certainly it was Michaux' success in America that lead the Paris Museum of Natural History to send forth Milbert, Bosc, and later Plee to the Atlantic seaboard, and Jules Remy to the Great Basin.

Audubon and then Rafinesque, both naturalists incarnate, came to the Mississippi Valley "in an ark," as those peculiar Ohio flatboats were called. The very genesis of these two figures excites the imagination! Their position in American natural history is secure. Let two friends of Audubon epitomize his place in history: first, Rev. John Bachman of Charleston: "[Audubon] taught me how much can be accomplished by a single individual who will unite enthusiasm with industry." Then there was Thomas Mayo Brewer, 1814–80, M.D., of New England, who established oölogy in this country. He wrote in April, 1857, shortly after Audubon's death, of Audubon "the gifted artist, the ardent and enthusiastic devotee alike of art and nature, the warm-hearted and kindly impulsive man."[15] Dr. James DeBerty Trudeau of New Orleans was a friend of Audubon and of Brewer and kept a close watch in his native Louisiana for novelties for Audubon.[16] Trudeau traveled in the Osage Country and painted bird

---

[13] Cf. F. Monaghan, *French Travellers in the United States 1765–1932* (New York, 1933), p. 27, for note regarding "probably a proof copy" at the New York Public Library of the original issue, printed and dated 1804, but not published.

[14] Georges Henri Victor Collot, *A Journey in North America* (Paris, 1826), I, 256: "Every season presents its peculiar vegetable productions. . . . We collected our information on this subject from Mr. Perron, who had resided in Upper Louisiana ten years, and who had been continually employed in the study of natural history." I suggest that "Mr. Perron" was Henri Peyroux de la Condrenière who wrote to Thomas Jefferson from New Madrid in 1804 mentioning his interest in natural history subjects. Caspar Wistar, as well as Collot, had difficulty with Peyroux' name, for when writing to Jefferson he mentioned Monsieur "Pirroux or Pierow" who had served as governor under Spain residing at New Madrid. Peyroux' known visits to New Orleans explain Collot's references to pomegranates, etc., growing in "Lower Louisiana," II, 175.

[15] Thomas Mayo Brewer, *North American Oölogy* (Washington, 1857, reissued 1859), preface.

[16] To references in Ewan, "L'Activité des premiers explorateurs français," p. 39, add "James Trudeau and the Recent Discovery of a Collection of Paintings of Eggs of North American Birds," *Tulane Studies in Zoology*, IX (1962), 259–263.

eggs for Brewer and together they projected an oölogy of North America, but though Brewer published the first installment, as a joint enterprise it did not materialize.

What brought the naturalists here?—the search for new products, new woods for naval uses, ship spars, and cabinet woods for the domestic arts (André Michaux was especially instructed in this quest); escape from hostile regimes; curiosities for the "cabinets" of patrons. Patrons have always been rare birds—some foresee their early extinction. William Maclure was the patron of Lesueur as well as of Thomas Nuttall. Certainly the appeal of the "New Founde World" was a magnet.

Besides governments and patrons certain social needs brought the naturalists to the Mississippi Valley. Europe's silk industry was seeking new horizons, and the American red mulberry was to be closely investigated as a food plant for the silkworm. Swedish "foundations" (we would call them today) had supported Peter Kalm in such an enterprise. A sinister disease had taken hold of European cities, first in her Mediterranean ports after the return of Columbus, and a search was pushed for antisyphilitics. "This dreadful disease," wrote Jonathan Carver in 1781, "is supposed to have originated in America, but the literary contest still remains undecided."[17] According to the logic of the day, if American by origin, then the remedy must also be American and Man must seek the healing herb, for as John Josselyn insisted "we have the Scriptures to back it that God created nothing in vain." What sarsaparilla was to the West India planter, sassafras was to the colonist to the north. Le Page du Pratz pointed out that Louisiana produces sassafras,[18] sarsaparilla, esquine— a second *Smilax* species—and "copalm" or liquidambar; thus Louisiana is to be esteemed for its full complement of medicines to meet its needs. The ethnobotany of sassafras remains to be brewed with the same vigor that maize has been researched in the great herbals.

Besides new caches for old furs, there was the search for new fur products. From the narratives it would seem that in the 1800's the

---

[17] Jonathan Carver, *Travels Through the Interior Parts of North America in the Years 1766, 1767, and 1768* (3rd ed., London, 1781), p. 392.

[18] Le Page du Pratz, *Histoire de la Louisiane* (Paris, 1758), "salsafras," as given in both legend and text, II, 36; sarsaparilla, II, 56; esquine, II, 57; and copalm, II, 28. The vernacular name in Swedish is salzenfras or saltenbras, because it makes sparks in a fire like salt; see W. L. McAtee, "Names of American Plants in Books on Kalm's Travels," *Torreya*, XLI (1941), 151–160. The note on salzenfras is on p. 156.

whole of trans-Mississippi America was swarming with beavers. Father de Smet said "the Beaver seems to have chosen this country for his own." The Paris documents of 1718 stated that "from the summit of the hill at Ouitenon [Tippecanoe County, Indiana] nothing is visible to the eye but prairies full of buffaloes."[19] Then, too, new perfumes, new dyes, new garden flowers, and after all the girasole, *Helianthus tuberosus*, that took the misshapen vernacular "Jerusalem artichoke," came from the Mississippi Valley. Perhaps there were other root crops to be found? Auguste Adolphe Lucien Trécul,[20] 1818–96, came to the Mississippi Valley in June, 1848, on a French mission to study and collect farinaceous root crops known to the native tribes that might be of use to the European farmer. His travels extended from New Orleans, which he visited both in April and again in September, 1849, to Missouri, Kansas, and Texas. He returned to France in February, 1850. Trécul's collections are preserved at Paris.

As early as 1721 or four years after the founding of New Orleans, Diron D'Artaguette reported that the country could supply quantities of medicinal plants for "all sorts of maladies," but added, "very few Frenchmen have any knowledge of them. . . . The savages who know their properties use them with success, but zealously guard the secret from the French."[21] John Duffy has brought together more information on the two brothers, Drs. Louis and Jean Prat, who came to Louisiana and evidently had genuine enthusiasms for botanical studies. The exact arrival date of Dr. Louis Prat is not

---

[19] B. W. Evermann, "Century of Zoology in Indiana, 1816–1916," *Proceedings of the Indiana Academy of Science* (1916 [1917]), p. 189.

[20] Paul Jovet and Robert Willman, "A. Trécul, botaniste français (1818–1896). Biographie sommaire. Voyage en Amérique du Nord (1848–1850)" in Centre National, *Les Botanistes français*, pp. 83–106. Another Frenchman concerned with collecting edible tubers in the upper Mississippi Valley was Christophe-Augustin Lamare-Picquot (b. 1785); see Grace Lee Nute, "Lamare-Picquot en Amérique du Nord," Centre National, *Les Botanistes français*, pp. 159–170, and "Founder of Minnesota's First Natural History Museum," *The Minnesota Naturalist* (Minneapolis), VIII (1957), 23–25.

[21] *The Rudolph Matas History of Medicine in Louisiana*, ed. John Duffy (Baton Rouge, 1958), I, 116. A continuity of contact between the two countries from the seventeenth century is notable. Gabriel Rollo in *Transactions of the American Philosophical Society*, n.s., XXXVIII (1948), 144, suggests that John Ray may have influenced Bernard de Jussieu. There was also a mutual exchange of influences between Tournefort and British botanists; Tournefort visited Oxford in 1687 where he met Jacob Bobart the younger, keeper of the physick garden. Cf. Chinard, "André and François-André Michaux," p. 345, and others.

certain but was probably the fall of 1724. He evidently brought medicinal plants from France though no list seems to be extant. By 1726 the population of New Orleans, including slaves, numbered 855. The first need was for medicinal plants to satisfy the needs of the colonists, but evidently Dr. Prat maintained a botanical garden during the ten years he remained in the colony. He returned to France in 1734 and the next year his younger brother, Dr. Jean Prat,[22] arrived to assume the duties Louis had begun. It is reported that Jean Prat came at the intervention of the distinguished Bernard de Jussieu, "founder" of the natural system of plant classification. Letters between Prat and Jussieu passed from the arrival of the physician in January, 1735, until 1746. Count Maurepas wrote to Prat in 1737 commending him on his zeal in making shipments of seeds and plants which "will be of use for the King's garden in Paris." Prat, according to John Duffy, was instructed to keep up the herb garden for the needs of the hospital, and Prat's petition for an assistant to permit him to devote more time to his botanical studies was denied. He was also instructed to pay close attention to the wax-bearing plants, which would mean *Myrica cerifera* and possibly its relatives. Dr. François LeBeau was Prat's successor at New Orleans and he was "physician and botanist of the King" until at least 1774. There is a record that Jean Louis Guérin was commissioned by the King of France to carry on plant studies in Louisiana for the royal garden in March, 1737, but that Guérin's death the following year curtailed the appointment.[23]

Not only did the Jardin des Plantes, which became in the nineteenth century the Parnassus of naturalists, welcome specimens but the British Museum sought them as well. The bird skins and dried plants of Auguste Sallé,[24] a professional natural history collector, were purchased by the British Museum. Sallé's largest collections were made in Mexico where he took 233 bird skins, but between February 11 and October 20, 1844, he was at least intermittently in New Orleans finding plant specimens in the swamps about the city. His field notes are unusually full, written in careful French.

Nicholas Marcellus Hentz,[25] born in Versailles July 25, 1797,

---

[22] *Rudolph Matas History*, ed. Duffy, p. 120.

[23] R. J. Usher, "Some Notes on the Botanical History of Louisiana," *Home Gardening* (New Orleans), I (no. 6, 1941), 12–13, 19–20.

[24] Ewan, "L'Activité des premiers explorateurs français," pp. 30, 38.

[25] H. B. Weiss, *Pioneer Century of American Entomology* (New Brunswick, N.J., 1936), pp. 99–101, *et passim*.

specialized in spiders. His father's flight from Paris for political reasons and from the country on the fall of Napoleon brought young Nicholas to America. He taught languages at the University of North Carolina and elsewhere, and studied and collected spiders at every opportunity. He moved to Covington, Kentucky, in 1830 to superintend the Female Seminary there. He was friend of both Lesueur, who loaned his etching tools that he might prepare his spider illustrations, and of Thaddeus William Harris, the entomologist, for whom Hentz named one of his sons. He married Miss Caroline Lee Whiting, the novelist and poet, whose *Mob-cap, The Parlor Serpent, Love After Marriage*, etc., were unquestionably better known to the public than his pioneer studies in arachnology.

Political exiles continued to enrich the cultural milieu through the nineteenth century. The highly popular Louis Agassiz created a waiting audience for the natural sciences through his skills in lecturing and fostering field courses, and, we may add, defending the Faith against the wiles of Darwinism. One of the forty-eighters who came under the influence of Agassiz was Jules Marcou.[26] Marcou's position in American geology is controversial, and yet he did bedrock work on several problems in stratigraphy. He met suspicions, jealousy, and governmental dishonesty. I think of Hesketh Pearson's words for the future biographer of Marcou: "I must confess to a partiality for discord since the conflict gives colour to the biographer's work."

Another exile, Leo Lesquereux,[27] Swiss-born but with French friends, contacted the moss specialist W. S. Sullivant of Columbus, Ohio, soon after his arrival in this country. Sullivant paid half of Lesquereux' expenses for a collecting trip through Tennessee, Alabama, and Georgia in 1850, about which he published commentary in his home-town journal back in Switzerland. He collaborated with Thomas Potts James in an identification guide of North American mosses and his fossil plant studies similarly opened fresh exposures.

How did the French naturalists come? Overland, as did the Michaux, father and son, or up river from New Orleans, or down the Ohio, the Illinois, or the Wisconsin. Among the Ohio voyageurs with natural history baggage first place goes to that "boatload of knowledge" that set out from Pittsburgh in 1825 in the keelboat *Philanthropist*. The destination: New Harmony, idyllically poised on the banks of the Wabash recently purchased by Robert Owen. In

[26] See G. P. Merrill, *First One Hundred Years of American Geology* (New Haven, 1924), pp. 308–310, *et passim*.

[27] Ewan, "L'Activité des premiers explorateurs français," pp. 31, 36

addition to the three brothers, Robert, David Dale, and Richard Owen there were the Maclure brothers, Gerard Troost, Thomas Say and his wife Lucy May, and Lesueur. Troost,[28] a Dutch naturalist, educated in Paris, was one of the seven founders of the Academy of Natural Sciences of Philadelphia in 1812. He served for five years as its first president. After living at New Harmony for two years Troost moved to Nashville in 1827 and remained there the rest of his life, teaching and collecting fossils, minerals, birds (including four hundred species of Java birds), and an excellent library, Alas! irretrievably lost. Proficient in several languages, he was not a recluse in the Tennessee wilderness but a polished scholar who had lived in Paris among savants. Like another unlucky naturalist, Riddell of New Orleans, Troost submitted a manuscript to Professor Joseph Henry of the Smithsonian Institution for publication, but Henry submitted it in turn to a reader who suppressed and pirated it!

Charles Alexandre Lesueur came to America accompanying William Maclure on a primarily geological foray. Lesueur had circumnavigated the globe with Péron[29] and was already a scientist and artist of distinction. He traveled the Ohio and Mississippi rivers and their tributaries down and up several times, and his unpublished observations with pertinent sketches are penetrating and accurate.[30] He stayed twenty-one years and left for Le Havre with a portfolio of the finest drawings of North American fishes that had been seen.

Arriving at New Orleans and proceeding upstream came Le Page du Pratz in 1718 and Captain Bossu in 1751. Though not natural-

[28] Ewan, "L'Activité des premiers explorateurs français," p. 39; S.W. Geiser, *Naturalists of the Frontier* (2nd ed., Dallas, 1948), pp. 261–263.

[29] An unexpected appearance of François Péron, wearing greatcoat and field cap, by the American artist, David William Moody, was published by A. B. Strong, *Illustrated Natural History* (New York, 1850), as a frontispiece. Strong's choice from many subjects to lead off a miscellany of natural history anecdotes designed for young readers opens new bibliographic questions. Moody's portrait is a copy with minor changes in background detail of the frontispiece to volume II in F. Péron's posthumous *Voyage de découvertes aux terres australes* (Paris, 1816) by C. A. Lesueur done "fifteen days before the death of his friend." In Deleuze's *Éloge* (p. 457) the circumstances of its production are elaborated: "M. Lesueur avoit exécuté le dessein de ce monument avec le goût qui caractérise tous ses ouvrages; il l'a formé de la corvette *le Geographie*, démâtée et recouverte d'une voile. Cette ingénieuse idée de donner à un homme pour tombeau le vaisseau même ou il exécuta taut de traveux, est pleine de sentiment et de délicatesse."

[30] Professor Gilbert Chinard, dean of French scholars in the United States, is editing Lesueur's journal.

ists and making no known collections, they are often quoted for their natural history observations which sometimes are unreliable. François Pagés[31] paused in lower Louisiana in 1767 on his tour around the world. Pagés proceeded upstream, as did du Pratz and Bossu, but only as far as the place of the papaw eaters, Natchitoches, and then proceeded westward over the old Camino Real to the place of the persimmon eaters, Nagadoches, Texas.

What did the naturalists find?

The garden favorite *Gaillardia* was first introduced and described in France from an unknown source in Louisiana. It was evidently sent to France about 1786 through the offices of the local consul.[32] Similarly the source of the first bird to be described from Louisiana, the loggerhead shrike, alias butcherbird or French mockingbird, is not certainly known. We have no such detailed account of American plants introduced into France as William Aiton published for England, *Hortus Kewensis*, with dates and sources.[33] But there is no doubt that the largest importation of *Magnolia grandiflora*, Louisiana's state flower, came from the vicinity of New Orleans from the early days of the port. It seems equally certain that on the basis of local intraspecific races[34] this Magnolia was reintroduced into Louisiana from French plantings, a step more easily and safely taken than seeking seeds or young plants in the difficult swamps. Bald cypress was first discovered along the lower James River of Virginia about 1610, but the French in the next century took the liveliest interest in its commercial uses. Charlevoix assigned balsamic and healing properties to the resin from *Taxodium* stems and cones. Simon Louis Pierre de Cubières[35] published a memoir on the bald cypress illustrated with a habit sketch of the curious "knees" and a drawing of their vascular anatomy. De Cubières evidently based his memoir

---

[31] Ewan, "L'Activité des premiers explorateurs français," plate IV, p. 37.

[32] Ewan, "L'Activité des premiers explorateurs français," p. 23.

[33] A. Guillaumin and V. Chaudin, "L'Introduction en France des plantes horticoles originaires de l'Amérique du Nord avant 1850" in Centre National, *Les Botanistes français*, pp. 123–135, provides dates and localities, but no collectors.

[34] R. A. Howard, "The Genus Magnolia in the West Indies," *Bulletin of the Torrey Botanical Club*, LXXV (1948), 348: "The population is extremely diverse and has been divided into several varieties. Since the chromosome count is 114 it is a high polyploid (hexaploid) population and extremely complex."

[35] Simon Louis Pierre de Cubières, *Mémoires sur le cypres de la Louisiane (Cupressus disticha, de Linné)* (Versailles, [1809]), pp. 1–30. Reprinted from *Soc. Agric. Seine-et-Oise Mem.*, 1809 (1809), 43–68. 2 plates.

on a report by Brydone, and the memoir was reviewed by the botanists Desfontaines, Thouin, and Mirbel. Adolphe Brongniart distinguished the upland cypress, *Taxodium ascendens*, in 1833. It was a pleasure to see the fine veteran of the species growing in Adanson's garden in France when I visited it in 1956, for it had not lost its distinctive habit since it was planted one hundred and fifty years before over that of the typical bald cypress growing with it.

Osage orange, bow wood tree, *bois d'arc* or *bois jaune* (from its producing a yellow dye), first enters the literature with the Lewis and Clark period though it must surely have been known to the French voyageurs some time before. Meriwether Lewis opened his letter to President Jefferson dated March 26, 1804, from St. Louis with the report he was sending some slips of Osage apples, as he called them, from Pierre Chouteau "who resided the greater portion of his time for many years with the Osage nation."[36] Lewis says the Osage apple is "perhaps a nondescript production" meaning that it had not been described in botanical literature and that it was brought to St. Louis about 1799 but that the trees had so far not produced flowers. He also told Jefferson that so highly do the Indians prize the wood for the long bow "that they travel many hundreds of miles in quest of it." Thomas Nuttall saw the Osage orange growing in Pierre Chouteau's garden in St. Louis in 1810 at which time it had come into fruit.[37] The slips Lewis sent to Jefferson from wild trees reached Bernard M'Mahon the pioneer nurseryman of Philadelphia.[38] M'Mahon planted some in front of his seed store on Fourth Street and today a row may be seen beside the Episcopal Church adjacent, which almost certainly date from that planting. Dr. George Hunter, "the renowned Man of Jefferson," also encountered the Osage orange in 1804 from St. Catherine's Landing on the Mississippi to the Washita River.[39]

Pierre Chouteau deserves a word at this point: Chouteau and the American Fur Company with which he and his sons were associated as well as the other companies in the field expedited the travels of

---

[36] *Letters of the Lewis and Clark Expedition with Related Documents 1783–1854*, ed. Donald Jackson (Urbana, 1962), pp. 170–171.

[37] Thomas Nuttall, *North American Sylva* (Philadelphia, 1865), I, 141.

[38] See Joseph Ewan, "Bernard M'Mahon (c. 1775–1816), Pioneer Philadelphia Nurseryman, and His *American Gardener's Calendar*," *Journal of the Society for Bibliography of Natural History*, III (1960), 369, 373.

[39] John Francis McDermott, *Transactions of the American Philosophical Society*, n.s., LIII, pt. 4 (1963), 94n., 111, 114, 121.

many naturalists into the wild trackless interior. Maximilian, Nuttall, Bradbury, Audubon, Nicollet, Catlin, and many others profited by the sympathetic offices of the fur traders.

One of the first plants made known from the Mississippi Valley by the French was the buffalo bur, *Solanum rostratum*, which in the wild is visited by a beetle that, with the introduction of the white potato, moved from the buffalo bur to the potato with calamitous results for the plains farmer. The collector of the original specimen of the buffalo bur from which the French botanist Dunal described *Solanum rostratum* is unrecorded. It may have been an accidental introduction as a propagule clinging like a cocklebur to an old buffalo robe.

Arriving with the French colonists from Santo Domingo and as supercargo in general were many unheralded introductions among the insects. Two Old World cockroaches, human body lice, bed-bugs, carpet beetles, dog and cat fleas, tropical rat fleas, house flies, stable flies, clothes moths, granary weevils, rice weevils, and one special notoriety, *Aedes aegypti*, the yellow-fever mosquito, all appeared almost at the founding of New Orleans and early years of the colony.[40]

The French colonists bestowed folk names on the birds and flowers they encountered in Louisiana which were counterparts of those they knew back home.[41] The indigo bunting was *évêque* or bishop, until the blue grosbeak proved to be larger, when it became the big bishop, *gran évêque*. Du Pratz noted that for good and sufficient reasons the French colonists applied the titles of ecclesiastical dignitaries to some of the more conspicuous native birds. On this principle the redbird could be named only the cardinal, with its cassock and biretta. The painted bunting became the Pope, etc. Remedies came with the language, some certainly from the French colonies in the West Indies. Every spring and fall for a week the slave children were dosed with a potion made from the seeds of "Amaranthus" (probably *Chenopodium ambrosioides*, although the identity does not seem to be recorded). Bossu mentioned the use of maidenhair as a valued pectoral remedy.

---

[40] G. H. Penn, "Brief Chronology of the History of Entomology in Louisiana," *Proceedings of the Louisiana Academy of Science*, XIV (1951), 72–87.

[41] W. L. McAtee, "Ecclesiastical Bird Names in Louisiana-French," *Names*, II (1954), 269–271.

Perhaps more important than individual garden subjects introduced was the role of the nurserymen in dispersing American discoveries abroad. Louis Claude Noisette, 1772–1849, the Paris nurseryman, for example, sold Carolina plants grown by his brother, Philippe-Stanislas,[42] at Charleston, and they were responsible for the introduction of some plants from the Michaux gardens as well.[43] David Baillie Warden, then serving as American consul in Paris, compiled a catalog of Louisiana's principal trees and shrubs, numbering 121 species including four medicinal species and six "which serve as nourishment for beasts."[44] The first garden guide for the lower Mississippi Valley was published by J. F. Lelievre, native of France, who came to St. Louis and later moved to New Orleans where from rue Royal et St. Anne in 1838 appeared the two-hundred-page duodecimo entitled *Nouveau jardinier de la Louisiane.*

A casual inspection of fourteen "Vegetables (perhaps nondescript) from the River Washita"[45] prepared by William Dunbar of Natchez and/or Dr. George Hunter, the Philadelphia chemist and mineralogist, reveals that the list is bilingual, or if with one name, it will be French. What is "L'Herbe à Joseph—a very efficacious vulnerary"? And what is "L'Herbe au Crocodile" also noticed as a "very efficacious vulnerary"? "Cabin wood" of this list, so called from its use in the weaving of Indian huts, was fully described down to its position in the Linnaean system in 1804, yet was not scientifically noticed until Professor Sargent described *Hamamelis vernalis* as new in 1911, 107 years afterward! 

We may consider French influences on Mississippi Valley insti-

---

[42] Ewan, "L'Activité des premiers explorateurs français," pp. 18, 28, 30, 37.

[43] Chinard, "André and François-André Michaux," p. 347. The activity of the Compagnie des Indes in naturalizing French plants abroad deserves close attention. The Celeste fig is the only French fruit that has persisted in Louisiana which has come to the author's notice.

[44] David Baillie Warden, *Description, statistique, historique et politique des États-Unis de l'Amérique septentrionale* (Paris, 1820), IV, 216–235, based on C. C. Robin's "Flore Louisianaise" in *Voyages dans l'interieur de la Louisiane* (Paris, 1807), III, 313–551; and C. S. Rafinesque, *Florula Ludoviciana* (New York, 1817), in turn a commentary and translation of Robin. Warden provided another catalog of 139 trees and shrubs for the country as a whole, acknowledging his debt to F. A. Michaux in its preparation (vol. V, pp. 649–660). These catalogs do not appear in the original Edinburgh edition of 1819 in this expanded form.

[45] McDermott, *Transactions of the American Philosophical Society*, pp. 120–122.

tutions springing from naturalists' energies. The first institution of higher learning, the Collège d'Orléans, in New Orleans, designed to perpetuate French influence, was founded in 1811. In 1821 Joseph Lakanal,[46] 1762–1845, who had come to New Orleans in 1815, became its first president. No natural history instruction or collections existed before his coming and though we lack precise information on this point it is likely from his interest in the sciences that some science was fostered at the college. Letters between Lakanal and French savants have survived. It is unfortunate that what promised to be a stout burgeon of culture died so soon, for the college "sank in a sea of troubles." In 1826 the Louisiana state legislature passed a law prohibiting any but an American citizen from teaching in the schools of the state and this brought the closing of the college. After some years spent on the Tombigbee River in Alabama at the French colony called the "Vine and Olive Colony," during which period he was in correspondence with Geoffrey St. Hilaire, and after another stay at a plantation he had purchased on Mobile Bay, Lakanal returned to France in 1837.

Where Lakanal had met disappointment with his American townspeople, another Frenchman Louis Frank Tainturier[47] of New Orleans found the British interested in the local natural history materials, and eight letters and some specimens passed between him and William Jackson Hooker of Kew between 1824 and 1836.

The first scientific journal in the strict sense had been founded in 1822 in Cincinnati, called *Western Quarterly Reporter of Medical, Surgical and Natural Science,* and to the first volume—it survived only into the second volume—J. Dorfeuille[48] contributed two papers on insects including one on what he called an "insect plant"—probably a Cordiceps fungus growing from the larva of a cicada, found near Natchitoches, Louisiana, and though previously known to naturalists, startling at the time, 1803. An insect changing into a plant!

The first scientific society west of the Appalachians was founded in 1837 in St. Louis and was called the Western Academy of Science. From inadequate funds it dissolved. At the turn of the century there was a physician in St. Louis, Antoine François

---

[46] Ewan, "L'Activité des premiers explorateurs français," pp. 18, 26, 27, 35.
[47] Ewan, "L'Activité des premiers explorateurs français," pp. 18, 29, 39.
[48] A Lyonnaise amateur naturalist who followed the trade of typefounder in Cincinnati, according to Geiser, *Naturalists of the Frontier,* p. 255.

Saugrain,[49] who was primarily interested in the physical sciences and medicine. However, of a library of four hundred and fifty volumes, five of his books were botanical in the strict sense and others, like Bomare's *Dictionnaire raisonne universel d'histoire naturelle,* contained general natural history.[50] But though Dr. Saugrain was active up to the year of his death in 1820, he worked alone. It was not until 1857 that the Academy of Science of St. Louis was incorporated, again with George Engelmann and Adolphus Wislizenus, who had unsuccessfully launched the Western Academy of Science, now joined by eight other citizens and Charles P. Chouteau of the fur-trading dynasty.

"They pass," writes Professor Samuel Wood Geiser, "these naturalists of the frontier, one by one, across the stage of history; some of them men of brain and heart and honor; others there are of whom we cannot speak with admiration. Yet they are not all to be gauged by the same standards; their environments, diverse and tortuous, helped to make them all. They were one in their devotion to the advancement of our common knowledge, and for their labors we are grateful."

---

[49] M. J. Klem, "History of Science in St. Louis," *Transactions of the Academy of Science of St. Louis,* XXIII (1914), 80–82. Two young Parisian friends, Piquet, "Botaniste," and Raguet, accompanied Saugrain to this country in 1787, ostensibly to explore the Ohio and Kentucky regions, carrying a letter of introduction to Benjamin Franklin. Piquet (or Pique) was wounded by Indians and drowned in an attempt to escape during the early part of the trip, March 19 to May 11, 1788. Evidently no botanical collections survived, if indeed any were made.

[50] John Francis McDermott, *Private Libraries in Creole Saint Louis* (Baltimore, 1938), pp. 90–107.

# A Kingdom Beyond the Rockies:
# The El Dorado
# of Mathieu Sagean

## Richebourg Gaillard McWilliams

On May 27, 1701,[1] the fire ship *Enflammé*[2] dropped anchor at Ship Island, bringing food and medicine for the garrison[3] at Biloxi, which was located to the north, across Mississippi Sound from the anchorage.[4] In that spring, France's new post on the lower Mississippi was a

---

[1] Sauvole to [Pontchartrain?], Biloxi, La., Aug. 4, 1701, in *Mississippi Provincial Archives, 1701–1729* (hereafter *M.P.A.*), ed. and trans. Dunbar Rowland and Albert Godfrey Sanders (Jackson, Miss., 1929), II, 11.

[2] For identification of the *Enflammé* as a fire ship, see Minister to the Sieur de St. Sulpice, Versailles, Feb. 22, 1702: AM., B2, 160:389. Archival descriptions of documents in Paris archives and libraries conform to the numbering system used in *Calendar of Manuscripts in Paris Archives Relating to the History of the French in the Mississippi Valley to 1803*, ed. Nancy Marie Miller Surrey (Washington, D.C., 1926). A few documents carry the numbers of the Bibliothèque Nationale system as used in Waldo G. Leland, *Guide to Materials for American History in the Libraries and Archives of Paris* (Washington, D.C., 1932), I.

[3] Iberville had left 122 men at Fort Maurepas, Biloxi, on his second voyage (Pontchartrain to Bégon, Fontainebleau, Nov. 3, 1700: AM., B2, 149: 149).

[4] Ship Island had been called Ile Surgères and then Ile-aux-Vaisseaux.

little over two years old. Even though Iberville, who had established Fort Maurepas at Biloxi, had revisited the post the year before, bringing more supplies, there never seemed to be enough food, and illnesses due to the unhealthful location of the post had become a problem to the commandant.[5]

If the men at Biloxi experienced a sudden surge in spirits when the *Enflammé* landed her cargo of food and medicines, back in France a small group of men more influential than those at Biloxi and close to the ministry and the crown were less concerned about revictualing the Biloxi garrison than they were about one passenger who arrived on the *Enflammé*. That man was a certain Mathieu Sagean, an illiterate Canadian[6] whom Pontchartrain,[7] the minister of marine, had sent to Biloxi to lead an expedition to the area where Sagean reported that he had located gold.

At Brest, France, Sagean had told that he had discovered and visited a nation south-southwest of the upper Mississippi and had found gold in such abundance that the natives, having so much, permitted Sagean and his companions to carry away as much as they wanted. This nation was called Acaaniba. With this great wealth the party of Frenchmen had returned from Acaaniba to Canada, from which Sagean was forced to take a long journey, by the longest route possible, that finally brought him to Brest. In Brest he told his story

---

[5] Iberville had written Pontchartrain that the 122 men had food that would last until February, 1701, and had suggested that a new supply for four to five months be sent. As for medicines, Pontchartrain approved the request for "Quelques Cordiaux que le Sr. d'Iberville demande pour eux [the men at Biloxi]" (Pontchartrain to Bégon, Fontainebleau, Nov. 3, 1700: AM., B2, 149:149; Minister to Bégon, Versailles, Nov. 24, 1700: AM., B2, 149:249). Thirty of the men were sick owing to tertian fever and sapped strength when Sauvole wrote his letter of August 4, 1701 (*M.P.A.*, II, 12).

[6] "Ledit Mathieu Sagean sçait un peu lire, mais non pas escrire." This is a statement that Mathieu Sagean made while probably under oath telling his *Relation*, later published as "Découverte et aventures de Mathieu Sagean, 1683–1699," in Pierre Margry, *Découvertes et établissements des français dans l'ouest et dans le sud le l'Amérique septentrionale (1614–1754)* (Paris, 1886), VI, 95. This narrative was dictated to the secretary of Desclouzeaux, the intendant of marine at Brest, presumably in the presence of the intendant. Michel Bégon, who interrogated Sagean at La Rochelle, referred to Sagean's narrative later as "la relation qu'il avoit dicté a Brest au Secretaire de M. Desclouzeaux" (Bégon to Villermont, La Rochelle, July 7, 1701: BN., MSS. fr., 22810:257). Sagean's narrative will be cited hereafter as *Relation*.

[7] Jérôme Phélypeaux, Comte de Pontchartrain, who succeeded his father in the ministry on September 6, 1699, and took his father's title, Comte de Pontchartrain.

of discovery to M. Desclouzeaux,[8] the intendant of marine. When Sagean's dictated account came to the attention of Pontchartrain in the spring of 1700,[9] the excitement about Sagean's fabulous discoveries began.

The tale Sagean told at Brest was, in a way, a sequel to La Salle's exploration[10] of the Mississippi River, for Sagean reported that he had been one of the La Salle party on that historic voyage. Sagean said that when the expedition reached Fort St. Louis[11] on its way back upstream, the great explorer set out for Canada with Father François, a Récollet, and fifteen men on his way to France to report his discoveries to the court. Before leaving Fort St. Louis, he had assigned the command of that French post to his lieutenant, Henri de Tonty. Among the men left at the fort was Sagean, who soon asked Tonty for permission to go on adventures and make discoveries of his own. Tonty granted the request, and Sagean set out with three bark canoes, eleven Frenchmen, and two Mahegans[12] to ascend the Mississippi River.

Two hundred and fifty leagues above Fort St. Louis, they came to a waterfall,[13] which forced them to make a six-league portage. After going forty more leagues up the river, the party stopped to hunt. During this hunting trip, being fourteen leagues from their camp on the Mississippi, they came to a river that, strangely, flowed in the direction opposite to the flow of rivers that emptied their

---

[8] For further evidence about Desclouzeaux' role in the history of Sagean's *Relation,* see Pontchartrain's instructions and the eight questions prepared by the minister for Desclouzeaux to use in testing Sagean further (Pontchartrain to Desclouzeaux, Versailles, Mar. 10, 1700: AM., B2, 146:325, and Pontchartrain to Desclouzeaux, Versailles, Apr. 7, 1700: AM., B2, 147:8).

[9] Before March 10, when Pontchartrain first requested Desclouzeaux to prepare the *mémoire,* i.e., the *Relation.* Pontchartrain's letter of March 10, 1700, is the earliest document in which I have seen Sagean's name mentioned.

[10] In showing how the narratives told or written in France about La Salle kept the explorer's name before the public, Marcel Giraud mentions Sagean as contributing in an oblique way to the memory of La Salle in *Histoire de la Louisiane française, tome 1er: Le Règne de Louis XIV, 1698–1715* (Paris, 1953), pp. 3–4.

[11] Located on Starved Rock and erected by La Salle and Tonty in 1682–83 (*Dictionary of American History,* ed. James Truslow Adams [New York, 1940], V, 161).

[12] The same as Mahican (*Handbook of American Indians North of Mexico,* ed. Frederick Webb Hodge [Washington, D.C., 1912], part 2, p. 1085).

[13] Anyone casually acquainted with the upper Mississippi in 1700 would be inclined to identify the falls as the Falls of St. Anthony.

waters into the North Sea.[14] This unfamiliar river flowed south-southwest; therefore, the French reasoned that it emptied into the South Sea.[15] Deciding to explore this stream, they returned to their camp, made the fourteen-league portage with their canoes, and launched them on the new river.

They proceeded two hundred and fifty leagues downstream, until they came to a large nation called Acaaniba,[16] whose territory extended for at least two hundred leagues. In Acaaniba, Sagean and his companions visited for about five months, so pleasant did they find this kingdom. And during their long sojourn among the Acaanibas, they learned a great deal about the blissful life led by these agreeable people. What Sagean reported to Desclouzeaux in France about the culture of the Acaanibas, he had learned partly by observation, one may assume, and partly through his two Mahegans, who served as interpreters, being adept at sign language.

The climate of Acaaniba was never too hot, never too cold, but so temperate that greenery lasted throughout the year. Perfect climate and rich soil provided everything needed by man, bird, or beast. Food for all creatures was supplied by nuts, cereals, and all fruits known in Europe or the Indies. Among these were almonds, chestnuts, potatoes, oats, maize, apples, peaches, strawberries, melons, grapes, bananas, oranges, and "lemons sweet and sour," all bigger and better than the ones known in Europe. And none of these nutritious and delicious foods growing on plant, vine, or tree required cultivation—none except maize.

Of the many animals grazing on the natural pastures on the plains, Sagean singled out several for detailed description: the *bœuf sauvage*, with a hump on its back, was domesticated as a work animal; and the *pitchitiou*, resembling the *bœuf sauvage* but smaller, having short legs and drooping ears, not only supplied the people with meat as good as mutton but also supplied them with a very fine wool, curly "comme les cheveux des nègres d'Afrique." The big red par-

---

[14] The Atlantic Ocean, for all the waters alluded to finally débouch through the St. Lawrence River.

[15] From the position of the upper Mississippi, a river running south-southwest would have to empty into the Gulf of California, which was often called the Vermilion Sea.

[16] N.B. the spelling of this name, which is the penman's spelling of a spoken name. Although Sagean never departed from this pronunciation or the penman of the *Relation* from this spelling, soon the circle of people in France who knew the *Relation* were writing the name as Caniba or Caaniba, which was a misleading linguistic error.

rots inhabiting the green forest could be tamed and trained to talk. Fowl that appealed to the appetites were chickens, partridges, ducks, geese, turkeys, and swans. In this Kingdom of Acaaniba, life was so suitable for man, Sagean observed, that the people lived to advanced age; during all his sojourn among the Acaanibas he was not aware of any deaths except those caused by the decay of old age. As there were no diseases in Acaaniba, the inhabitants had neither doctors nor surgeons.

The history of the Acaanibas[17] was preserved in monuments and in hieroglyphics done on stone and metal and, to some degree, in Acaaniba songs. King Hagaazen, a descendant of Montezuma, was the ruler of the kingdom. At one time the ancestors of this nation had inhabited a region close enough to the Spaniards to suffer from Spanish cruelties.[18] At that time the king was Attibala, who had three sons; the three princes were named Attibala, *fils*, Montezuma, and Acaaniba. When the Spaniards killed the two Attibalas, father and son, and captured Montezuma, the surviving prince, Acaaniba, fled with some of his people and established the nation that later bore his name. Acaanibas continually sang, and taught their children to sing, songs about the cruelty of Spaniards. In the short time that the Acaanibas had occupied their new land, they had flourished, and, as will be presently inferred, there had been a population explosion such as may occur in an area where people are well fed and there are no diseases to afflict them.

Although King Hagaazen was an absolute monarch, his government was ingenuous and benevolent; still, as punishment for certain seditious, cantankerous individuals, the king made use of an engine of punishment comparable to the pillory, in which the criminal lay almost entirely naked on the ground, with his head poked through a hole in the engine of punishment; there he lay, the object of derision of the people in the public square, deprived of food for the duration of the sentence. Sagean saw one person punished for two weeks in this fashion. The king, being an absolute monarch, could decree extreme punishment, which he did when a certain soldier of the

---

[17] Recalled by Sagean when he was being asked Pontchartrain's eight questions. The questions and answers appear as the *Enquête*, in Margry, *Découvertes et établissements*, VI, 162–166. This inquiry or deposition has a marked legal tone. Sagean almost certainly was under oath when he was being questioned.

[18] *Enquête*, Margry, *Découvertes et établissements*, VI, 165–166. These facts of Acaaniba history are not told in the *Relation*.

guard failed to show proper respect to a prince of the blood. Sagean reported one other instance of extreme punishment inflicted upon some girls, because of an infraction of royal decree.

As said earlier, the population of Acaaniba had grown rapidly, as may be inferred from the size of the armed forces serving the king, although Sagean made no estimate of the population itself. In the army there were nearly one hundred thousand men,[19] cavalry as well as infantry, of whom three-fourths were cavalrymen camping around Hagaazen's capital city, Miali, located six leagues from the river by which the French had come among these people.

The inhabitants of this great nation occupied both villages and cities; village houses were constructed of wood and bark; the cities were enclosed by palisades and earthworks and were further protected by forts, although the peace-loving King Hagaazen was at war with no nation, not even with the Spaniards, whom Acaanibas hated. But no Spaniard had so far entered Hagaazen's domain; Sagean and his companions were, of course, the first Europeans to visit this nation.

Acaaniba society was stratified to this extent: King Hagaazen and, presumably, the princes of the blood, were the superior class; otherwise, the people enjoyed equality, although two marks of status were evident. Hirsute people, who were recognized to be the handsomest, the most beautiful,[20] had status, and so did people with long fingernails. Surpassing all others in length of nails was the king himself.[21]

These people worshipped idols and believed in the transmigration of souls. One animal called bichihilly, meaning "la beste belle"—a big jet-black ape with a white ruff that surrounded its head, creating the effect of raising the ape's chin—was held in such veneration by the Acaanibas that no one dared to kill a single one of these apes. To kill one was an offense considered more heinous than homicide; it might be patricide or even "avocide," for the Acaanibas commonly said that the white-ruffed apes might be their ancestors and

---

[19] An army of one hundred thousand men suggests a population of over a half-million souls—perhaps a population nearly as great as the Indian population (in 1492) in all the area of the present-day United States.

[20] Most Indians had an attitude contrary to this one; indeed, Indians were generally depilators.

[21] Toward the end of the *Relation*, Sagean tells of living for a while on Formosa, where he met the grand mandarin and some lesser mandarins (Margry, *Découvertes et éstablissements*, VI, 155–157).

that perhaps they, too, after death might return in the form of apes. Despite the idolatry and the veneration of apes, there was still some evidence that the people believed in a Creator: each morning after the king and his people had shown adoration to their idols, they began to shout, "Ibella ouac Sima houally!" and from sunup to sundown continually shouted the same words, which were similar to an invocation of the One who made everything,[22] as Acaanibas put it.

The Acaanibas liked to dance, to smoke tobacco, and to drink palm wine, although they disapproved of intoxication. They had big appetites and ample food with which to indulge them, and they did indulge by eating both day and night, but at no fixed time.

The men practiced polygamy, each man being permitted to have as many wives as he desired. Parents often arranged engagements for their daughters when the girls were quite young. Fidelity was demanded, and if a married woman or an engaged girl broke the law of fidelity and the infidelity was discovered by husband or fiancé, the girl ran the risk of losing her own life, and the gallant could lose his. But single women and unpromised girls could indulge in promiscuity without criticism. The king himself, far from being a celibate, could hardly be emulated by any polygamist, however ambitious. King Hagaazen had many wives who occupied palace rooms adjoining the king's apartment, which was three stories high. No one entered his quarters except his wives, and then only the one chosen for the night. Next morning the favored wife was rewarded by being given the privilege of cooking the king's breakfast in her room and then serving it in the king's room, where she ate with him.

Sagean thought Acaaniba men were ugly; they were sunburned, and their heads were unnaturally long and narrow, deformed by the Acaaniba mothers' practice of pressing boy children's heads between two boards. "Mais pour les femmes"—ah, what a difference! In the first place, they were white, as white and as beautiful as European women, and were given to modesty, "se cachant certains endroits." The only criticism Sagean offered of the women was that they had huge ears, which they pierced and loaded with bones and heavy gold

---

[22] The use of the capital *S* on *Sima* suggests the pious nicety that Sima is the true deity. Not even a learned Jesuit could have identified the word meaning God in the shout of the Acaanibas.

rings. Both the women and the men liked the French visitors and regaled them with the *agréable* as well as the useful. King Hagaazen vied with his subjects in making life *agréable* for his guests: he decreed that any girl—presumably, a girl not engaged or married—who was indifferent to the visitors would be put to death. When one of Sagean's companions, Turpin, who was inclined to get drunk on palm wine, was rebuffed by six girls, he, in his frustration, registered a complaint. The six girls soon found that the king had meant what he had decreed: all six were stabbed to death.

Such hospitality reached its zenith in the king's treatment of Sagean. As Sagean makes no mention of his own indulgence in palm wine, perhaps he was more acceptable than Turpin as lover or husband; too, Sagean had the distinction of being the leader of the expedition. Whatever the cause, King Hagaazen offered his own daughter, twelve years old, to Sagean, but Sagean, giving the excuse that he would have to be leaving soon, declined this proposal, which probably was meant to be a tender of a marriage contract. The king's reaction to the rejection was not anger, but patient persistence: he would, he said, save his daughter until Sagean could return to Acaaniba.

In such a paradise as Acaaniba, perhaps one should not expect people to work for a living. Although Sagean's report shows him to be strangely indifferent to the way such a large population made use of their time, he did describe some works of art that had to be the creations of artificers and artisans. Weavers surely had to be busy producing the garments to clothe the Acaanibas, and some specialist on furs had to prepare the ermine worn by the king. There were sculptors, too, whose medium was not stone but gold. Before the palace stood two idols, statues of heroic size, both having hideous faces. One was the statue of a conquering Acaaniba king, shown as a warrior armed with lance, arrows, and quiver, and having one foot on the ground, the other raised while the warrior's hand grasped the horse he was mounting. In his mouth this warrior king held a carbuncle, or ruby, as big as a goose egg. Sagean reasoned that the big red stone had to be a carbuncle because it shone brilliantly at night, like fire. The other idol, or statue, was of a woman, some former empress or queen, riding a horse, or unicorn, having one horn six feet long in the center of its forehead. Around this equestrienne were statues of four dogs. Every idol, every statue, was of massive gold.

In the king's apartment, or cabinet, where only his wives could visit him, but where Sagean was permitted to go on one occasion, the artificers had used wood and gold to create the great room, twenty-eight by thirty feet, and three stories high. The walls, eighteen feet high, were constructed of gold, not gold sheets or thin gold plates, but gold tiles or panels, bound together by golden clamps and gold rods. Of pure gold were the trumpets used by the army as well as the solid parts of drums, and all utensils were of pure gold.

Although the ermine worn by the king and the great ruby clamped in the mouth of the ugly idol suggested other wealth, Sagean's curiosity was directed chiefly to the source of all the gold that dazzled him at every turn. Although he did not get to go to the gold fields himself, two of his companions went, along with some Acaanibas, and from the two Sagean obtained a description of the location of the mines and of the mining methods employed.

The gold lay as nuggets in the beds of streams into which overflowing streams had washed it from hills and ravines in the mountains. Fortunately, the beds of the streams in which the nuggets lay were dry for four months each year; mining, then, meant picking up the nuggets from the dry beds of streams.

Sagean's companions told him that their journey to the mines and back had required three days, as the gold field was close to Hagaazen's capital city, Miali, which was only six leagues west-northwest of the river by which the French had come. The name of this river, Milly, meant *rivière d'or;* and the River Milly was wider and deeper than the Mississippi.[23] Although he had not reported such in his *Relation,* Sagean believed that he had seen gold dust along the banks of the River Milly.

If Sagean reported little evidence of work being done by the people in Acaaniba, he gave ample evidence to show that gold was the chief business of the kingdom. The people, he was sure, trafficked in gold with some nation, but he could not learn which one, unless it was the Japanese. He was told by the people that the distance from Acaaniba to their market was six moons' travel. Sagean himself witnessed the departure of one caravan—three thousand oxen

---

[23] The River Milly and the comparison of it with the Mississippi do not appear in the *Relation,* but in the *Enquête* (Margry, *Découvertes et établissements,* VI, 164). The *Enquête* did not discredit Sagean's *Relation;* instead, it offered Sagean the opportunity to add some attractive details he had not thought of before.

laden with gold[24] convoyed by three thousand cavalrymen bearing shields and armed with lances, arrows, and daggers. This commerce made use of at least one modern business practice: the leaders of the caravan carried bills of lading written in hieroglyphics on bark.

When Sagean's five-month sojourn in this paradise, this el dorado, came to an end and the French took leave of the king, King Hagaazen not only exacted from them a promise to return to Acaaniba in thirty-six moons, but specified the items of trade the French should bring back with them: coral, glass beads, porcelain, and other baubles to exchange for gold, which meant little to the Acaanibas because they had so much.

On departing from this generous, ingenuous king, the French were permitted to carry away all the gold they wanted. Accordingly, each Frenchman took sixty bars weighing about four pounds each.[25] To help the French with their heavy loads and to show them proper respect, certainly not to protect them, the king sent an escort of two hundred cavalrymen, who carried the 2880 pounds (*c.*) of gold to the three canoes left on the River Milly and, even more, rode for five days along the bank while the French paddled upstream. Finally, the escort bade the French adieu with horrible howls.

On the return journey, the French travelers were forced to throw away some of their gold, fourteen bars each, as sixty bars had proved to be too heavy a load for each man. Once they reached Montreal, Sagean discovered that his parents[26] and five brothers and

---

[24] In 1866 this three-thousand-ox load of gold in one caravan was estimated to weigh two million pounds and to be worth $560,000,000. In 1866, when the ox was common enough as a draft animal, there were, of course, men who could make authoritative estimates of what one ox could carry—in this reckoning, 667 pounds. The authority who made this estimate must remain unknown; I assume that he was the anonymous translator of a four-page extract from Sagean's *Relation*—an extract that had been among the papers of Father Léonard. Although the anonymous author knew almost nothing about Mathieu Sagean, he was the first writer in America to mention the name Sagean in a journal. See "Matthew Sagean and His Adventures" (anon.), *Historical Magazine*, X (Mar., 1866), 65–71. The estimate of the worth of the gold is given in a footnote, p. 67.

[25] The two Mahegans, who wanted no gold, were puzzled by the desires of the French—until the French told them that the gold would be used to make pots (*Relation*, Margry, *Découvertes et établissements*, VI, 110).

[26] According to his own statement, Sagean's parents were Jean Sagean, from Bordeaux, and Marie Larrante, from La Rochelle, who settled in the Lachine quarter of the Island of Montreal, where Mathieu was born (*Relation*, Margry, *Découvertes et établissements*, VI, 95). Note 1 on the same page, identified as a note from the manuscript, further identifies Marie Larrante,

sisters had been killed in an Iroquois irruption. After participating in this war to the extent of taking more than ten Iroquois scalps, Sagean proceeded with his companions in three canoes toward the mouth of the St. Lawrence, hoping to catch a French ship for France.[27] When they encountered an English corsair, *la Sainte Rose,* commanded by Captain Wilmessen from New York, all the French along with their gold were seized. The cruel and sadistic English captain, Wilmessen, not only appropriated their gold but also killed six of Sagean's companions. Sagean had had the forethought to cut some strips of gold from an ingot and tie them in his hair for concealment against future needs.

From this point on, his narrative turns into a story of hardships and adventures aboard one ship after another: he wandered down the Atlantic coast, to the West Indies, to the Cape Verde Islands, down the west coast of Africa and up the east coast, into the Red Sea, and by way of India to the East Indies. He participated in the life of a corsair, was made aware of cannibalism among Europeans starving in an open boat, and visited Portuguese and Mohammedan settlements. His *Relation* gives the names of ships and the names of their captains. The end of all of this adventure around the world was a shipwreck on the coast of Formosa that forced him to stay among the Chinese on the island until an English ship arrived nearby, took him aboard, and carried him to London on August 17, 1699. For two months, with the aid of seven guineas given him by the English captain, he lived in London until he could get passage on a ship bound for Nantes.

This ship put him ashore at Perros, from which he made his way to Brest, where he promptly called on M. Desclouzeaux,[28] the intendant of marine, to pay his respects.

---

the mother, as Marie Rende: "C'est Marie Rende; elle était de Marans." For a description of the massacre of Sagean's family, see *Relation,* Margry, *Découvertes et établissements,* VI, 112–113.

[27] On the journey to Canada, the two Mahegans had stayed among the Miamis (*Relation,* Margry, *Découvertes et établissements,* VI, 114).

[28] Two months after Sagean's arrival in London on August 17, 1699, would be October 17, 1699, the approximate date when Sagean called on Desclouzeaux, the intendant at Brest. Here is Sagean's statement, which, having been dictated in the presence of Desclouzeaux, should be accurate: "Il [Sagean] a eu l'honneur, à son arrivée, d'y rendre ses respects à M. Desclouzeaux, Intendant de la marine, et s'est enrôlé dans la compagnie de La Vieuville pour pouvoir subsister, en attendant quelque occasion de s'en retourner en Canada ou d'aller à la Louisiane, si la Cour trouve à propos de l'y envoyer" (*Relation,* Margry, *Découvertes et établissements,* VI, 161–162).

Between Sagean's arrival at Brest in late autumn, 1699, and March 10, 1700,[29] he had told about his discoveries, probably to Desclouzeaux, the intendant, for the news of his discoveries had already reached Pontchartrain. On March 10 Pontchartrain wrote Desclouzeaux that he was awaiting the *mémoire* Desclouzeaux must write about the discoveries made by a Canadian soldier by the name of Mathieu Sagean. The minister, already quite interested, requested a detailed account that would enable him to separate the true from the false. The intendant wrote, or had his clerk write, Sagean's dictated narrative, which he sent to Pontchartrain on March 29 or 30, for on April 7, 1700,[30] the minister, writing back to Desclouzeaux, showed himself to be familiar enough with the *Relation* to compose eight questions[31] that Desclouzeaux must use in holding an *enquête*,[32] a legal inquiry, about the truthfulness of Sagean's fabulous story. Pontchartrain instructed the intendant to hold Sagean at Brest until he could be transferred to the port from which he would be sent to the Mississippi. Even though he seemed to have made a decision, Pontchartrain still had some doubts and exercised caution in insisting upon the *enquête:* he wanted more information and wanted to test the veracity of the wonderful *Relation*, which he had just read.

Because Desclouzeaux as an intendant had judiciary powers, he almost certainly put Sagean under oath[33] while he was answering the eight questions. Having acted promptly on his superior's orders, Desclouzeaux finished the *enquête* and sent it back to Pontchartrain a

---

[29] Pontchartrain to Desclouzeaux, Versailles, Mar. 10, 1700: AM., B2, 146: 325.

[30] Pontchartrain to Desclouzeaux, Versailles, Apr. 7, 1700: AM., B2, 147:8. Writing from Versailles, Pontchartrain says: "J'ay receu vos lettres des 29 et 31 du mois passé avec les papiers qui y estoient jointes . . . J ay recu [?] la relation des voyages de M. de [?] Sagean . . . faites le rester a Brest Jusqua nouvel ordre."

[31] Included in the letter of April 7.

[32] In a letter to the Abbé Dangeau, August 15, 1701, Villermont, the king's counselor, refers to "l'article qui regarde la déposition de Mathieu Sagean," which the counselor had sent to the Abbé Bernou (extract in Margry, *Découvertes et établissements*, VI, 173). The important word in the quoted passage is *déposition*, which indicates the legal fashion in which the *enquête* was conducted and in which the *Relation* had been dictated by Sagean under Desclouzeaux' supervision.

[33] The language of the *Enquête* (Margry, *Découvertes et établissements*, VI, 162–166) is just as legal in tone as the *Relation* is in certain places. Here is a sample of the legal language in the *Relation:* "Il proposa audit Sagean et ses camarades de se joindre à luy pour aller entrer par ladite embouchure dans ledit fleuve" (Margry, *Découvertes et établissements*, VI, 130).

week later. The replies Sagean made to one of the eight questions, the shrewdest one, show what a sharp mind and brilliant memory the minister and the intendant were trying to test.

As an attempt to identify witnesses who could verify or impeach Sagean's story, one question requested him to name the Canadians that had been with him on his journey. The answer was that there were four Canadians, including himself; but Sagean could not give the names, he said, except in Algonquin; he had known the three Canadians only by their Algonquin warrior names. It was customary in that country, he explained, for men to take warrior names when they set out to seek their fortunes, in order to make themselves more acceptable among Indians. He readily gave the warrior names of all four Canadians: his own, Routine, meaning "the Wind"; Micana, meaning "Duchemin";[34] Maramègue, meaning "Fish"; and Garahau, the meaning of which Sagean could not recall. Besides Sagean, only Micana, that is, Duchemin, was alive—perhaps; Sagean had left him at night in a prison in New York when he leaped from the wall and escaped. Maramègue had been killed by the English captain of the corsair that seized the explorers' gold, and Garahau had lost his life in the Iroquois irruption. As for the seven other companions, Frenchmen from the provinces, Sagean accounted for the deaths of five just as he had reported in the *Relation*. The remaining two Frenchmen, La France and Barrois, had stayed at the prison in New York, La France because he broke both legs in leaping from the wall and Barrois because he decided not to try to escape with Sagean. Although this answer must have been frustrating to both the minister and the intendant, they at least had the names of three men[35] whom they might locate as witnesses to Sagean's discoveries. The task was not to be easy.

---

[34] I have left this name untranslated for two reasons: in the first place, it is hard for one to translate, thinking of it in terms of the Algonquin warrior's life; in the second place, Pontchartrain himself remembered this name and referred to it when he wrote a letter to Martinique in an attempt to locate a witness to Sagean's discoveries.

[35] Micana ("Duchemin") and Barrois and La France. All other companions except the two Mahegans, who stayed among the Miamis, had been killed in one way or another. Turpin, who liked the palm wine of Acaaniba, had drowned during a shipwreck on the Barbary Coast. A *métis* named Turquoy, a native of Acadia, seems not to have made the journey to Acaaniba but to have joined the party later in Canada; he was killed by Captain Wilmessen aboard the corsair (*Enquête*, Margry, *Découvertes et établissements*, VI, 162–164).

Suddenly a clue developed about where one of Sagean's surviving companions might be located. A captain of a ship, Captain Belle-Issue, began to talk at Brest about a stranded Canadian who had come to him in Martinique, two and a half years earlier, seeking aid and a passage to France. Although Belle-Issue could not recall the man's name, he remembered well enough the strange tale the Canadian had told him. Failing to win the support of Belle-Issue, the Canadian stranger departed to call on the governor of the French Islands, the Marquis d'Amblimont, then staying at Fort Royal, Martinique, and to try to get help from him. While the Canadian was gone, Belle-Issue sailed away. The report he gave of the strange story told in Martinique[36] finally reached Pontchartrain; then the minister found himself examining an almost perfect abstract of Sagean's Acaaniba story.

Pontchartrain wrote a rebuke[37] to the Marquis d'Amblimont for failing to send the Canadian to him and ordered Amblimont to locate him in the area, if he could, and send him to St. Domingue to await further orders. This man, thought Pontchartrain, was the witness he had been lacking.[38] Not once, judging by the letter to Amblimont, did the suspicion enter Pontchartrain's mind that the Canadian stranded in Martinique a few years before might have been Sagean himself, telling his Acaaniba story, singing for his supper[39] and a passage to France.

Desclouzeaux had not just held Sagean at Brest, as he had been ordered to do; he had imprisoned him in the Château de Brest for no specified reason. Sagean had been in the Château for some time[40]

---

[36] "Un Canadien, à la Martinique, fait au Capitaine Belle-Issue un récit analogue à celui de Mathieu Sagean" (Margry, *Découvertes et établissements*, VI, 166–169).

[37] Le Ministre de la Marine à M. le Marquis d'Amblimont, 28 avril 1700 (Margry, *Découvertes et établissements*, VI, 169–170).

[38] Barrois or La France or Micana identified by Pontchartrain as "Duchemin" (Margry, *Découvertes et établissements*, VI, 169–170).

[39] In the *Relation* (p. 134) Sagean said that he had been to Cuba, St. Domingue, and Puerto Rico with the corsair commanded by Captain Cras. He had been quite close to Martinique. If the stranded Canadian was indeed Sagean, he may have had, besides the purpose of getting a handout, a strange compulsion to tell his story of Acaaniba, somewhat like the Ancient Mariner's compulsion, but for a different reason. Sagean's inclination to tell his story is revealed by Pontchartrain in the letter of instructions he wrote to Sauvole about Sagean: "Il dit qu'il a esté chez une nation ou il y a grande abondance d'or; il vous en entretiendra luy meme ainsy je ne vous en dis rien de plus" (Minister to Sauvole, Versailles, Nov. 24, [1700]: AM., B2, 149:282).

[40] Pontchartrain to Clairambault, [Versailles?], Sept. 22, 1700: AM., B2, 148:523.

when Pontchartrain ordered that he be transferred to La Rochelle so that Iberville could interrogate him. And Pontchartrain warned against Sagean's trying to escape along the way.[41]

The minister wanted Iberville to interrogate[42] Sagean because Iberville knew Canada well and knew Lachine, Sagean's birthplace. Although Iberville's report of his interview seemed satisfactory to Pontchartrain,[43] the results appear to be no better than Desclouzeaux' report of the *enquête;* for Pontchartrain asked Iberville to quiz Sagean again, this time specifically about China. During the first interview, Iberville had apparently failed to get Sagean even to tell who he was. In his next letter to Iberville, Pontchartrain sent word to Bégon, the intendant at La Rochelle, to lock Sagean up again to force him to tell his real name. Furthermore, the minister, in some frustration and calling upon more authority, wrote Bégon directly in the name of the king to lock Sagean up until further notice.[44]

All of Pontchartrain's measures—the *enquête,* the two interrogations by Iberville, the imprisonment, the locking up again and again—show that the minister was cautious about accepting Sagean's discoveries; nevertheless, he was planning to send Sagean to the Mississippi just the same.[45] While Sagean waited, incarcerated though he was, he was probably well treated and well fed. The imprisonment may have been no more than a measure to provide protective custody for an illiterate man who happened to have precious information important to the crown.

The story Sagean had started had created some excitement among a small circle of men interested in the Mississippi and in

[41] "Il est necessaire que vous fassiés passer ce soldat [Sagean] à Rochefort par la première occasion sure que vous aurés. [R]ecommandez bien à celui que vous en chargerés d'avoir soin qu'il ne s'evade."

[42] "Il [Iberville] pourra nous dire plus certainement que personne si on doit faire quelques fonds sur le raport de cet homme" (Pontchartrain to Desclouzeaux, Versailles, Aug. 25, 1700: AM., B2, 148:297).

[43] Pontchartrain to Iberville, Fontainebleau, Nov. 3, 1700: AM., B2, 149: 155; Pontchartrain to Bégon, Fontainebleau, Nov. 3, 1700: AM., B2, 149:149.

[44] For the whole discussion of interviewing Sagean, making him tell his real name, and keeping him under lock and key, see these two letters: Pontchartrain to Iberville, Fontainebleau, Nov. 3, 1700: AM., B2, 149:155; Pontchartrain to Bégon, Fontainebleau, Nov. 3, 1700: AM., B2, 149:149.

[45] "Le Roy trouvoit bon que vous l'envoyassiez [Sagean] au Mississipy par le premier vaisseau que vous y ferez passer" (Pontchartrain to Bégon, Versailles, Nov. 17, 1700: AM., B2, 149:216). The title of section IV, of Margry, volume VI, in which Sagean's *Relation* is printed, admits that, although the *Relation* seems "extraordinaire," yet, "aux yeux de l'Administration, mêlé de faits dont elle reconnait la verité" (Margry, *Découvertes et établissements,* VI, 93).

Louisiana in general. They were chiefly men of learning or of responsible position, close to the ministry or the crown. The circle was probably kept small because the minister did not want Sagean's discoveries to be known.[46] The important men in the informed group were Villermont, king's counselor; the abbés Bernou and Dangeau; and Father Léonard, the librarian of the convent of the Petits Pères in Paris. Father Charlevoix,[47] whose interest may have developed later, showed the *Relation* first to Delisle and then to the Duke of Orleans, after he became regent.

The manuscript of the *Relation* became important to these men. How many copies there were is unknown. Everybody who did not have a copy or an extract wanted one. Perhaps there were between one and three copies; the original was in Pontchartrain's possession[48] for a while; he sent it to Iberville to read.[49] La Touche seems to have had another copy.[50] The king's counselor, Villermont, had to content himself with an extract, sent him from Brest.[51] The librarian, Father Léonard, owned an extract[52] at some time, and so did the Abbé Bernou.[53]

---

[46] For evidence that secrecy was desired, if not attained, in the Sagean affair, see "Conclusion à Tirer du Voyage de Mathieu Sagean," extrait d'une lettre de M. de Villermont à M. l'abbé de Dangeau (Margry, *Découvertes et établissements*, VI, 173–174). For further evidence, taken apparently from manuscript notes on Father Léonard's extract from the *Relation*, see "Matthew Sagean and His Adventures" (anon.), pp. 65–71. The editor and translator of this extract gained the impression that the French administration was unwilling for more than the few pages to be extracted.

[47] Father Charlevoix went to the Mississippi some twenty years later, hoping to find a waterway through North America. He had studied Sagean's *Relation*, as the manuscript printed by Margry must show. See Margry, *Découvertes et établissements*, VI, 93: "Ce Mémoire, Communiqué par le Père Charlevoix à Delisle, est soumis plus tard par lui au Duc D'Orléans, Régent."

[48] Informative abstract of Bégon to Villermont, Romegou, Aug. 7, 1701: BN., MSS. fr., 22810:304, and Pontchartrain to Desclouzeaux, Versailles, Apr. 7, 1700: AM., B2, 147:8. See also Pontchartrain to Iberville, [Versailles], Sept. 22, 1700: AM., B2, 148:518.

[49] Pontchartrain to Iberville, [Versailles], Sept. 22, 1700: AM., B2, 148:518.

[50] Informative abstract of Bégon to Villermont, Romegou, Aug. 7, 1701: BN., MSS. fr., 22810:304, given in Surrey, *Calendar;* and extract of Villermont's letter to Dangeau, Aug. 15, 1701, Margry, *Découvertees et établissements*, VI, 173–174.

[51] "Il faudra que je me contente de l'extrait qu'on m'en a envoyé de Brest" (extract of Villermont's letter to Dangeau, Aug. 15, 1701, Margry, *Découvertes et établissements*, VI, 173–174).

[52] "Matthew Sagean and His Adventures" (anon.), pp. 65–71.

[53] BN., MSS. Clair., 1016. Informative abstract, Leland, *Guide to Materials*, p. 177.

These men were all far from being foolish men, yet they tee-tered between faith and doubt in Sagean's story. They attempted to prove him right by means of their scholarship, and one of the first errors they made was to use a variant spelling for Acaaniba: they began to use *Caniba*, which Sagean used in neither the *Relation* nor the *Enquête;* he always said Acaaniba. The *Caniba* form was espe-cially misleading in the hands of scholars searching for supporting evidence in books, because *Caniba* is only a variant of Spanish *Canibal. Caniba* was likely to be found in works of early Spanish exploration among American Indians.[54] Furthermore, the French scholars not only searched for *Caniba* but obtained books and fol-lowed leads about the nearness of Acaaniba to Japan.

There was a need for secrecy[55] about Sagean, now being held in protective custody. Suppose Sagean was telling the truth about Acaaniba, as he was about his further travels about the world. Some evidence on the extract owned by Father Léonard, possibly manu-script notes, made a nineteenth-century writer conclude that the few pages from the *Relation* were all the French government would allow "to go forth." One of Villermont's letters, to the Abbé Dangeau, shows the need of the secrecy in which the Sagean affair had been referred and entrusted to the abbé. Needless to say, such an exciting secret, which apparently Sagean was willing to tell anyone who had something to give in return, could hardly be kept. The importance that several of the circle attached to Sagean's discoveries is patent in the title of the extract owned by the Abbé Bernou: "Account of the Finest Discovery Made in More Than a Thousand Years, by the Sieur Sagean, of the Kingdom of Caaniba [*sic*]."[56]

[54] Although not listed in most dictionaries, the word *caniba* appears in *A New English Dictionary on Historical Principles,* ed. Sir James Murray (Oxford, 1893), II, 71, where it is given as a variant of Spanish *canibales,* a plural form for the Carib Indians. When Columbus heard the name of the Carib Indians in Cuba, he explained it as "los de Caniba." He associated *Caniba* with the Grand Khan, saying, "Caniba no es otra cosa sino la gente del Gran Can [*sic*]." *Handbook of American Indians North of Mexico,* ed. Hodge, part 2, p. 83, gives *Canibas* (also *Cannibas* and *Kanibals*) as a name of the Norridgewock Indians in Maine. Sagean may have heard the word in Maine and have adjusted it slightly to his purpose. He had been in New England.

[55] In writing about the Sagean discoveries, Villermont used these words: ". . . le secret, soubs lequel vous me mandés que cette affaire vous a esté confiée et renvoyée" (extract of Villermont's letter to Dangeau, Aug. 15, 1701, Margry, *Découvertes et établissements,* VI, 173–174).

[56] "Relation de la plus belle découverte que l'on ayt faite depuis plus de mil ans, par le Sieur Sagean, du Royaume de Caaniba" (Leland, *Guide to Ma-terials,* p. 177). N.B. that M. Mathieu Sagean is, in this title, Sieur Sagean and that the syntax of the title practically makes him a nobleman of that realm.

Perhaps the average Frenchman would not have been inclined to believe Sagean's description of a kingdom where the remnant followers of Prince Acaaniba had, in less than two hundred years, increased to a population of more than a half-million white people, judging by the hundred thousand men in the army, and where gold was so plentiful that the yearly caravan must have transported more than a billion dollars' worth of gold to a market, possibly Japan. Ironically, the men that appraised Sagean's discoveries were so intelligent, so curious about the world, that they were deceived[57] by Sagean's story.

There were more specific reasons, too: (a) for a long time the ministry and the scholars in France had been intermittently active in trying to discover a waterway through North America, as the name Lachine on the Island of Montreal always reminds one; (b) the area west of the Mississippi and north of Spanish settlements in the southwest was unknown in 1700 and would, in great part, remain unexplored until after the Louisiana Purchase; (c) the French, who had never made a great gold strike in North America, were jealous of Spanish successes among the Incas, the Aztecs, and the Chibcha Indians[58] of Colombia; (d) English explorers and traders having reached the Mississippi River, the French were suspicious that the English had found gold west of the river and were bringing it back to their settlements on the Atlantic coast;[59] (e) Pontchartrain and Villermont had little to show for the two French ventures on the lower Mississippi—the La Salle debacle on the Texas coast and Iberville's post at Biloxi—except some worthless freshwater pearls, different kinds of hides and some furs of an inferior quality, a shipment or so of timber and ores of questionable value, plus some cunning but

---

[57] Villermont, king's counselor, concluded that the Acaanibas' commerce with other parts of the world (Sagean had mildly suggested Japan) by means of the three thousand oxen in a caravan proved that the four parts of the world were one continent (extract of Villermont's letter to Dangeau, Aug. 15, 1701, Margry, *Découvertes et établissements*, VI, 173-174). To support this conclusion, Villermont cited the story of a Mexican woman who, after being abducted into slavery in Mexico, was passed from nation to nation until she finally arrived in China, having crossed only a narrow *détroit* of the sea on her way to the Orient.

[58] The original el dorado, the myth of the gilded man, had already originated near or at little Lake Guatavita, close to Bogotá, among the Chibcha Indians.

[59] Bégon to Villermont, La Rochelle, July 27, 1702; brief abstract of BN., MSS. fr., 22811:198, given in Surrey, *Calendar*, I, 90.

valueless animals indigenous to America;[60] they needed a bonanza of gold to vindicate their counsel and decisions and to bring riches to a royal treasury depleted by the extravagances at Versailles; and, finally, (f) Villermont and the learned clerics were ready to exercise their learning by putting it to some practical as well as religious and scientific use in exploiting Louisiana.

Sagean's motive in telling his story is clear enough:[61] he wanted to persuade some official to feed him and send him back to America, either to Canada or Louisiana—to any spot on the Mississippi, he bravely declared, promising to build canoes on the river and lead a party to his el dorado. Although he liked storytelling for its own sake, as shown in the imagination displayed in his *Relation* and exemplified by his artistic selectivity to win an audience, his was primarily a limited, selfish motive, perhaps with some hope of gaining personal fame.

He deceived minds better than his own by his skill in narration, his cunning in covering his tracks, his appeal to what Frenchmen wanted, and his amazing memory, which retained an infinite variety of facts about geography, shipping, and the rivers and ports of the world and was accurate enough to withstand the interrogations he was subjected to by Pontchartrain, Desclouzeaux, and Iberville. In the *Relation* and the *Enquête*, such details as the Aztec ancestry of King Hagaazen, the long fingernails as a status symbol, the yearly caravan of three thousand oxen making the six-moon journey to a market, possibly Japan—all must have appealed strongly to those who read the *Relation* when the world was much bigger and stranger than it is today. And the simplicity of the Acaanibas,[62] especially King Hagaazen's request that, when the French returned, they should bring trinkets and baubles to trade for Acaaniba gold, surely

---

[60] From Fontainebleau, Pontchartrain wrote Iberville, giving him permission to come to court and asking him to bring "avec vous tout ce que vous avez ramassé de curieux dans le voyage que vous venez de faire et ce qui vous reste d'animaux" (Pontchartrain to Iberville, Fontainebleau, Nov. 3, 1700: AM., B2, 149:155).

[61] *Relation*, Margry, *Découvertes et établissements*, VI, 111.

[62] Delisle's Carte de la Louisiane, 1718, shows a legend in which one may perceive some of the condescension that the European assumed toward the Indian's innocence of the value of gold: "Vers ce lieu au rapport des Indiens les Espagnols le passent à gué sur leurs chevaux le Missouri allant traiter avec les Nations Situées vers le Nordouest d'ou ils aportent du fer jaune cest ainsi quils lexpriment."

invoked cupidity in the hearts of the men who learned of the secret discovery. Although no document supports the supposition, there is still the possibility that Sagean intended for the incontinence of Acaaniba girls to attract all men with a prurient attitude toward *amour*.

The reception Sagean got at Biloxi is in cruel contrast to the response in France.[63] More than two months after Sagean arrived on the fire ship *Enflammé*, Sauvole, the commandant at Biloxi, described him as being very much embarrassed. A number of people at the fort, having known Sagean in Canada as an enlisted soldier, contradicted him about his claiming to have gone with La Salle to the mouth of the Mississippi and denied that he was the son of a sergeant named Duplessis, "as he tried to assure me," Sauvole wrote.[64] Nevertheless, even in the presence of men who possessed the information to impeach him, to expose the golden hoax, Mathieu Sagean, despite the embarrassment, clung to his story of Acaaniba, declaring that he would go back by the Missouri River to find it again.

Le Sueur was more indignant and scornful than anyone else was about Sagean's claims. Le Sueur reported[65] that Henry de Tonti, being at Biloxi, had never known Sagean "anywhere except here."[66] But Le Sueur had known him in Canada under the name of Mermande. Perhaps Le Sueur was proud of his own familiarity with the upper Mississippi, for he seemed to take delight in disproving the

[63] Bégon, who sent Sagean to Biloxi, wrote Villermont: "Je crois qu'on luy donnera un détachment de vingt hommes pour aller reconnoitre le pays dont il parle." Bégon had interrogated Sagean four or five times, with the *Relation* before him as well as Father Coronelli's globe map, and he had been able to discover only minor discrepancies between the *Relation* and Sagean's responses to questions. Iberville, Bégon reported, had learned no more than he himself had learned (Bégon to Villermont, La Rochelle, July 7, 1701: BN., MSS. fr., 22810:257). Hopes that Sagean would find his way back to Acaaniba must have been nurtured in France until the *Enflammé* returned to Europe, having to put in at Weymouth because of a storm. Then, from Weymouth came some news in a letter written by the purser on the *Enflammé;* Bégon had had other news written from Biloxi. Sagean was persisting in his claims and demanding men to take with him to Acaaniba, but nobody in Louisiana believed him (Bégon to Villermont, Rochefort, Jan. 31, 1702: BN., MSS. fr., 22811:24).

[64] Sauvole to [Pontchartrain?], Biloxi, La., Aug. 4, 1701, *M.P.A.*, II, 17.

[65] The same letter from Sauvole places Pierre Charles Le Sueur at Biloxi (*M.P.A.*, II, 16 and n. 2).

[66] "Here" places both Tonty and the writer, Le Sueur, at Biloxi. For Le Sueur's opinions of Sagean, see the extract from the Mémoires of Le Sueur, Aug. 13, 1701, Margry, *Découvertes et établissements*, VI, 171–172.

accuracy of Sagean's description of Fort St. Louis[67] and the portage beginning below the Falls of St. Anthony. Rising to sarcastic irony, Le Sueur called Sagean "le fameux aventurier" who claimed he could find a river where there was more gold than it would take to buy all Paris. Le Sueur was particularly exasperated that Sagean should have said that he failed to see a single Indian during the winter he passed above the portage.[68] To Le Sueur this observation was as absurd as someone's saying that he had spent a whole day on the Pont-Neuf in Paris without seeing a single person.

When Iberville moved the French post from Biloxi to the Mobile River in 1702, Sagean was doubtless transported to Dauphin Island[69] and then up the bay to the new site on which Fort Louis de la Louisiane was being erected on the Mobile River. A map of Fort Louis,[70] commonly called Fort Louis de la Mobile, shows that in 1711 one Mathieu Sajan [sic] owned the middle lot of the three lots fronting on rue de Bienville; presumably he had a house on the lot and was living in it, for the map is of the village, La Mobile, whose streets were laid out close to the fort fronting the river. Perhaps Mathieu Sagean was still trying to convince people that he really had discovered Acaaniba, a kingdom beyond the Rockies and near the Vermilion Sea.

---

[67] In the *Relation* (Margry, *Découvertes et établissements*, VI, 99), Sagean said that the French built Fort St. Louis "sur un islot adjacent de la grande terre, à laquelle on communique par le moyen d'un pont, qui se tire dans ledit fort." "Rien de tout cela," wrote Le Sueur. "Le fort que M. de La Salle avoit fait construire aux Illinois estoit sur la grande terre, sur une montagne de roche fort escarpée" (extract from the *Mémoires* of Le Sueur, Aug. 13, 1701, Margry, *Découvertes et établissements*, VI, 171).

[68] This criticism of Sagean's *Relation* appears inaccurate; of course, once he got to Biloxi, Sagean may have told some new details that he had not put either in the dictated narrative or in the *Enquête*.

[69] The anonymous author who translated Father Léonard's extract believed that Sagean died at Biloxi of yellow fever when "Sauvolle [sic] and most of the French" died there ("Matthew Sagean and His Adventures" [anon.], pp. 65–71).

[70] In Peter J. Hamilton, *Colonial Mobile* (2nd ed., Boston, 1910), p. 84. This map, called "Fort Louis de la Mobille, 1706 (?)," is dated dubiously. More recent and more authoritative scholarship has fixed the date of this map as 1711 and has identified it as the work of the Sieur Chevillot (Giraud, *Histoire de la Louisiane Française*, p. 201 and n. 1). Information in a letter to the author from Professor Marcel Giraud of the Collège de France, Feb. 12, 1964, gives further support to the date 1711. Professor Giraud wrote: "The map you refer to, by Chevillot, as quoted by Hamilton, dates from 1711 rather than 1706."

# The Seminary of Quebec: Resources for the History of the French in the Mississippi Valley

## Noël Baillargeon

### THE SEMINARY OF QUEBEC AND ITS MISSIONS IN THE MISSISSIPPI VALLEY IN THE EIGHTEENTH CENTURY

The Seminary of Quebec is a community of diocesan priests which was founded by Msgr. François de Montmorency-Laval, first bishop of New France, to prepare young men for priesthood and to assure parochial ministry. Bishop Laval promulgated his decree of erection in Paris on March 26, 1663, and King Louis XIV granted confirmatory letters-patent the following month.[1] Since the population of New France was not more than twenty-five hundred people, the provident bishop realized that his young institute needed strong supporters in France to be able to survive and expand. He therefore decided to unite it with the Seminary of Foreign Missions recently founded in Paris. The act of affiliation was signed in the capital of

[1] Decree of Erection of the Seminary of Quebec by Msgr. de Laval, Mar. 26, 1663, Archives of the Seminary of Quebec (hereafter ASQ), Séminaire, XI, 36 (original parchment signed and sealed); Confirmatory letters-patent granted by King Louis XIV to the Seminary of Quebec, Apr., 1663, Séminaire, XI, 1 (original parchment signed and sealed).

France on January 25, 1665.[2] The Seminary of Quebec then added to its name that of Foreign Missions and henceforth considered the conversion of the natives of this country one of its essential objectives. And throughout the French regime the Seminary of Foreign Missions of Quebec never wavered before any sacrifice to send to and to provide for the maintenance of its priests in the missionary outposts in Acadia, on the Atlantic coast, and even in the Mississippi Valley.

However, more urgent works in Quebec, as, for instance, the parochial ministry and the education of young men for priesthood, prevented for many years the Seminary of Quebec from devoting itself to missions among the Indians. It was not before 1685 that Msgr. de Laval and his seminary found the means to establish their first Acadian mission.[3]

The missions of the Seminary of Quebec in the Mississippi Valley date from 1698 and were given by Msgr. Jean-Baptiste de Chevrières de Saint-Vallier, who had succeeded Bishop Laval on the Seat of Quebec.[4] Msgr. de Saint-Vallier by two letters-patent, dated April 30 and July 14, granted the Seminary of Quebec the right to establish any mission it wanted "dans les lieux qu'ils jugeront les plus propres" and, specially, among "les Sauvages dits Tamarois qui sont entre les Illinois et les Acansas."[5] Two days after the grant of the second letter-patent, the three priests chosen for the founding of the intended missions, François de Montigny, superior,[6] Antoine

---

[2] ASQ, Polygraphie, XVII, 7.

[3] This first mission was founded among an Abnaki tribe called the "Crucientaux." They had their village at Miramichi in the Province of New Brunswick.

[4] Msgr. de Laval resigned in 1685 but remained in Canada. He retired to the Seminary of Quebec, where he died on May 6, 1708, at the age of eighty-six.

[5] Letters-patent of Msgr. de Saint-Vallier to the Seminary of Quebec for the establishment of missions in the Mississippi Valley, Apr. 30, 1698, ASQ, Polygraphie, IX, 3 (original signed and sealed). See also the same original letters-patent dated May 1, 1698, ASQ, Polygraphie, IX, 2.

Letters-patent of Msgr. de Saint-Vallier to the Seminary of Quebec for the establishment of the Mission of the Tamaroa, July 14, 1698 (original signed and sealed). This document has been reprinted in *Old Cahokia*, ed. John Francis McDermott (St. Louis, 1949), pp. 57 ff.

[6] François de Montigny, born in Paris in 1669. came to Canada in 1692. His nomination as superior of the future missions is dated May 12, 1698. Cf. ASQ, Missions, 61. Father de Montigny did not stay very long in Louisiana; he embarked at Biloxi and went back to France on May 28, 1700. He then joined the Society of Foreign Missions and was appointed to China. Cf. Amédée

Davion,[7] and Jean-François Buisson de Saint-Cosme[8] left Quebec for Montreal. The departure of the expedition took place at Lachine, near Montreal, on July 24. The party was fifteen men strong and included, besides the three fathers, Brother Alexandre, a member of the Hospitaliers-de-Saint-Joseph-de-la-Croix,[9] three servants, and eight voyageurs, all in four birchbark canoes.[10] The expedition by way of the Ottawa River, Lake Nipissing, and the French River reached Lake Huron and arrived at Fort Michilimackinac on September 8. There the missionaries had the good fortune to meet the former lieutenant of Cavelier de La Salle, the famous Henri de Tonty, who offered to be their guide as far as the Arkansas River.[11] Father Buisson de Saint-Cosme has told in his letter of January 2, 1699, how the party managed to reach safely the first Arkansas village on December 27, 1698.[12] This was not the end of the journey, for the Arkansas Indians were far less numerous than the missionaries had expected them to be.[13] Father de Montigny then decided to go

---

Gosselin, "M. de Montigny," *Bulletin des Recherches Historiques,* XXXI (1925), 171–176; Pierre Margry, *Découvertes et établissements des Français dans l'ouest et dans le sud de l'Amérique septentrionale (1694–1703)* (Paris, 1879–88), IV, 431.

[7] Antoine Davion came to Canada in 1690. He did not quit the lower Louisiana region until 1724; he died in France in 1726. See François de Montigny to Monsieur ———, May 22, 1726, ASQ, Lettres, M, 48: 4.

[8] Jean-François Buisson de Saint-Cosme was born in Lévis, near Quebec City on January 30, 1667. He studied at the Collège des Jésuites and at the Seminary of Quebec and was ordained on February 2, 1690, by Bishop Saint-Vallier. He had been a missionary in Acadia before being chosen for the Mississippi missions. His younger brother Michel was sent to Louisiana by the Seminary of Quebec in 1700 but came back to Canada in 1703. Cf. Amédée Gosselin, "Les Buisson de Saint-Cosme, prêtres," *Bulletin des Recherches Historiques,* XXX (1924), 195–198.

[9] This order, dedicated to the care of the poor and the sick, was founded by François Charon de la Barre in 1691. The members were better known by the name of "Frères Charon." The order ceased to exist in 1747.

[10] For the names of all who were employed by the missionaries during the 1698–99 expedition, see the memorandum drawn up by Father de Montigny, ASQ, Missions, 107. This document was published in English under the title: "Memorandum of Engagees and Their Wages for a Party Which Left Montreal for the Gulf Coast, 1699" in *Old Cahokia,* ed. McDermott, pp. 60 ff.

[11] Saint-Cosme to Laval, September 13, 1698, ASQ, Lettres, R, 27.

[12] Saint-Cosme to Laval, January 2, 1699, ASQ, Lettres, R, 26.

[13] See "Letter of Thaumur de la Source" in John Gilmary Shea, *Early Voyages up and down the Mississippi* (Albany, 1861), p. 79. La Source was the chronicler of the second part of the journey to the Arkansas. See also M. de Montigny to Monsieur———, May 3, 1699, AN, K 1374, n. 82 (copy); M. de Montigny to Monsieur———, May 6, 1699, AN, 3 JJ, vol. 387; and Montigny's letter of January 2, 1699, in Shea, *Early Voyages,* pp. 75–79. That letter, in fact, was not written before the middle of April or the beginning of May.

farther south, and, with the exception of Tonty and his men who were on their way back to the Illinois Country, the expedition started once again on January 4, 1699.[14]

The first half of the year 1699 was one of extensive travels back and forth on the Mississippi River. De Montigny and Davion even went as far as the Gulf of Mexico where they paid a visit to Fort Maurepas, which Pierre Lemoyne d'Iberville had built on the bay of Biloxi (now Ocean Springs, Mississippi).[15] By mid-summer three mission posts had been founded: Davion was among the Tonica on the Yazoo River, Buisson de Saint-Cosme had been in charge of the Holy Family Mission of the Tamaroa since the month of May, and François de Montigny had chosen the Tensa and the Natchez, nearly ninety leagues south of the Arkansas. In his report to the bishop of Quebec, August 25, Father de Montigny was optimistic, for he had learned at Fort Maurepas that the French were going to establish a settlement at the mouth of the Mississippi River. "I do not believe," he wrote to Saint-Vallier, "that any [Indian] nation would dare oppose the French in their plans . . . it is to be anticipated that so many nations having lived for so long in ignorance and infidelity will know and will love the true God and their Saviour and Redeemer Jesus Christ."[16]

Unfortunately, the Seminary of Quebec was not rich enough and did not have enough recruits to be able to provide with efficiency for the remote missions of the Mississippi Country as well as its other missions in Acadia. On the other hand, the Foreign Missions in Paris had other commitments in China and in Indochina, and they could not be of great help. Nevertheless, both seminaries managed to maintain some of their missionaries for twenty odd years in lower Louisiana. The Gentlemen of Foreign Missions, as they were called, performed their duty, mainly in Biloxi and in La Mobile (Fort Louis de la Louisiane) where a parish was erected July 20, 1703, and united to the Seminary of Quebec.[17] Farther north, along the Mississippi River, the two missions were not successful. Father Davion could not convert even one of his barbarous Tonica, but it

---

[14] Shea, *Early Voyages*, p. 80.
[15] François de Montigny to Saint-Vallier, Aug. 25, 1699, ASQ, Missions, 41.
[16] François de Montigny to Saint-Vallier, Aug. 25, 1699, ASQ, Missions, 41.
[17] Decree of Erection of the Parish of La Mobile, July 20, 1703, ASQ, Missions, 65.

was not that he did not try, for he was still with that tribe in 1719.[18] As for the Tensa and the Natchez, Father Buisson de Saint-Cosme, who had succeeded de Montigny in 1701, tried also in vain to convert them until his assassination in 1706 by a band of marauding Chitimacha Indians.[19]

In 1721, the missionaries of Foreign Missions learned that the time had come for them to retire from the lower Louisiana regions. At the request of the West Indies Company, the bishop of Quebec gave his consent to a division of the jurisdiction in the Mississippi Valley. The Capuchin Fathers were given the New Orleans area and, a little later, in 1726, the Jesuits received the ecclesiastical authority on all the lands between the Natchez and their mission of Kaskaskia.[20] Thereafter, the Mission of the Holy Family of the Tamaroa and the Cahokia was the only one left to the Foreign Missions of Quebec. They were to take good care of it until the end of the French regime.

How the Seminary of Quebec lost its mission in 1763 is a sad story. On learning of the conquest of New France, the panicked missionary Forget du Verger promptly sold for the cheap price of 32,500 livres the properties of the mission, which were estimated at at least 400,000, and he ran away.[21] The following year, steps taken by the Seminary of Quebec to have the sale canceled had no success, and when, in 1768, the directors were asked by the bishop of Quebec to send again a missionary to Cahokia, it was too late. In their meeting of May 8 they declared that the seminary, being reduced to five members and half-ruined by the last war, was now unable to resume its apostolate in the Parish of the Holy Family. On the same occasion they decided to renounce forever in favor of the church of Cahokia whatever property could be recovered.[22]

---

[18] See "Journal de Bénard de La Harpe" in Margry, *Découvertes et établissements,* VI, 247.

[19] Bénard de La Harpe, *Journal historique de l'établissement des français à la Louisiane* (New Orleans, Paris, 1831), p. 43; see also "Relation de Pénicaut" in Margry, *Découvertes et établissements,* V, 433.

[20] *Rapport sur les archives canadiennes pour l'année 1904,* appendice K, pp. 10, 16.

[21] ASQ, Missions, 25, 25a. Certified copies, on February 22, 1766, by Garic, notary at New Orleans, of the deeds of sale made by Father Forget du Verger, November 5, 1763. See also Forget Duverger to de Villars, Apr. 3, 1764, ASQ, Missions, 36; Pierre-François de Volsey (French commandant at Cahokia) to Messieurs ———— (probably the directors of the Seminary of Foreign Missions), New Orleans, Jan. 25, 1764, ASQ, Missions, 40: 2.

[22] ASQ, Grand Livre du Séminaire de Québec, p. 35.

The Seminary of Quebec has never changed that decision and so, by a last act of generosity, ended its apostolic works in the Mississippi Valley.[23]

## Notes on the Resources in the Archives of the Seminary of Quebec for the History of the French in the Mississippi Valley

The Seminary of Quebec has never forgotten this heroic period of its long history, for there are in this order's archives many documents which refer to its accomplishments in upper and lower Louisiana. There are but a few records which may be considered as useful information for the general history of the Mississippi and Missouri regions. Such are the Jean-Baptiste Trudeau manuscripts and Pierre-Antoine Tabeau's *Voyage dans le Haut Missouri en 1803, 1804 et 1805*.[24] The greater part of our documents are, therefore, of religious nature or pertain mostly to religious matters. These documents, relating to the missions, both in Acadia and in Louisiana, are

---

[23] On May 14, 1768, the directors of the Seminary of Quebec gave Father Pierre Gibault, the new missionary appointed by the bishop of Quebec to Cahokia, a proxy in order to cancel the sales of the mission's real estate (ASQ, Missions, 22). Father Gibault did not succeed in fulfilling his mandate, because of the ill-will of the British commanding officer of Cahokia (Gibault to Monsieur —— [probably the Superior of the Seminary of Quebec], June 10, 1771, ASQ, Lettres, P, 19: 1). Twenty years later, the citizens of Cahokia sent the Seminary of Quebec a letter in which they said that they had recently heard of Father Gibault's proxy (see "The Deputies and Church-Wardens of the Parish Mission of Cahos to the Seminary of Quebec, 6 June, 1787," in *Old Cahokia*, ed. McDermott, pp. 83–87; the original of this letter is in ASQ, Missions, 30). In his reply, Superior Henri-François Gravé said that it was true that the Seminary of Quebec had given up all its property in favor of the parish of Cahokia and that the decision taken on May 8, 1768, would not be changed (Gravé to the Parishioners and Church-Wardens of Cahokia, Aug. 6, 1789, ASQ, Missions, 19b).

[24] Description abrégée du haut Missouri addressée à Monsieur don Zenon Trudeau lieutenant Gouverneur de la partie occidentale des illinois, &c, &c, &c. Par J B^te trudeau voyageur, ASQ, Fonds Verreau-Viger, carton 50, nos. 70, 71, 72, 73; Extraits des journaux du voyage to J. B^te trudeau Sur le haut Missouri adressés a Mess^rs les directeurs de la Compagnie a S^t Louis des illinois, carton 50, no. 74. These are being edited for publication (in English) by John Francis McDermott. Voyage dans le Haut Missouri en 1803, 1804 et 1805 par M. Pierre Antoine Tabeau, ASQ, Fonds Verreau-Viger, La Saberdache rouge, cahier C, pp. 1–139. This is a copy made by Jacques Viger in 1848 after a copy made in 1820. This narrative was published in English by Annie Heloise Abel under the title *Tabeau's Narrative of Loisel's Expedition to Upper Missouri* (Norman, Okla., 1939).

distributed in a rather arbitrary way, I must say, in carton boxes entitled: *Évêques, Lettres, Missions, Polygraphie,* and *Séminaire.*[25] I have no doubt that the most important documents are well known to you, for they have been reprinted by the St. Louis Historical Documents Foundation or in other noted historical collections. Therefore, I find it more expedient to underline some types of less-known documents, such as memoirs and letters which were exchanged between the seminaries of Paris and Quebec from the last quarter of the seventeenth century and later.

There was a regular and continuous correspondence between France and Canada, depending on navigation. Correspondence was due in Quebec at the beginning of June and could not leave later than the end of October. During the long winter months communications were at a standstill. It is easily understood that everyone was eager to include in his letters all the news and events he could think of. It will always be of profit to historians to consult the letters written by the directors of both seminaries, but two of them certainly deserve a special mention: Father Jean Dudouyt and Father Henri-Jean Tremblay, who were successively the *chargés d'affaires* of the Seminary of Quebec in Paris, the former from 1677 to 1688 and the latter from 1693 to 1740. Both were experienced businessmen and perfectly informed of the political and religious questions of the time. The letters written by Dudouyt to Msgr. de Laval in 1634, for instance, supply very useful information, not only about Cavelier de La Salle's plan regarding the founding of a colony on the Gulf of Mexico coast, but also about the demand made to the Holy See by the Franciscan Fathers to obtain exclusive powers of jurisdiction in Louisiana.[26] As for Abbé Tremblay, let us say that during his long career he wrote nearly one hundred letters, some of them more than fifty pages long. From 1699 on there is hardly any letter from him which does not mention, one way or another, the affairs of the Mississippi.

However, the letters from the missionaries are the ones to be consulted, because, though an echo may be heard in the corre-

---

[25] Each title on these boxes is followed by a letter or by a number. For instance, Lettres, R, Polygraphie, IX. The documents contained in the boxes are also numbered, 1, 2, 3, and so on.

[26] Dudouyt to Laval, Mar. 11, 1684, ASQ, Lettres, N, 77; Dudouyt to Laval, Mar. 16, 1684, ASQ, Lettres, N, 78; Dudouyt to Laval, Mar. 28, 1684, ASQ, Lettres, N, 79; Dudouyt to Laval, May 2, 1684, ASQ, Lettres, N, 83.

spondence of their fellow members in Quebec or in Paris, nothing can replace the testimony of the pioneers of the Faith themselves. Those humble priests, isolated among barbarous people, miles and miles apart in the wilderness, had to maintain contact with their superiors and friends to get advice, support, and even the material aid they needed to survive and to fulfill their duty. As well as telling the events of their daily life, their moral and physical ordeals, their letters are also full of pertinent observations on the land and its inhabitants, which are of great interest to the ethnologist and the geographer. Because they were in those days almost the only ones to keep such records, we cannot exaggerate the contribution to history made by missionaries like Jean-François Buisson de Saint-Cosme, François de Montigny, Marc Bergier, Henri Roulleaux de La Vente, and Jean-Paul Mercier, whose letters, at least a good part of them, have been preserved in the Archives of the Seminary of Quebec.

From Father Buisson de Saint-Cosme we still have sixteen letters addressed to Msgr. de Laval, Msgr. de Saint-Vallier, and Father Henri-Jean Tremblay, written from 1698 to 1706. Three of these letters, dated August 30, 1698, September 13, 1698, and January 2, 1699, tell of the journey from Montreal to the Arkansas River made by the founders of the very first missions in the Mississippi Valley. As for the other letters, two of them are dated from the Tamaroa, March, 1700; one from Lake Peoria, also March, 1700; another from the fort at Biloxi, August 1, 1701; and the remainder from the Natchez where Buisson de Saint-Cosme had succeeded Father de Montigny.[27] All Buisson de Saint-Cosme's letters are autographs with the exception of the one of January 2, 1699, which is a copy made from the original now lost. This narrative is a well-known document and, of all his letters, it is the only one which has been printed. John Gilmary Shea published it from a copy given to him by Francis Parkman, first in French, and a second time in English. The copy held by the Seminary of Quebec has also been published, in an English translation, by Louise P. Kellogg in *Early Narratives of the North West.*[28]

---

[27] ASQ, Lettres, R, 26–40. It must be noted that the letters are not placed in chronological order.

[28] Tremblay to Laval, June 12, 1700, ASQ, Lettres, N, 113: 3; Tremblay to Saint-Vallier, June 12, 1700, ASQ, Lettres, N, 6: 1; John Gilmary Shea, *Relation de la mission du Missisipi du Seminaire de Québec en 1700* (New

Father François de Montigny has left three original manuscripts: a memoir containing the names of the men employed by him
for the 1698–99 expedition and their wages and other expenses, and
two letters from the Tensa Village, dated August 25, 1699 and
January 27, 1700.[29] The memoir is without title, author, or date, but
the handwriting and other internal and external evidence clearly
show that it was drawn up by de Montigny in 1700 and was addressed to Father Tremblay. This document has been printed in an
English translation under the title: "Memorandum of Engagees and
Their Wages for a Party Which Left Montreal for the Gulf Coast,
1699," by Joseph Donnelly, S.J., in *Old Cahokia*.[30] The letter dated
August 25, 1699, is a narrative, sent to Msgr. de Saint-Vallier, in
which de Montigny tells the bishop of Quebec of the establishment
of the Holy Family Mission among the Tamaroa at the end of May,
1699, and of his long trip to Fort Maurepas on the Gulf of Mexico
coast. There are also in it descriptions and commentaries about the
religious and other practices of the Tensa and the Natchez Indians.
This letter was brought to France by Pierre Lemoyne d'Iberville in
1700. Father Tremblay, in Paris, had some copies made of it and
forwarded back the original to Quebec. Today there is but one copy,
somehow incomplete, which is in the Bibliothèque Nationale in
Paris, with a copy, also incomplete, of another letter written by the
same de Montigny to de Saint-Vallier from New York, July 17,
1700. These two copies, however, are not signed, and the addressee is
not otherwise indicated than by the title of "Monseigneur." Waldo
G. Leland, who ignorant of the existence of the original letter, has
erroneously attributed both copies to a certain "Father François
Jolliet de Montigny, S.J." The third letter of Father de Montigny,
dated January 27, 1700, is a short but useful one giving additional
details about the engagés and the expenses of the expedition of
1698–99.[31]

---

York, 1861), pp. 13–45; Shea, *Early Voyages*, pp. 45–75; Louise Phelps
Kellogg, *Early Narratives of the North West, 1634–1699* in *Original Narratives
of Early American History*, ed. J. Franklin Jameson (New York, 1917), XVI.
Kellogg seems to have believed that the copy held by the archives of the
Seminary of Quebec is the original manuscript (p. 340).

[29] ASQ, Missions, 107, 41, 41a.

[30] *Old Cahokia*, ed. McDermott, pp. 60 ff.

[31] Tremblay to Laval, June 12, 1700, ASQ, Lettres, N, 113: 3. BN MSS fr.
n.a., Renaudot 7485, part II, fols. 121v–127v, 127v–131v; Waldo G. Leland,
*Guide to Materials for American History in the Libraries and Archives of
Paris* (Washington, D.C., 1932), I, 97. These two copies have been printed by

Father Marc Bergier arrived at the Tamaroa mission in the month of February, 1700, and stayed there till his death in 1707. He was an educated man, and his thirty-four letters are of great interest. They were written, from 1699 to 1705, to the bishop of Quebec, to the directors of Foreign Missions in Quebec or in Paris, and to Father Tremblay.[32] All but two are autograph letters. Father Bergier is also the author of a manuscript map, showing the Mississippi and its tributaries, which is also in our archives. That map has been erroneously attributed to Father Jean-Paul Mercier. A comparison of Father Bergier's handwriting with the handwriting on the map shows without any doubt that both are the same.[33]

Father Henri Roulleaux de La Vente performed his apostolic work in lower Louisiana only. His thirteen letters to the superior of the Seminary of Paris or to Father Tremblay were written at Fort La Mobile, also called "Fort Louis de la Louisiane," from 1704 to 1709. The writings of that missionary give useful accounts on the early history of the Gulf coast settlements. As for Father Bergier, we may take the opportunity to mention that the archives of the Seminary of Quebec holds a manuscript map of the Mississippi and Missouri rivers, drawn by Father de La Vente. That map, like Bergier's map, is without title, date, or signature, but its identification is made possible by the handwriting which is undoubtedly that of de La Vente.[34]

Father Jean-Paul Mercier is well known for his "Plan de la Seigneurie et Etablissement de la Mission des Tamarois" and for the "Explication du Plan," which accompanied his survey of the

---

Isabel MacBreath Calder in *Colonial Captivities, Marches and Journeys* (New York, 1935). Calder has mistaken "Monseigneur" for Count Pontchartrain.

[32] ASQ, Lettres, R, 41–73. Chronological order. There is also from Father Bergier a short memoir about the opposition made by the Jesuits to his jurisdiction at the Tamaroa mission. Cf. Mémoire touchant la mission des Tamarois, et la jurisdiction du pays, 5 mai 1702, ASQ, Missions, 69.

[33] ASQ, Polygraphie, IX, 43. This map has been reproduced by Sara Jones Tucker in "Indian Villages of the Illinois Country," *Scientific Papers*, Illinois State Museum (Springfield, Ill., 1942), vol. II, part 1 atlas, plate XVIII. Tucker did not share Father Amédée Gosselin's opinion according to which Father Mercier could be the author of this map, but Tucker was unable to identify the real author either, because she did not know Father Bergier's handwriting.

[34] ASQ, Lettres, R, 74–86; ASQ, Polygraphie, IX. This map is also reproduced in Tucker, "Indian Villages," plate XIX. As for Bergier's map, the editor could not identify the handwriting.

Seigniory.[35] We also have from this missionary a letter dated May 21, 1735, to the directors of Foreign Missions of Quebec; another one to the Marquis de Vaudreuil, governor of Louisiana, April 20, 1743; and the copies of four letters to Father Jean Lyon de Saint-Ferréol, then superior of the Seminary of Quebec, in the years 1732 and 1733.[36]

To complete the present list, and in order to give justice to everyone, three other missionaries who have contributed one letter each should be added: Antoine Davion, from Ile Dauphine in the Gulf of Mexico, in 1711; François Lemaire, also from Ile Dauphine, in 1717; Nicolas Laurent, from Cahokia, June 27, 1756.[37]

I am well aware that this short account is far from being exhaustive. Nevertheless, it is my hope that, with these few data, I may bring forth new light on the role played for more than sixty years by the Seminary of Quebec in the history of the French in the Mississippi Valley.

[35] ASQ, Polygraphie, IX, 42; Original manuscript, in the handwriting of Father Mercier, 36 × 49 cm., Explication du plan et Etablissement de la Seigneurie de la Mission des Tamarois, ASQ, Polygraphie, IX, 18. N. 18a and n. 18b are two copies of the same memorandum.

[36] ASQ, Polygraphie, IX, 15; ASQ, Missions, 28; see also Governor Vaudreuil's answer in ASQ, Missions, 27, 27a. These letters deal with the seigniory grant to the Holy Family Mission made in 1722. ASQ, Missions, 43; Father de Saint-Ferréol himself copied the four letters in Quebec on October 8, 1733, and, presumably, sent the originals to France.

[37] Davion to Monsieur ———, Oct. 20, 1711, ASQ, Missions, 46; François Lemaire to Monsieur et tres cher Confrere ———, May 28, 1717, ASQ, Missions, 47; Nicolas Laurent to Monsieur ———, June 7, 1756, ASQ, Missions, 26.

# Resources in Detroit for the History of the French in the Mississippi Valley

James M. Babcock

Fifty years ago this month, Clarence Monroe Burton, a public-spirited collector of books and manuscripts, presented his library to the people of Detroit. The Detroit Public Library eagerly accepted Mr. Burton's collection which was rich in the resources for the study of American history. Particularly rich were the sources for the history of Detroit and Michigan and the entire Great Lakes region.

For seven years the collection remained in Mr. Burton's home which he had also presented to the library. In 1921 the collection was moved into the new main library building. Just last year the collection was once more moved, this time into a new wing of the main library building.

In 1914 the collection numbered perhaps thirty thousand volumes, several hundred thousand manuscripts, and hundreds of maps, prints, and pictures. Now there are approximately one hundred and fifty thousand books and over three thousand collections of manuscripts. The map collection has grown accordingly, as have the picture and print collection. Additions to the library have been made possible through an endowment fund established by Mr. Burton.

Within the basic scope of the history of the Great Lakes region, the era of the French in North America has been the subject of collection and study since the inception of the library. Greater emphasis has been upon Canada, although Louisiana and the Mississippi Valley French have necessarily been considered.

In the absence of a detailed guide and of extensive calendaring, my discussion will be in general terms with some specific citation of sources. The fur trade in the upper Mississippi Valley is reflected in our holdings of records of traders and merchants. Events in the Illinois Country from the French and Indian Wars to the American acquisition of Louisiana Territory may be traced in several collections. Our holdings of materials which may be classed as Old Northwest obviously have some relation to the Mississippi Valley.

The sources available consist of original manuscript records of every description, contemporary publications of travel accounts and missionary activity, and contemporary maps. The original manuscripts derive from official government groups, old families, and organizations and institutions.

Antoine de la Mothe Cadillac, founder of Detroit, was a governor of Louisiana. Under the direction of Mr. Burton and others, the French archives were searched for documents relating to Cadillac and his activities in America. Twelve volumes of Pierre Margry's transcripts of Mississippi Valley documents were ordered collated with the originals and translated by Mr. Burton. This translation has never been published. A portion of these pertain to Cadillac's tenure in Louisiana. Photostats of other miscellaneous documents from the French archives which relate to Canada and the upper Mississippi Valley have been collected.

Another source in the Burton Collection for the study of the French in the Mississippi Valley is the group of fur-trading archives. Most extensive are the American Fur Company Papers. Our portion of these are for the period 1805–43.

Among the chief sources for this discussion are the parish registers, notarial records, and other official series. Many of the families who later settled in the Mississippi Valley were first in Canada.

The parish registers available in transcript include Assumption Church, Sandwich (now Windsor), Ontario, 1752–1824; St. Francis Xavier's, Vincennes, 1704–1838; St. Anne's Church, Mackinac, 1695–1799; St. Anne's, Detroit, 1704–1848; St. Antoine, Monroe,

Michigan, 1794–1849; St. Joseph, Michigan, Roman Catholic Mission, 1720–73. They include baptisms, deaths, and marriages.

In addition to the Margry transcripts from the Archives Nationales in Paris, we have a translation of his six-volume collection of *Mémoires et documents pour servir a l'histoire des origines françaises des pays d'outre-mer* . . . *(1614–1794)* (Paris, 1879–88).

The records of the French Consulate of Norfolk, Virginia, would also be useful. They consist of births, marriages, deaths, wills, inventories, and business transactions for the years 1784–1866, in eleven volumes.

Father Christian Denissen, on commission from Mr. Burton, compiled a twenty-six-volume work in typescript, "Genealogy of French Families of Detroit." He searched many sources of vital records and family papers in compiling the genealogies.

A related collection of note is the papers of Father Pierre Potier (1708–81). Father Potier came to Canada in 1743 and from Quebec to the Detroit River in 1744, where he labored as a missionary to the Huron Indians, and subsequently as pastor to the Assumption Church at Sandwich, Ontario, until his death in July, 1781. The papers consist of (1) the original manuscript of the "Livre de compte de la Mission des Hurons du Detroit," 1733–81, (2) typewritten copies of his account book of Assumption Church, 1775–81, which include a list of the inhabitants of the Petite Côte, in 1778; and (3) typewritten copies of "Les Itineraires conserves par Pierre Potier [1743–44]," taken from the original manuscript in St. Mary's College, Montreal. The "Livre de compte" is an account book, mostly in the handwriting of Father Potier, with baptismal entries, 1789–91, in the handwriting of Father François X. Dufaux. It is invaluable for its record of the Jesuit mission to the Hurons and as a catalog of the French families resident at an early date on the Detroit River, and to some extent, for the beginnings of the Assumption Church. The "Itineraires," which include descriptions of the journeys from Quebec to Detroit, Detroit to St. Joseph, to the Illinois Country, to Mackinac, and to posts on Lake Superior and the lower Mississippi, afford, as a whole, a body of information concerning the primitive routes of travel of unusual historical value.

In the Isadore Chene Papers is an account of the capture of Fort Sackville, Vincennes, February 24, 1779, as reported to Chene who was in Vincennes at the time (photostat from Public Archives, Ottawa).

The personal and business papers of John Askin comprise several thousand letters and a large number of manuscript business and other record books. Askin was a native of Ireland who came to America as a soldier in the Seven Years' War, and upon its termination he became a merchant and trader at Albany. From 1763 to 1780 he resided at Mackinac, from 1780 to 1802 at Detroit, and from 1802 to 1815 at his country home opposite Belle Isle in what is now the city of Windsor. His papers as preserved by himself must have comprised a vast quantity. The neglect of descendants and the ravages of time have destroyed much of the original collection. The portion remaining is relatively scant prior to 1780 and relatively abundant from that date onward. Taken in their varied aspects, they mirror almost every aspect of life in the Great Lakes area for the period to which they pertain. Selections of the more important of them, as judged from the Detroit point of view, have been published as Volumes I and II of the *Burton Historical Records* (Detroit, 1928, 1931).

Within the Cicotte Family Papers is found an important ledger[1] containing the contemporary accounts of the French government with settlers brought to Detroit, 1749–52, in an effort to build up this place as an effective center of opposition to the English efforts at colonizing the upper Ohio Valley. Although the enterprise proved futile, it brought a considerable increase of population to Detroit, and the book is an interesting memento of this particular government-promoted settlement.

Some census records for Detroit and Michigan in which are enumerated persons who migrated farther into the continent are available for the years 1701, 1710, 1749, 1750, 1760, 1765, 1773, 1779, 1782, 1796, 1799 (election roll), and 1805. Four volumes, A–D, 1737–95 (records for July 11, 1784, to May 24, 1786, are missing) of Detroit notarial records are available. Volumes A–C are in the Wayne County, Michigan, archives and Volume D is in the Dominion Archives, Ottawa, Canada. Transcripts of all of them are in the Burton Collection. Mr. Burton commissioned the transcribing of the Montreal notarial records from 1678 to 1819 which consist of twenty-two volumes. The transcripts were made from 1895 to 1898.

Among our manuscript collections are the papers of several

---

[1] Rev. George Pare, "The Cicotte Book," *Detroit Historical Society Bulletin*, XIV (Feb., 1958), 10–15.

early Detroit French families, such as the Campaus, the Rivards, the Morans, the Chenes, the Chapatons, the Navarres, and the Cicottes, which include letters, accounts, receipts, deeds, marriage contracts, parish records, and other material.

For the English period of Detroit, 1760–96, we have the papers of John Askin (whose many volumes of account books have not been published), William Edgar, Sampson Fleming, Alexander D. Fraser, John Porteous, Thomas Williams, Henry Hamilton, William Kirby, Angus Mackintosh, Alexander and William Macomb, William Robertson, Solomon Sibley, James Sterling, James and Robert Abbott, Henry Bird, William Burnett, and others.

In addition, we have a few original papers together with transcripts of such officials as Sir Jeffrey Amherst, Lord Dartmouth, Lord Dorchester, Henry Gladwin, Jehu Hay, John Montresor, Patrick Sinclair, and General Thomas Gage. The records of military officers and units, for example, Henry Hamilton, provide a source for the study of French-British rivalry in Illinois. Included in the Henry Hamilton papers are the original articles of capitulation at Vincennes, signed by George Rogers Clark and Hamilton, together with a report to General Haldimand containing a report of the Vincennes campaign. An individual document of significance to this period may be quoted. Captain Harry Gordon wrote from Philadelphia to Thomas Thoroton, Secretary to Lord Granby, May 20, 1766:

> By General Gage's orders I am thus far in my route to Fort Chartres on the Mississippi. The representations of the commanding officer there of the chance that Fort has of being carried off by the river. The projects for the construction of several others to prevent the French Traders intercourse with our Indians, and disturbing our trade; by penetrating into our country, to the eastward of the River Mississippi, thro the Illinois above and the Ohio below Fort Chartres. The description wanted of these communications and the proper situation of our affairs in ye Floridas which can hardly be seen thro by the so differing accounts the commander in Chief has received of them. These with some other affairs of a political nature are the cause of my being ordered upon so distant service.
>
> My opinion of the impropriety to attempt to support ourselves along the Mississippi, by an overruling force, will naturally make me cautious of forwarding projects, to multiply Forts along that Frontier. On the contrary I am convinced it is much more the interest of the publick to carry on our possession by the good will of the Natives, to negotiate with them, and apply ourselves to gain them, at least for some time, till their fighting spirit subsides, than by erecting new posts, to curb all at once their beloved intercourse with their old friends and to keep the natural jealousy they do

entertain of our design to enslave them. Besides if awe is to be exerted over them it would be improper there. Detroit is in the midst of the leading nations and there only it is proper to shew our force. Let Pondiac, a western, or northern chief, hold up their hand it is enough for a Mississippi Indian so that while we keep strength at Detroit and speak fair for the rest we shall do well with those people.

I would have transmitted you for my lords perusal a copy of our estimate for works for the season but as it consisted of some insignificant repairs which will not amount to £3000 curr$^{cy}$ I did not think it worth troubling you with. The engineer at Hallifax has made representations of many repairs wanting there. But Mr. Gage does not allow of much to be done till he hears of the result of the project for fortifying at Newfoundland. The affair of our back forts is now properly fixt, I wish it was the like of our front Forts. I assure you sir was my opinion of much import I would be at no great expence about Hallifax. Since the demolition of Louisburg and the conquest of Canada I can view Hallifax in no more usefull light than its being a good harbour. The port of New York is not a bad one, and it is from thence we shal for the future operate. It is to that ground we should abutt our bridge to America, and it must be from thence. Enterprises must proceed against the French and Spanish West Indies in case these neighbours disturb our tranquility or prove refractory. 12,000 good troops with a superior fleet rendezvoused at New York, will almost imprint as great awe as a conquering army in the heart of France or Spain. Besides enterprizes of a more domestick kind point out this place as a proper spot. Protection for our Fisheries on Newfoundland, a force at New York, and a superior fleet in the gulph of Mexico and we may spit upon Spain. They would lose Mexico in a twelve months war.

I beg your excuse for this Freedom of expression but it would I am persuaded prove a just picture of such a future event, and my ardent desire is to write you sir with impartial truth and be ingenuous. I hope the route I have to perform will afford something curious, if not important to send you, and that I shall go thro with my commands to the satisfaction of my General, and thence entitle me to my Lords and your future protection. My will is good.

The expence I have been obliged to put the Board to for a boat and crew in this long water expedition I hope will not be taken amiss, as it is unavoidable.

I have nothing further to add but my most sincere respects and that I am. . . .

Our collection of Jonathan Carver (1710–80) consists of a photostatic copy of his original journal (1766–67) from Boston via Detroit and Mackinac to the upper Mississippi area and back to Mackinac.

In the Jacob Schieffelin papers is a typescript of the original entries in his diary. He was a lieutenant in the British Army, military secretary of Lieutenant-Governor Henry Hamilton of Detroit. He was captured by George Rogers Clark at Vincennes. His diary discloses incidentally that when Governor Hamilton left Detroit in 1778 his objective was "to possess New Orleans then under Don Galves for Spain; to proceed with all the force he could collect and force his way down the Mississippi."

Among the original papers of Hugh Heward (d. 1803) is a journal of his voyage from Detroit to the French Illinois, March 24 to May 21, 1790, which has been printed in *Burton Historical Records* (Detroit, 1928), I, 339–360.

The French colonies, as was France itself, were governed under a series of administrative acts: *arrêts, édits, ordonnances, déclarations, mandements, récrits, instructions, règlements,* and *mémoires.* More than thirteen hundred were issued separately from 1540 to 1791. Of the several hundred which deal directly with the colonies, the Burton Collection has 138. The administrative acts were of several types: *édits,* spontaneous royal acts, usually concerning only one subject; *ordonnances,* laws of the king, usually called forth by petition and of a more general nature than the *édits; déclarations,* interpretations or modifications of the law; *mandements, récrits,* and *instructions* were orders to execute the law; *règlements* were actual administrative acts. Navigation, trade, commerce, and finance in Canada and Louisiana were regulated by these acts.

Most of my discussion has been of manuscript and archival sources available in Detroit, either in the original or in transcript. In Ann Arbor are two other repositories within the University of Michigan deserving of notice: The William L. Clements Library and the Michigan Historical Collections. Published guides for each are available.

The Burton Collection has also the important editions of contemporary accounts by Champlain, Sagard, Hennepin, La Hontan, Charlevoix, Kalm, Carver, and many others. We have also more than forty of the original published editions of the *Jesuit Relations,* as well as the publications of the Leopoldine Society.

The map collection is extensive and includes most of the significant items for our present period of study. Recently we acquired an original manuscript map on vellum, 1756, of the middle British colonies. This map, though similar to the 1755 Lewis Evans map, has certain new information.

Another recent acquisition of marginal interest to us here is a group of papers of Louis Antoine de Bougainville from his Canadian period.

All of the resources of the Burton Historical Collection are

216

freely available to any qualified scholar who makes application in our reading room. We encourage the use and publication of our collections. Reference and research service by mail must be limited to bibliographic assistance and specific questions.

In conclusion, may we pay tribute to Clarence Monroe Burton, whose paramount interest as a collector was in the research value of what he collected. While the library was still in his possession he welcomed scholarly use of it. The administration of the Detroit Public Library has continued to emphasize research values in its collecting and has perpetuated Mr. Burton's purpose of collecting research materials for scholarly use.

# Manuscript Sources in Louisiana for the History of the French in the Mississippi Valley

## Winston De Ville

To say that Louisiana's colonial records are valuable to researchers in French colonial history would be an understatement—they are essential. To say that they are among the least studied would be sadly true—in most cases, their pages were last read over two centuries ago by the men who wrote them.

This paper will focus attention on the major archival collections in Louisiana, emphasizing the earliest records and giving the researcher some knowledge of their scope, present condition and availability, and possible plans for their preservation.

One group of records often neglected by researchers is the New Orleans Notarial Archives, located in the Civil Courts Building in the new Civic Center. For the French period, they are the least organized and most elusive of the thousands of volumes in that depository.

In an index prepared in 1944 by the custodian of notarial archives,[1] the twelve notaries who would interest us are listed with impressive location symbols. In reality, however, only three notaries

---

[1] Available in handwritten form at the notarial archives.

have volumes primarily devoted to their records and labeled with their names. Only these are readily found: Almonaster, Garic, and Maison. The records of Andres Almonaster date from 1770 through 1782, and are contained in sixteen large and well-preserved volumes. Those of Jean Baptiste Garic are in twelve volumes, the first of which covers 1739–66, and the remainder divided between 1767 and 1779. Both of these notarial groups have tables of contents in their opening pages. The records of the third notary, Charles J. Maison, date from 1766 through 1769 and are bound in one volume without a table of contents.

What has become of the records drawn by the nine other notaries—Bunel, Chantalou, Ducros, Henri, de Kernion, La Mothe, Raquet, Rossard, and Salmon? Although the 1944 guide to the notarial archives does not indicate the irregularity, the records of these nine notaries are not in separate volumes, but are scattered through the miscellaneous books as well as bound into the volumes of the three notaries mentioned first. The de Kernion records, for instance, are bound into the Maison volume. "Miscellaneous Records, Volume I" contains records dating from 1731 through 1741, while Volume II dates from 1733 with some documents as late as 1807. Two of the most important volumes in this depository do not appear in the guide to the notarial archives. These are two succession books: Volume I, 1731–92, and Volume II, 1735–68, which contain the succession papers of many men prominent in early Louisiana history—de la Chaise, for example. In these four books, too, will be found some of our lost notaries.

For the use of researchers, Table I is a list of the notaries with marginal notes I have found useful.

Less available than the notarial archives are records known as the "Cabildo records." This false title includes not only Spanish documents and territorial papers, but Louisiana's earliest and largest single colonial record group, the records of the Superior Council—in 1956, totaling almost 12,000 pieces.[2] These are the records which are of considerable interest to us today. They are probably the most talked about and least understood, the most quoted and least often consulted of any in the nation.

Until recently, these records were housed in the damp vault of the Presbytère, one of the buildings of the Louisiana State Museum

---

[2] John C. L. Andreassen and Edwin A. Davis, *Louisiana Archives Survey, Report Number 2, Findings and Recommendations* (Baton Rouge, 1956), p. 20.

TABLE I

| Name of Notary | Records Begin | Records End | Location |
|---|---|---|---|
| Andres Almonaster | March 10, 1770 | May 28, 1782 | 21-L and 29R |
| Antoine Bunel | Sept. 14, 1735 | Feb. 25, 1738 | See Arthur Meigner book |
| Augustin Chantalou | March 24, 1759 | July 19, 1762 | Miscellaneous and Succession books (especially Miscellaneous, pp. 56840–67485) |
| Joseph Ducros | Oct. 17, 1764 | Nov. 10, 1766 | Miscellaneous and Succession books |
| Jean Baptiste Garic | June 6, 1739 | Sept. 23, 1779 | 21-L and 23R |
| Nicolas Henri | Oct. 11, 1745 | Oct. 6, 1749 | Miscellaneous and Succession books |
| Huchet de Kernion | July 8, 1766 | Feb. 20, 1769 | Charles J. Maison book |
| Guillaume La Mothe | Oct. 23, 1766 | Feb. 18, 1769 | Miscellaneous and Succession books |
| Charles J. Maison | July 8, 1766 | May 29, 1769 | 16-L |
| Jean Baptiste Raquet | March 18, 1739 | April 13, 1739 | Miscellaneous and Succession books |
| Michel Rossard | March 21, 1735 | April 8, 1735 | Miscellaneous and Succession books |
| Gatien Salmon | Sept. 26, 1739 | Oct. 24, 1739 | Miscellaneous and Succession books |
| Miscellaneous Records (2 vols.) | 1731 | 1770 | These are known to the attendant simply as the "oldest records" and should be so designated when requested. |
| Succession Records (2 vols.) | | | |

complex, just off Jackson Square in New Orleans. Within the past two years, however, during the renovation of the building, the papers were removed for storage. Two years ago (that is, in 1962), upon briefly examining these records, I was told that they were not available to researchers; no satisfactory answers have been received to various inquiries regarding their return to the museum or their future availability.

What *is* known about these records? The "Black Books" in the Louisiana State Museum Library (to be discussed later) indicate that the records of the Superior Council date from 1714 and are a continuous record of official and personal legal activities throughout the French period.

Several attempts have been made to prepare guides to these French and Spanish records. A discussion of each effort may clarify research procedure. The most popular guide appears in the *Louisiana Historical Quarterly*, beginning in 1917.[3] This calendar, unfortunately, is not complete and fails to include many documents of rare importance to Louisiana history, such as a group of documents discovered last year tucked away in a corner of the Louisiana State Museum Library giving much detail on the 1768 Rebellion in Louisiana and dealing with Nicolas Denis Foucault in particular. Another unusual find, again not mentioned in the *Quarterly*, is a short manuscript poem, which I hope to publish.[4]

The *Index to the Louisiana Historical Quarterly*,[5] published in 1956, is useless to researchers who wish to use the records that *do* appear in the *Quarterly*, for it does not include the Superior Council Records or the Spanish Judicial Records. However, Helen De Ville of Alexandria, Louisiana, a former editorial secretary for the journal *Louisiana History*,[6] has been preparing for two years a comprehensive index to the Superior Council Records as they appear in the *Quarterly*, and upon publication, will begin work on the Spanish Judicial Records. Still other guides are available to the original records. The "Black Books," previously mentioned, are ninety-four small ring-binders on the shelves of the Louisiana State Museum

---

[3] *Louisiana Historical Quarterly*, I (Jan., 1917), 103.

[4] This poem describes the various nations of slaves represented in Louisiana and their passion for the *Calenda, Bamboula*, and other primitive dances.

[5] *Index to the Louisiana Historical Quarterly*, comp. Boyd Cruise (New Orleans, 1956).

[6] Quarterly publication of the Louisiana Historical Association, with editorial offices at Louisiana State University, Baton Rouge, Louisiana.

Library.[7] The entries in these notebooks are essentially the same as the *Louisiana Historical Quarterly* series, for a typical entry includes document number, date, document title, and a two- or three-line description. The principal parties in the document appear in bold print and those who signed are listed last. If the document was listed or published in the *Quarterly*, that fact is stated. These small volumes are being reprinted in the quarterly genealogical publication called *New Orleans Genesis*.[8]

A last, and for biographical data more useful than the "Black Books," guide is the unnamed card file in the rear room of the Louisiana State Museum Library. These cards attempt to give a genealogical digest of the data appearing in all these colonial records, including those of the Superior Council. Arranged in alphabetical order by the name of the principal party named in the document, the cards indicate the date and give an index number which is supposed to correspond with the original in the Presbytère. It is doubtful, however, if either this number or the number indicated in the "Black Books" would serve the researcher without fail, considering the present disorganized state of the records. These cards are open to the public, are not supervised, and consequently are rapidly becoming as disheveled as the documents they purport to index.

The Louisiana State Museum Library, mentioned so often in this paper, contains many guides to research, duplicates of records in France, many W.P.A. typescripts, and copies of some church records. Here, with some controversial exceptions, are found the books and bound manuscripts which once formed part of the Louisiana Historical Society Collection. Included in this group are the volumes copied in France at the Archives de la Marine and Archives des Colonies by Félix Magne. Purchased for the state in 1845 by Governor Mouton, most of the important documents copied by Magne have since been published and are readily available in print—Pénicaut's story, for example, and the La Salle papers which so intrigued Margry.[9]

Another useful file is the card index of church records from St.

---

[7] 547 Ste. Anne Street, New Orleans, Louisiana.

[8] Published by Genealogical Research Society of New Orleans, Box 30312, Lafayette Square Station, New Orleans 30, Louisiana.

[9] *Fleur de Lys and Calumet*, ed. Richebourg Gaillard McWilliams (Baton Rouge, 1953); Pierre Margry, *Découvertes et établissements des français dans l'ouest et dans le sud de l'Amérique septentrionale, 1614–1754* (Paris, 1879–88), II.

Charles Parish, called the "Little Red Church" file. These entries record the baptisms, marriages, and deaths of the French and German population of the "Côte des Allemands"[10] in the 1740's and 1750's.

Four very useful handwritten volumes copied from originals in France are "Recensements, 1707–1741," "Louisiane: Correspondance Générale," "Concessions" (a volume which details land grants in Louisiana during the earliest period of settlement), and the "Louisiane: État-Civil, 1720–1734," which includes baptisms and funeral notices of not only settlers in the lower Mississippi Valley, but also those of the Illinois Country. These are also available at the Library of Congress and are well worthy of full publication.

The parish registers of the St. Louis Cathedral in New Orleans contain the vital records of many of the earliest Frenchmen who came to Louisiana. Although the records suffered from the various New Orleans fires, destroying the pages between 1733 and 1764, the first volume of marriage records is useful for the earlier period, dating as it does from 1720. The volume labeled "Baptisms and Marriages" dates from 1731 through 1733 and contains a large section of funeral records. Upon recommendation of a high church official and/or the pastor, it is possible for serious researchers to use the records.

Because they are so readily available and well known, I shall not dwell on the Tulane University archives, the Archives Department of Louisiana State University, or the collection in New Orleans Public Library. The Tulane Archives Department is noted for its Kuntz Collection on Louisiana history, including many original manuscripts dating from the founding of the colony. Valuable, too, are the "Prairie Parish" papers, including documents which somehow strayed from their original place of deposit in Opelousas or St. Martinville. One of these documents, a land grant, was useful in determining the date of the establishment of the Opelousas Post. The Louisiana State University archives contain some of the Opelousas documents, as well as a few documents from La Balise, below New Orleans. The holdings of these three important institutions are outlined in Hamer's *Guide* and the holdings of Tulane and L.S.U. are discussed in Volume I of *Louisiana History*.[11] It is well

---

[10] Now St. Charles and St. John the Baptist Parishes, to be discussed later.

[11] *A Guide to Archives and Manuscripts in the United States*, ed. Philip M. Hamer (New Haven, 1961), pp. 202–204, 205–208; Connie G. Griffith, "Col-

to note here that these are the only archival depositories in Louisiana where inquiries are answered with satisfaction.

At this point it should be in order to outline the collections in the Louisiana State Archives and Records Commission in Baton Rouge. But, except for the two record groups of Opelousas and Avoyelles posts which will be discussed later, the state archives have nothing to offer the researcher in French colonial Louisiana.

Private collections in Louisiana are few. I claim no knowledge of the Alexander Parsons Collection now peacefully resting in Texas,[12] except that, to quote many, it is "fabulous." The Kuntz family of New Orleans, with generous foresight, has made an extensive collection available to scholars working at the Tulane archives, as we have just seen. Father Blaise D'Antoni of Ste. Theresa's Catholic Church in Shreveport is the fortunate heir of Roger Baudier in Louisiana's Catholic Church history.[13] He is building a remarkable collection around the Catholic clergy of Louisiana from Father De Ville to all the present-day priests. His files include many of the Baudier notes, photostatic and microfilm reproductions of many early church records, and a valuable card index which this young priest has made on all the Louisiana ecclesiastics known to him with references to his sources.

Let us leave the present limits of Louisiana now and investigate the sources for research in Mobile, Alabama, so vitally a part of colonial Louisiana. The first inquiry is usually about the civil records quoted so liberally by Peter J. Hamilton in his *Colonial Mobile*.[14] When Hamilton used the records, they dated from 1710 and were housed in the Mobile County Court House, stored in black cypress boxes. Today, all that remains to remind us of the records are these black boxes—handsome enough but of little use to historians. After two years of questioning and one year of turning each proverbial stone in Mobile County and at the state archives in Montgomery, I have concluded that the records have been destroyed—perhaps inadvertently—or stolen—not so inadvertently.

The only written remnant of Mobile's colonial past of use to

lections in the Manuscript Sections of Howard-Tilton Memorial Library, Tulane University," *Louisiana History*, I (Fall, 1960), 320–327; V. L. Bedsole, "Collections in the Department of Archives and Manuscripts, Louisiana State University," *Louisiana History*, I (Fall, 1960), 328–334.

[12] Department of Archives, University of Texas, Austin, Texas.

[13] Roger Baudier, *The Catholic Church in Louisiana* (New Orleans, 1939).

[14] Peter J. Hamilton, *Colonial Mobile* (2nd ed., Boston, 1910), p. 155.

researchers is the Catholic Church records of the Basilica of the Immaculate Conception. The records are now in the vaults of the Chancery Office of the Diocese of Mobile. The registers were poorly laminated some years ago, and are now difficult to use because of warping, fading, and torn pages. However, in the manuscripts division of the Alabama State Department of Archives, the researcher has access to W.P.A. typescripts of these church records which begin in 1704. Peter A. Brannon, state archivist, assured me that, until I pored over them last October (1963), these copies had never been used, although they were deposited there approximately twenty years ago. I have compared the copies with the originals in Mobile, and, except for variances in spelling, easily enough recognized, they seem to be complete and carefully transcribed.

Once again in present-day Louisiana—but in the "country," as New Orleanians would say—there are seven fertile fields for the historian of Louisiana's French period. These are the colonial posts whose records give us details of life in eighteenth-century Louisiana. Although these archives contain few singularly important manuscripts, they do include wills, various conveyances, suits, some important correspondence, marriage contracts, successions, bonds, receipts, depositions, and many other types of legal documents of importance. Although it would seem difficult to write an authoritative and complete state or regional history without knowing the history of each part of that area, absolutely none of these parish records were consulted in the field by many of the historians who have so unsuccessfully tried to capture Louisiana's past in print.

The records of Avoyelles Post, now Marksville, located between New Roads and Alexandria, date from 1786, but actually are a continuing record of settlers from the older French post at Pointe Coupée. In the summer of 1961, the clerk of court of Avoyelles Parish authorized their removal from the local courthouse, where they were fast deteriorating, to the Louisiana State Archives and Records Commission in Baton Rouge. When this transfer was completed, the State Archives Commission sorted, organized, and calendared the colonial records and published a small booklet entitled *Calendar of Louisiana Colonial Documents, Volume I, Avoyelles Parish*. Providing a quick reference to the 413 items comprising this collection, the booklet also reflects the plight of the state's old records, for gaps appear from 1787 to 1789, and again from 1801 to 1802. This printed guide contains two major faults: it does not make it clear that the Avoyelles records will be deposited permanently at the state archives and the number of pages in each document is not indicated. But, as the editor said in the preface to this little volume: "Many observers will view this publication without realizing its value. Others will realize its value but begrudge its failure to contain translations of all the documents described. A few will be thankful that, at last, a project has been started which eventually will preserve and catalogue the extant chronicles of Louisiana's colonial history. These few will help to determine the success of the emprise."[15] Some vital records for the Avoyelles population are to be found in St. Paul the Apostle Catholic Church at Mansura, near Marksville. They do not begin until 1796, and at last report were unavailable.

The mother-post of the Avoyelles settlement was at Pointe Coupée on False River. The site of Pointe Coupée post was visited by Bienville in 1699 and it is likely that unorganized or temporary settlement began soon thereafter. By the late 1720's, at least, the area was so populated as to require a priest,[16] and the earliest records drawn at this post are dated at this time. The documents dating prior to 1762 are interfiled with documents of a later date and do not appear in an index which, with the extant documents, is deposited in the local parish courthouse at New Roads. Five years ago they were contained in more than fifteen ancient leather volumes, bound chronologically. Today, however, some of the volumes are missing. To my knowledge, there are no organized plans to preserve the Pointe Coupée records.

The church records are now filed in the diocesan offices in Baton Rouge and, upon formal written request, may be used by researchers.[17] They are an excellent group of ecclesiastical papers and date from September, 1737, with only minor skips. I have handwritten copies of these records through 1750, and these are available for the use of scholars.

The post of St. Jean Baptiste in northwest Louisiana was founded in 1714 by Louis Juchereau de St. Denys at the site of present-day Natchitoches. The colonial records of this French post

---

[15] *Calendar of Louisiana Colonial Documents, Volume I, Avoyelles Parish*, comp. Winston De Ville (Baton Rouge, 1961), p. ix.

[16] Etat des Missions desservices et a desservoir . . . April 24, 1787, Mississippi Provincial Archives (transcripts in Mississippi State Department of Archives [Jackson], XVI [1725–27], 289–308).

[17] The address of the diocesan archives is Diocesan Archivist, St. Joseph's School, Fourth at North Streets, Baton Rouge, Louisiana.

remain in the offices of the clerk of court in the courthouse. Usually cited as dating from 1716, I have been unable to find even one record antedating the 1720's. With no further large gaps through the entire colonial period, the records are divided into two groups: a small box in the personal office of the clerk of court contains the "important" papers as designated by some of the local historians. These include the 1744 will of St. Denys and his succession papers, as well as those of his wife, a high-born Spaniard of Mexico. Other papers in this group relate to locally important individuals or events—such as the publishable manuscript telling of dissension between a priest, Father Valentin, and his parishioners in 1759. The other group of Natchitoches records are in the clerk's vault office. These papers are bound into volumes divided by years and are in relatively good order. A guide called "Index to Conveyances" serves as a table of contents to the more than twenty large volumes. In these records will be found much source material, for the most part untouched, on French relations with the Spaniards of Mexico and Texas, and on early prominent French families such as the De Blancs, Coulon de Villiers, Derbannes, Layssards, Dauterives, and, of course, Juchereau de St. Denys. Careful study would also reveal some important references and some full documents on the two other north Louisiana posts whose own records are not extant—Rapides and Ouachita.[18]

Mild efforts in 1961 by the state archives to have the Natchitoches records transferred to Baton Rouge met with more-than-mild opposition. Fortunately, the Genealogical Society of the Church of Jesus Christ of the Latter Day Saints, Salt Lake City, has just completed a filming program in Natchitoches. It has been reported that the colonial records and the valuable guide or index have been microfilmed. Libraries may purchase copies of the film.

Although it is very difficult to obtain entry to the church archives in Natchitoches, we are fortunate that at the Public Archives of Canada, a microfilm copy of the complete Natchitoches church records is available at nominal cost. These registers are some of the state's oldest and date from 1729.

The records in the parishes of St. Charles and St. John the

---

[18] Katherine Bridges, Louisiana Librarian, Northwestern State College, Natchitoches, Louisiana, a scholar in her own right, is well acquainted with these, and other colonial Louisiana records. Her "St. Denys and Father Hidalgo," *Louisiana Genealogical Register*, VIII (Mar., 1961), 19–20, is a gem of historical writing.

Baptist on the Mississippi River just above New Orleans are in a deplorable condition. The records of St. Charles date from 1734, while those of St. John begin in 1753. Here one will find—if one is willing to work his way through unorganized papers—records relating to the John Law settlement of Germans and the French who settled among them, particularly after the Natchez Massacre of 1729. The church records for St. John the Baptist parish do not begin until 1771, although those of St. Charles record the births, marriages, and deaths of both settlements during the French period. As we have seen, copies of the St. Charles church records are available in the Louisiana State Museum Library.

The Poste des Attakapas in south-central Louisiana had jurisdiction over two distinctly different groups of Frenchmen—the humble Acadians and the aristocratic families that turned this frontier settlement into what is still known as "Petit Paris." The site of the old post is now St. Martinville, seat of St. Martin Parish. The colonial records are found in the office of the clerk of court and are in remarkably good condition. They date from the late 1750's, when the post was established, and have no significant gaps.

The Public Archives of Canada again can provide aid to those unable to see the church records in St. Martinville, for they hold microfilm copies of these registers. They date from 1756 and are complete.

Some thirty miles to the north of Attakapas Post is the site of the last French settlement established in Louisiana—the Poste des Opelousas. Founded in 1763, Opelousas soon became a cosmopolitan center. The church records in St. Landry Catholic Church date from 1771 and record Spaniards from San Antonio, Englishmen—later Loyalists—from the East, free Negroes from as far away as Boston, Germans, Italians, Danes, and, of course, French—from France, Canada, and Acadia.

The colonial records of the Opelousas Post which date from the year of establishment were until recent years in disarray in the attic of the St. Landry Parish courthouse, in the town which today bears the name of the early post. In 1961, the parish clerk gave his consent for the removal of the Opelousas colonial and territorial records to the State Archives and Records Commission. It was my pleasure to supervise this transferral and the broad organization of the records into colonial and territorial groups, later arranging the colonial records in more detailed order. This project, however, was being conducted simultaneously with the Avoyelles records project, and for two years after the publication of the calendar for the Avoyelles papers, I was told that funds were not available for Volume II which would guide researchers to the Opelousas records. During these two years, I was in almost daily contact with the records, and, while taking notes for a thesis, was able to construct a calendar for the first twenty-one years of the post's existence, correcting the faults found in Volume I. In December, 1963, plans were made to publish this portion of the calendar with private funds, as the publication of the complete calendar by the state archives was not in sight. These plans stirred the state officials into action, for only last week (February 4, 1964) I was formally asked to submit my manuscript calendar for publication by the State Archives and Records Commission—a seemingly small victory for Louisiana history, perhaps, but one that we should hope will grow in significance.

This paper has attempted to call attention to the major manuscript collections in Louisiana. I cannot know if it has been thorough, for who would guess that valuable documents were once found in a barrel outside the doors of the Cabildo—or, in a dustbin in Natchitoches, ready for the fire—or, I am assured, under a camellia bush in Audubon Park! Louisiana is still our frontier as surely as it was a frontier to our eighteenth-century Frenchmen.

# The Contributors

James M. Babcock, as chief of the Burton Historical Collection in the Detroit Public Library, is happily seated in one of the greatest manuscript depositories ever assembled by a private collector for the history of an American city and its regional connections.

Abbé Noël Baillargeon, professeur titulaire d'histoire moderne in the Faculté des Arts, Université Laval, and professeur de l'histoire du Canada in the Petit Séminaire of Québec, has a special interest in the part played by the Séminaire de Québec in the Mississippi Valley in the eighteenth century and has published articles concerning it in the *Revue de l'Université Laval*, the *Revue de l'Instruction Publique*, and the *Rapport de la Société Canadienne d'Histoire de l'Église*.

Pierre H. Boulle, a French citizen, is working on his Ph.D. in history at the University of California. He has taught at Stanford University and is now teaching at the University of Delaware. His paper here is an extension of the research for his dissertation on "The Colonies in French Public Opinion, 1748–1763."

WINSTON DE VILLE, formerly director of the Special Collections Department at Mobile Public Library and now associated with Harper & Row Publishers, traces his ancestry in Louisiana to Juchereau de St. Denis. His interest in colonial records has resulted in the publication of a series by the Louisiana State Archives Commission titled *Calendar of Louisiana Colonial Documents*. His *Louisiana Colonial Marriage Contracts*, now in its fourth volume, *Louisiana Colonials: Soldiers and Vagabonds*, and *Acadian Church Records, 1679–1759*, are other highly useful compilations for the history of French Louisiana.

JOSEPH P. DONNELLY, S.J., now on a research appointment in Chicago, was until 1955 a member of the Department of History and librarian of St. Louis University and was later professor and head of the Department of History at Marquette University. He is the author of a bibliography on the fur trade of the American colonies and of a history of Holy Name Parish at Cahokia, and he has contributed several chapters of documents to *Old Cahokia, a Narrative and Documents Illustrating the First Century of Its History*. He has also translated and edited the diary of Father Nicolas Point, who traveled in the Rocky Mountains with Father De Smet.

JOSEPH EWAN, since 1947 a member of the faculty at Tulane University and now professor of botany there, has wandered with his subjects over wide territory. He is the author of *Rocky Mountain Naturalists* and of many studies in scholarly journals; his latest book is *John Lyon, Nurseryman and Plant Hunter, and His Journal, 1799–1814*, published by the American Philosophical Society. In 1956 he was an official delegate of the French government to a Paris conference on the history of Franco-American botany to 1850; to it he contributed a valuable paper on "L'Activité des Premiers Explorateurs français dans le S.E. des États-Unis."

CHARLES GUENTHER, chief of the technical library at the Air Force Aeronautical Chart and Information Center in St. Louis, has contributed poems, criticism, and translations to *The New Yorker; Kenyon Review; Partisan Review; Perspective; Poetry; The Quarterly Review of Literature;* and other periodicals. He has published volumes of translations of contemporary French, Spanish, and Italian poets.

Dorothy Garesché Holland (Mrs. William K. Holland) is a descendant of some of the people she has written about on this occasion. A graduate of Maryville College of the Sacred Heart in St. Louis, with a master's degree in English from Washington University, she has taught English at Maryville but is now executive secretary of the alumnae there. She is the author of an *Annotated Checklist of Magazines Published in St. Louis Before 1900* and of *The Garesché, de Bauduy, and des Chapelles Families: History and Genealogy* (1964), a volume based on a large collection of letters and memoirs.

Jack D. L. Holmes, associate professor of history at the Birmingham Center of the University of Alabama, has worked extensively as a Fulbright scholar in the Spanish archives. He has edited *Documentos Inéditos para la Historia de la Luisiana, 1792–1810* (Madrid, 1963) and is about to publish a biography of Gayoso de Lemos, governor of Louisiana 1797–99, and a volume of his letters. Professor Holmes has also contributed to scholarly periodicals many articles concerned with the Spanish decades of French Louisiana.

John Francis McDermott, research professor of humanities at Southern Illinois University (Edwardsville) has long been interested in the French in the Mississippi Valley. McDermott, whose family has been St. Louisans since 1764, has contributed many articles to periodicals on this subject. Among his books are *Private Libraries in Creole Saint Louis; A Glossary of Mississippi Valley French; Old Cahokia, a Narrative and Documents Illustrating the First Century of Its History;* and *The Early Histories of St. Louis.* He is now at work on a biography of Pierre de Laclède and plans an edition of the Louisiana portion of the memoirs of Pierre Clement de Laussat, colonial prefect of Louisiana, 1803–4.

Richebourg Gaillard McWilliams by his given name displays an ancestral interest in early Louisiana. Professor of English at Birmingham-Southern College, he has translated and edited the journal of Pénicaut, Mississippi River traveler in 1700, under the title of *Fleur de Lys and Calumet.*

CHARLES E. PETERSON, F.A.I.A., entered the National Park Service in 1929 and in 1954 became supervising architect for historic structures, EODC. He has now a consulting practice in architectural restoration and historical preservation and has just accepted an appointment as adjunct professor of architecture at Columbia University. Assigned to the Jefferson National Expansion Memorial project in St. Louis in 1935, he served here for eight years (broken by service in the Navy). Important scholarly results of the great interest aroused in him by French colonial architecture have included *Colonial St. Louis* and "Notes on Old Cahokia." He has published many other papers and since 1950 has been editor of "American Notes" in the *Journal of the Society of Architectural Historians.*

FREDERIC E. VOELKER, a native St. Louisan, has conducted extensive research in materials on the far western fur trade and the men who carried it on and has contributed many articles on these subjects to historical journals and other publications. He is now engaged in preparing a number of sketches for a forthcoming biographical dictionary of western mountain men.

SAMUEL WILSON, JR., F.A.I.A., practicing architect in the New Orleans firm of Richard Koch and Samuel Wilson, Jr., is also an architectural historian with a scholarly reputation resting solidly on numerous publications including his edition of *Impressions Respecting New Orleans, the Diary and Sketches of Benjamin Henry Latrobe, 1818–1820* and studies of eighteenth- and nineteenth-century buildings in New Orleans such as *A Guide to the Architecture of New Orleans; The Capuchin School in New Orleans, 1725; The St. Louis Cemeteries of New Orleans; Baroness Pontalba's Buildings;* and "Louisiana Drawings of Alexander De Batz" (some of these with the collaboration of Leonard V. Huber).

# Index

238

240